TROUBLES OF CHILDREN AND PARENTS

TROUBLES OF CHILDREN AND PARENTS

SUSAN ISAACS

SCHOCKEN BOOKS · NEW YORK

First SCHOCKEN PAPERBACK edition 1973

First published 1948
Copyright © 1973 by Schocken Books Inc.
Library of Congress Catalog Card No. 72-95661
*Published by arrangement with
Routledge & Kegan Paul Ltd.*
Manufactured in the United States of America

INTRODUCTION

TROUBLES OF CHILDREN AND PARENTS is a book of questions and answers. It is a book of advice in the form of replies to letters received from mothers and nannies. Although a social document of the 1930's, it is just as relevant today: the nannies and maids have vanished from the scene, but children's problems remain today what they were forty years ago. Mothers and all those surrogate mothers who come in contact with children in daycare centers, Head Start programs, nursery schools, early-learning centers, and play groups—all will immediately recognize the depth of concern and wisdom of Susan Isaacs' advice.

D. E. M. Gardner, former head of the Department of Child Development at the University of London, said of Susan Isaacs that, in helping parents, "she brought all her knowledge and experience to bear: giving deep consideration to the nature of any problem and offering advice with discernment and sympathy in a way which helped parents to understand for themselves and therefore to feel more confident and less anxious, though she never minimized the difficulties either of the child or the parent. It was her respect for both, together with her vivid appreciation of the reality and intensity of a young child's feelings, which made her advice so acceptable and fruitful to parents." *

Re-publication of this book comes at a particularly auspicious time in the United States, inasmuch as Susan Isaacs is recognized as having laid the foundations for the modern

* *Susan Isaacs: The First Biography* (London: Methuen, 1959), p. 77.

British infant school. The Malting House School, which she founded in Cambridge in 1924, was, in effect, the first open classroom. It embraced the ideas of both the integrated day and family grouping. It addressed itself to the three areas of education that are still our primary concerns today: intellectual growth, freedom, and emotional hygiene. Its aim was to "foster in every possible way the child's joy in discovery. . . . When one of them put out an intellectual feeler an attempt was made to insure that the feeler met the kind of situation which would encourage it to go on." The school also attempted to find the right balance between freedom and control, and it sought to gain a fuller understanding of the young child's emotional needs.

TROUBLES OF CHILDREN AND PARENTS, Susan Isaacs' last book, was first published in 1948. But the material it contains was collected during her most active years of writing. From 1927, when she left the Malting House School where she collected the data for *Intellectual Growth in Young Children* and *Social Development in Young Children,* until 1937, when she became head of the newly formed Department of Child Development at the University of London Institute of Education, she wrote her most important books. During those same years she also undertook additional training in psychoanalytic work, following the lead of Melanie Klein. It is most characteristic of Susan Isaacs that during this very busy and productive time she concerned herself with the daily problems of mothers and nurses.

The answers to the problems presented appeared in the British journal *The Nursery World* between the years of 1929 and 1936. But after that, until her death in 1948, Susan Isaacs continued to receive and personally answer letters. The quality of her concern is evident throughout. She will continue to speak for present and future generations of children in this very clear presentation of their normal development, the reality and intensity of their feelings, and the troubles which inevitably are part and parcel of growth.

EVA S. GLASER

Department of Elementary Education
City College, City University of New York
January 1973

PREFACE

PARENTS have many problems. Those dealt with in this book are mainly the social and emotional difficulties arising in the development of children in their early years. The material is selected from a much larger bulk of actual letters from parents and nurses which I answered under the pseudonym of "Ursula Wise" in *The Nursery World* (published by Benn Bros.) during the years 1929–36.

The letters and replies have been shortened but not otherwise changed. I felt that the "local colour" giving the picture of the actual children and parents, and of the living relationship between them, was much more likely to make the replies helpful than any artificial summary of the questions could do.

Similar questions crop up every year with each new family of children. Not only so. Many of these problems are transient and normal, however trying to the parents they may be. They pass away with sensible handling and with the further development of the child. Worried young parents seldom realize this. It is often a great help to them to learn how frequent and typical such happenings are in the developing child. Often the mere lessening of anxiety in the parent through the knowledge that the early years of childhood are bound to have such storms and crises will do much to ease the difficulties of the parents, and hence of the children.

What I always tried to do in my replies to these anxious enquiries, and what I hope this book will do for its readers now, is to give parents and nurses some sense of children's normal development and at the same time a greater awareness of the reality and intensity of the child's feelings in his various relationships—how human he is, even as an infant, and how necessary it is to be aware of this if one is to treat him reasonably.

From the practical point of view I do not suggest that one can be as useful to parents through the medium of letters as by means of a first-hand diagnostic interview, but there are many cases of children with urgent problems of behaviour where circumstances do not justify or may even preclude a visit to a Child Guidance Clinic. This was especially so at the time when these letters and replies were written. Now there are many more clinics available. Even at that date, whenever I judged that first-hand diagnosis and advice was required, I suggested this to the parents and gave them the name and address of the nearest Child Guidance Clinic. (For want of space few of these letters are republished in this volume).

As regards the value of the book to systematic students, the material offered is not based on a representative cross-section of the population. The children described are mostly middle-class. But I have seen enough myself, and have received enough confirmation from those working in Clinics, Nursery and Infant Schools, and people familiar with children from poorer homes, to know that the same problems occur, with differences in "local colour", in children of all classes. The difficulties described are mostly the typical difficulties of development during these years.

When I first drew this tentative conclusion and published it, some psychologists considered that I was describing what happened in a few "abnormal" cases, and that the "ordinary" child did not plague his parents in these ways. Since that date, however, trustworthy evidence has accumulated on every hand that this criticism was unsound, and that emotional difficulties are part of the normal picture of the developing child in his early years.

PREFACE

This point stands out most clearly in regard to difficulties in cleanliness and the need to ask what are the proper standards to be applied to the child. I have, however, left that series of problems out of this volume, mainly because of the very large number of letters raising the issue—these would require a volume to themselves; but also because I have already dealt with the problem elsewhere. (See list of references). Fortunately the climate of opinion on this subject has changed a little in recent years, and children now are not so often subject to the fantastic demands which parents generally had been taught to make upon their babies at the time when I began this work in *The Nursery World*.

Many other problems dealt with at some length in the original correspondence (such as feeding difficulties, bedtime troubles, lying, toys and play materials, etc.) have had to be omitted as such from the present book. But they are not altogether left out, as will be noticed. One of the striking things about children's problems is the way in which they overlap. It was often quite difficult to classify these letters, since in most cases they raised several issues, occurring in the day-to-day life of the same child. This observation—familiar enough to child psychiatrists and child guidance workers—is important for parents too: the fact that an underlying state of conflict and anxiety in a child will usually show itself in a variety of symptoms; and may have been stirred up by events which it has not occurred to the mother or nurse to link with the obvious troubles. This will be seen again and again in the quoted letters, and is one of the points I found it helpful to bring out in my replies. It gave me further reason to believe that it would be more useful to publish the actual letters as fully as possible, showing the details of the child's circumstances and family setting, rather than short summarized statements of a series of apparently unrelated questions.

The vivid pictures of actual families and of the attitudes of parents and nurses which the letters afford as they stand may also prove a useful source-book to students of family life and relationships.

SUSAN ISAACS

February, 1948

ACKNOWLEDGMENTS

MY GRATEFUL acknowledgments are due, first, to Messrs. Benn Bros., Ltd., and the Editor of *The Nursery World* for their kind permission to re-issue these letters and replies in book form.

Secondly, to my friend Miss D. E. M. Gardner, Head of the Department of Child Development, University of London Institute of Education, without whose most generous and unfailing help and many practical suggestions I should not have been able to complete the arduous task of sorting and arranging this material.

Also to Miss Eunice Webb and Miss E. Bremer, who gave me most valuable help in the work of classifying the letters; and to Miss D. Withers and Miss M. Horrocks, who assisted in preparing them for the press.

CONTENTS

	PAGE
INTRODUCTION	i
PREFACE	v
ACKNOWLEDGMENTS	ix

CHAPTER

I. RELATIONSHIPS WITH PARENTS, NURSES AND CHILDREN 1
Clinging to mother after change of nurse—training in politeness—the importance of father—should children play alone?—spoiling the youngest child in the family—a toddler among strange children—explaining about an adopted child—over-dependence upon mother—should parents take a holiday?—can we train children not to shirk responsibility?

II. OBEDIENCE, DISCIPLINE AND PUNISHMENT . . 24
Should children obey?—the "strong-willed" child—should they obey instantly?—"it hurts me more than it hurts him"—should we smack a two-year-old?—the seven-year-old who "forgets" requests—two stubborn children—"playing up" to a new nurse—is a "hard time" good for children?

III. LACK OF SELF-CONTROL AND CRYING . . . 55
Fussing about small hurts—hysterical crying in an eight-year-old—the child who "makes scenes"—the child who cannot bear disappointment.

xii TROUBLES OF CHILDREN AND PARENTS

IV. TANTRUMS AND STUBBORNNESS 66
An excitable three-year-old—a two-year-old's tantrums with her nurse—dislike of changes in routine—tantrums when parents and nurse are together—contrariness in a boy of four—temper at two years—tantrums in a three-year-old boy—wilfulness at two years—dislike of being dressed and undressed—obstinate slowness in a boy of nine—tantrums after illness—resistance to going out.

V. SHYNESS 92
Fear of strangers—shyness at two years—fear of other children—shyness at seventeen months—a child who will not say "Good-morning"—a self-conscious five-year-old—an unsociable boy—a sensitive girl—fear of a strange house at nine months—"showing off" after shyness has been overcome.

VI. JEALOUSY 111
A three-year-old's attacks on a baby brother—open jealousy in a girl of five and a half—jealousy affecting sleep—another girl of three and a half who hurts the baby—fear of strangers linked with jealousy—sudden destructiveness connected with rivalry—intolerance of thwarting—a nine-year-old bully in the family—jealousy of brother and dependence on nurse—two boys who are fond of younger brothers but often bully them—jealousy affecting meal-time behaviour—jealousy and fear of the dark—spitefulness to the baby—jealousy and nervous habits—jealousy and "fidgeting"—fighting between three two-year-olds.

CONTENTS xiii

VII. PHOBIAS AND ANXIETIES **144**
Fear of imaginary biting animals—a three-year-old's anxiety in the night—night-terrors at five years—acute fear of strange places—phobias of the vacuum-cleaner and of the dark—fear of medicines—fear of noises—two children with a phobia of hair-washing—horror of trains—fear of houses—fear of balloons and crackers—sleeplessness and excitability—how to deal with fears following on unpleasant experiences—fear of strange people at nine months—hysterical fear of doctor or dentist.

VIII. DESTRUCTIVENESS AND AGGRESSIVENESS . . **179**
Sudden attacks on people—destruction of toys—tearing wall-paper and cutting sister's hair—a two-year-old's cruelty to a dog—throwing beads on the floor—throwing objects about suddenly—biting younger children.

IX. VARIOUS SYMPTOMS OF DIFFICULTY . . . **195**
Cot-banging in the night—nail-biting at eighteen months—body-rocking—thumping movements at night—head-knocking—nervous sniffing—a habit of "screwing eyes up" after styes are cured—thumb-sucking cured in a boy of nine—two enquiries and a "horrified" protest about thumb-sucking—thumb-sucking and disturbed sleep—playing with nose—sucking blanket—tongue-sucking—finger-sucking—a boy of five years who pulls his nails off—nail-biting at four years—nail-pulling at three years.

X. SEX EDUCATION AND "WHERE BABIES COME FROM" **222**
How to explain the coming of a new baby to a

boy of three and a half—a three-year-old's interest in her own babyhood—can we "prepare" a child of nineteen months for the next arrival?—should mother make a "definite effort" to give sex knowledge to a boy of seven? how soon beforehand should children be told of a new baby to come?—is it useful to read a book about the origin of babies to a child of seven?—how to tell an older boy about the "facts of life"—when should a girl be told about menstruation?

REFERENCES FOR FURTHER READING 237

1. RELATIONSHIPS WITH PARENTS, NURSES AND CHILDREN

Q. My small girl M., aged four years and four months, has a brother aged ten months to whom she is devoted. At first she went through various difficult phases which we put down to jealousy. Two months ago we had to have a change of nannie, and I anticipated a lot of trouble as she adored *the girl who was leaving, and lavished all her affections on her. I told M. that nannie had to have a long holiday, and rather to my surprise she took the change fairly calmly, though she still asks occasionally when will the old nannie's holiday be over. She seems quite fond of the new girl, but I tried to show her more affection myself in order that she should not feel so "lost". Now, starting about a month ago, she simply clings to me, and we have scenes every time she has to go out with nannie, or be put to bed, meals, etc. I have to promise repeatedly to see her the moment she gets back, or the meal is over, and she works herself into a perfect panic and frenzy over this, having to ascertain exactly what time she can see me, and where I shall be. She seems quite unable to help these outbursts, and it is pitiable to see her; she works herself up to such a pitch of crying, and imploring to be with me. I have been firm over these scenes and insisted on her going out with nannie, having meals, etc. though she is sometimes left alone until she has "recovered". I have* never *deceived her, and I have reasoned with her and explained that I cannot always have her with me. But when the occasions crop up she seems quite unable to control herself. When I am out, or away for the day, she is nearly always perfectly good and happy.*

A. I would suggest that the chief trouble with your little girl is that you have *not* been strictly truthful with her about the loss of her nannie. She is terrified to let you go out of her sight because she does not feel sure that *you* will come back, even though you promise to do so. A child of her age knows perfectly well that holidays do not last as long as this, and that nannie's absence must mean much more than a holiday. You can be sure that she has sensed from your manner, whenever you have told her that nannie was on holiday, that this is not strictly true. Intelligent children are extraordinarily quick to sense signs of evasion of the truth in grown-ups. Moreover, it is more than likely that she has heard some comment from somebody else; for example, the new nurse, which makes her realize or half realize that the old nannie has really left and the new one taken her place. I would strongly advise you to talk to her quite frankly about the whole trouble and say that her old nannie is not coming back, and that you did not tell her the full truth because you were afraid she would be so unhappy about it, but that you think now it would help her best if you did tell her, and that you quite understand that she is so distressed when you leave her because she fears you will stay away a very long time like nannie has done, and does not feel really secure in your promise not to do so. It is surprising how readily children respond to real frankness and the full truth, and how much more they thrive on it than on evasions and half truths. A very admirable mother told me just recently a striking instance of this with her own small boy. When the boy was about two and a half the excellent nurse he had always had was knocked down and seriously injured by a motor car. The mother and father quite naturally feared to tell the truth about this to the little boy, and when he asked for his nurse they told him that she had gone on a long holiday. They were quite sure that the boy heard no conversations about the real facts of the matter, but after many months— nearly a year—they came to the conclusion that, in spite of their great care, the boy had sensed the fact that they had not told the truth. He had appreciated the subtle expression in their manner and voices that something serious had happened, and the fact that they were evading when they said that the nurse had gone on a holiday. This was brought home to the parents by the change in the boy's emotional attitude to life. From being a happy, stable child he became not merely rather difficult but characterized by a special quality of facetiousness and excessive light-heartedness, which hinted at strong anxiety and distrust underneath. When the mother saw this facetiousness settling down into a characteristic attitude and realized the strain the child was evidently feeling underneath, she took the first opportunity the boy gave her by asking again about his nannie to tell him about her accident and illness. She explained that she had not told him before because she had been afraid that it would worry him too much. But now, as he asked questions she answered them, without going into unnecessary details, but giving him the essential truth and showing that she felt seriously about it. After this conversation the boy lost the sense of undue strain and anxiety and completely lost this unpleasant quality of facetiousness which he had developed so strongly. He returned to a normal confident attitude, with complete trust in the grown-ups around him. I would not suggest, and this boy's mother would not suggest, that it is necessary to give every detail of such a tragic happening to a little child, but such evidence points to the fact that it is no use evading the essential truth of the situation to the child and pretending that something unimportant has happened when there has been a really tragic event.

Now in your little daughter's case the loss of the nannie is not so serious an event as happened to the nurse of this boy, but nevertheless it is serious from the child's point of view, and you can be sure she knows that you are pretending and under-estimating the reality of her feelings of loss. It would be far better to show frankly that you do appreciate her feelings of loss and sympathize with them and are to be relied upon as a completely truthful person.

You will probably find that the child will cling to you less than she has done when she has confidence in your promise to come back. It is, of course, clear from your letter that the child was specially sensitive to this type of situation and therefore all the more needs full understanding and help. If the outbursts still occur, I would handle them firmly and quietly. The fact that the child is happy when you are away although she finds the parting so difficult should reassure you.

Q. My little daughter, who is three years eight months is a perfectly bonny child, happy, lovable disposition, and I think quite intelligent for her age. There is just one thing that worries me, and that is when she is spoken to she nearly always pretends she has not heard, and the first word that follows is "Eh?" I've proved repeatedly that she does know what has been said; it just is a habit she has. Also I've corrected her and told her that if she must ask what has been said to say "Pardon", or "What do you say?" but she will not grasp it. Now I just ignore her when she says, "Eh?" and she immediately says, "Pardon". Do you think this is the best way of breaking her of it? I've been treating her this way for over a week, but she still continues. She also forgets to say, "Please", very often. When this happens I either say, "Is that the way to ask?" or "I should say please", and she at once corrects herself. She will say "Excuse me", "I'm sorry", and is quite polite in every other way without having to be told. It is so disheartening day in and day out to find that she does not improve. M. is an only child with no other companions.

A. The whole question of training in politeness is a delicate one. If one cares only for obtaining the form of politeness, the actual words "please", thank you", "sorry" and so on, one can as a rule get these by strict demands and punishments. But obtained in that way most of us would feel they were quite worthless. The whole point about these conventional modes of speech is surely that they indicate a real wish to please others, and a real sense of considerateness and friendliness. If one can ensure that state of mind, the conventional speech can be left to take care of itself. The state of mind, if genuine, will last on through life and ensure happy social relations wherever the child goes. The form of words, unless it springs from friendliness in the mind, will only last as long as we are there to enforce it.

This attitude of mind cannot be made to appear in the child on *demand*. It is a matter of growth, and it grows in response to our own friendliness and consideration. It will come naturally from the child's actual living experience of friendliness and consideration in the grown-up around him. If *we* are consistently polite and considerate, treating the child as a *person*, with all the personal respect we should give to a grown-up, it is very rarely indeed that he will not respond with equal courtesy.

From your letter it sounds to me as if your little girl had these general characteristics of lovableness and friendliness which you desire in her, but that for some reason she has developed this single habit that you find so tantalizing. Now I think that your suggestion of ignoring her "Eh?" is much the best. It is much more likely to lead her away from it than any scolding or reproach. But in any case if a little girl of three years and eight months were perfectly polite all the time one would surely suspect she was a little machine and not human at all! It would really be quite unnatural. I should not worry very much about her sometimes forgetting to say "please", but I should be very careful to say it to her myself. And I would not accede to any request she made in any domineering or tyrannical tone. I don't think, however, that it would do any harm occasionally to make your friendly request for her to say "please" without being distressed if she forgets, and without making too much of it. If you fuss about it, you run the risk of spoiling her whole relation with you.

Q. So much is said about the importance of the mother in the child's first years; what difference is it likely to make if, as in our case, the father tends to be the most important person to our small boy of just three? He is a tremendously active child and very capable for his age, but he cannot bear to be alone for more than half a minute not only because he is afraid but also because he must have someone to share what he is doing and take an active interest in it, and also he seems to find it necessary to say all his thoughts out aloud to someone. There is no other child in the family nor any at all in the vicinity, nor even a nursery school. For financial and other reasons we do all our own work and look after him entirely ourselves. We do find it rather exhausting sometimes to keep pace with him! My husband stands the pace better than I do and they get on very well working in the garden and in other male pursuits. My husband is one of those practical people who can do anything and everything, and it is no trouble to him to bath him or anything else that is required, and though very strong is also very gentle. If it did no harm, I think we should get along very well if I could leave the child to him a great amount (especially as I hope to have another child before long) and retire more into the background. At present there does seem to be sometimes a bit of conflict in his mind about which one of us he prefers to do things for him, though we try to occasion none, and as I seem to be one of those people who find life a strain unless I have a fair amount of time to think my own thoughts, and get rather exhausted in co-operating for long in his activities —I feel perhaps it would be a good thing to reduce any cause for conflict. At present he turns to me in trouble mostly, though I don't know that even that would happen were I to leave him more to his daddy—I have a feeling that he would prefer to concentrate on one of us and would find his daddy all sufficient. Would it do any harm?

A. Surely the father is always an important figure in the little child's life, at any rate after the first year? We cannot doubt that the mother is the most important during the first year, but a great many children in the second and third years turn to their father as a person whom they can admire and gain security from. When the father is an understanding person, interested in the child and sympathetic with him, in addition to all the qualities of a grown-up man which the small child so much reveres, he can be of enormous help even to the little child. It certainly could not do the slightest harm for you to leave the boy more to his father. But I would not go too far in that direction. I cannot see why the child should be in the hands of one or the other parent, why they should not share in his training and in companionship with him. In fact, most children find the greatest emotional stability if both parents do share, at any rate to some extent, in their upbringing and their daily companionship. To have either parent exclusively or to an excessive degree is liable to lead to one-sided development in the child. What he needs is parents who are in harmony, who can do different things but do them together, and who can both give freely of their special services and special qualities to the child. Many children go through a phase of wanting one parent more than another, and it may be that your little boy is at present in the stage when he so much admires what his father can do and so much wants to be like him that you are temporarily eclipsed in his feelings of interest. It is surely an excellent thing that father and son like working in the garden together and that the boy's father can bath him and tend him. I don't think you need have any anxiety on this point. Later on he may come back to you, but it is perfectly normal to want more of his father at this time. Let him see that you don't mind his spending his time with his father, but remain loving and friendly and helpful to him. That will lessen the conflict in his mind.

Q. Your remarks about children playing alone have amazed me, and it would be extremely interesting to hear the grounds for your views, as your opinion is certainly to be respected. It would be extremely bad for a child to have no companionship at all, but it seems to me that if he has companions for a large part of the time, a short time alone can only do him good, especially in a comparatively well-to-do home, where he has a mother and nurse devoting almost all their attention and energy to him, thereby providing a good deal of mental stimulus. A child of two has a day of about nine or ten waking hours. During that time he is constantly having new impressions thrust on him and new accomplishments suggested to him, either consciously or unconsciously, on the part of his companions. In other words, his mind is being constantly stimulated, except in sleep. No grown-up could stand so much mental stimulus; those who really use their minds almost always find they need a quiet time alone, and those who live constantly with companions usually cease to use their minds for useful purposes. Surely this would apply to a child too. An hour or so to try over his new ideas and achievements by himself will encourage habits of concentration and thought, and tend to fix his knowledge firmly in his mind. You have said too, that most children who enjoy playing alone all the time are usually dull and unintelligent or anti-social. My own experience is limited to my own child. But the qualities that seem to strike other people most are just his great busy-ness and concentration. He is usually completely absorbed in something, trying to puzzle out how it works, or trying to improve his skill.

And, secondly, his strong sense of humour and his insistence that everybody present must appreciate the joke, too. In most ways he seems to be up to the normal standard of accomplishment, and in some he is beyond it. Although he is quite happy playing alone, he is always pleased if someone joins him, and anxious to show what he has been doing. So I do not think, in spite of the slowness in learning to talk, that he is less sociable than most children.

A. I certainly do not mean to suggest that it is *never* desirable for little children to play alone. I fully agree that it is desirable that they should have the *opportunity* of occupying themselves quietly alone from time to time. It is a good thing in itself for both grown-ups and children not to be altogether dependent upon the presence of other people for content or interest. So that I would not deprive a child of the chance to play by himself, and, on the whole, I should be pleased if a child would be content to do so as an occasional thing. But that is very different from saying that *every* child *ought* to play alone, whether he wants to or not, and for a certain part of every day, right through the years of toddlerhood. It is this rigid idea for which there is no justification. To begin with, children differ very much in their temperaments, even from the cradle. What is easy and natural for one child will not necessarily be good or possible for another. Any idea of virtue or method of training which is built upon a rigid pattern for all children is certain to create more difficulties than it solves. Nor does this cut across what I am always saying about the value of a regular routine. A regular routine is absolutely essential as a background for the child's life, but, of course, it is more important in things like meal-times and bed-times and bath-times and training in cleanliness than in such a question as this. Here *regular* must not mean *rigid*. A child may be happy to play alone one day and not the next. I would always give him the opportunity, but

I would never consider that he was naughty if he preferred to be with mother or nurse on some days, or even if he were of such a temperament that he always preferred to be with someone else. Secondly, with some children it is not even a question of "temperament" but of positive fears of being left alone. As some of the letters to me dealing with this have shown, there are lots of children who are really terrified if they are left alone, or who, at any rate, feel so strongly the need for companionship that enforced solitude makes it impossible for them to interest themselves or to make their play happy and valuable. I should, therefore, think it most undesirable to compel such children to play alone, or even to suggest in any way that it was "naughty" not to want to do so. What I would do would be, as early as possible, to arrange for other little children to play with them, so that they could become more independent of the grown-ups.

My own general impression is undoubtedly that far more children between the age of one year and four prefer to play with others or with a grown-up than to be alone, though, of course, there are quite a number who will play happily alone. When they will it is fortunate, but it is neither a universal characteristic of the age nor a virtue that should be sternly enforced.

Thirdly, with regard to the suggestion sometimes made that infants should be trained to lie quietly awake for long periods. This, of course, I agree is of much value for health and development, and nothing I say about not enforcing *toddlers* to be alone applies to children under, say, six months. But the problem for children whose social interest is awakened and those who can walk and talk, who have become actively interested in people, and whose curiosity about the world is rapidly developing, is quite a different one from that of the infant under six months. Just as their diet changes and needs to change, so their needs of *mental* development change. I have known several children whose development has been definitely held up by enforced solitude. On the other hand, of course, I agree it would be a great mistake to be constantly stimulating them by talking to them, telling them stories, persuading them to play at this or that, or teaching them. But the presence of an adult is not necessarily over-stimulating. This depends, naturally, on the adult and on the way she behaves. Very many of the children described in the letters to me seem to need only the actual presence of a grown-up who can be busy about her own work, or sewing, or reading, while the child occupies himself with his own pursuits. If we just quietly respond to anything the child says to us or asks of us, there is no risk of over-stimulation. But he is certainly over-stimulated by his own imaginative terrors or tempers if we force him to stay alone against his real needs or the natural trend of his temperament. As against these fears and phantasies the presence of an adult may be not only soothing but encouraging to independence, to speech development and skills.

Q. I am nurse in a family of eleven children. I have entire charge of four dear babies, aged six, four and a half, three, and the baby, just turned two last week. The baby of two is a very healthy and strong little girl, but for two months she has been very difficult. In the nursery she wants all the toys for herself, and if one of the other children wants to take one, she howls for hours. I've tried to show her other interesting things, or to speak about her Teddy bear that she loves particularly, but it is no better. And very often when she wants a toy, if she gets it she is not contented, and screams for another. I think it is very bad for her and for the other children. I've tried also punishing her, putting her in the corner, and one day she was screaming for three hours, so I put her to bed in the end. I'm afraid it is not a good thing, as she is very excitable. As my nursery consists of several children, I try to teach unselfishness as much as possible; but I must say all the children rather spoil their baby sister. This, of course, makes it more difficult for the little one to understand when they want a toy or not. At the same time, the children are rather young to understand that it is bad for their little sister to be spoilt—the eldest being fourteen.

A. You certainly have your hands full with four small children, even if they are all contented and happy, but the problem of dealing with the youngest child in such circumstances especially if she is rather wilful, cannot be an easy one. She knows her own power to tyrannize only too well, and, on the other hand, seeing all the other children round her must be such a stimulus to her own envy and jealousy that it will not be easy to win her to friendliness and contentment. But obviously it will be very bad for her if she settles into the regular habit of tyrannizing over you and the older ones by her screaming fits, and if the other children are in this way led to spoil her by giving her all she demands. You will need to be very firm and yet patient and cheerful, simply not allowing her to get any favour or privilege as a result of her screaming.

I don't think that it will do her any harm to put her to bed when she has these severe screaming fits, as that will give her a chance to get calm. But I should not scold her sharply. I should try to talk to her pleasantly and easily and win her by positive suggestion to friendly acceptance of other people's wishes.

It would, however, be a very great help if you could get the other children to co-operate with you in being sensible with the child. The six-year-old at least should be able to understand the need neither to spoil nor to tease the little one. Many children, even of four and six, have a strong protective impulse towards tiny ones, and you might be able to call this out for your help. But, of course, they should all be asked to respect the little girl's own property. She should be allowed to have some of her very own toys, and these should only be used by the others if she really consents. However, I daresay she will still go on wanting the toys the others are playing with, even if she has some of her own. You will need to see that she gets her reasonable share and reasonable consideration without being either thwarted or spoilt. But all this will necessarily take time. One cannot train a wilful child to sense and contentment in a few days or a few weeks, even with the best methods in the world. One can only go steadily on in the right direction, knowing that time and growth are one's best helpers.

Q. Could you advise me upon small children making happy associations with other small children without learning too many selfish and unpleasant habits? Pat is a happy, healthy, normal infant of nineteen months. Although rather small for her age she is exceptionally bright, saying practically everything, including words like telephone and elephant, runs quite fast, and so far has been eager to share with others, giving the pup her biscuits and handing her toys to other little tots. However, we have had one or two unfortunate experiences lately which are beginning to leave their mark. Pat was playing quite happily with a small boy a few months older, when he suddenly decided to ride into her quite vigorously with his tricycle, causing a rather frightening fall. Later he threw a big rubber ball in her face, causing her to fall backwards. Another time we were playing happily on the beach when an apparently nice little girl joined us. After a few minutes' happy play, the visitor seized Pat's spade and pail and tried to make off with it. When Pat reached for it back she received a sharp crack on the head with the spade for her pains. Later on we went off in great glee to Pat's first party. Pat was rather small for the games, so she amused herself climbing up and down a small flight of six stone steps. Another wee tot was sitting on the top step crayoning, when suddenly, as quick as a flash, he stood up and pushed Pat backwards down the steps. I caught her halfway fortunately, but she had already received a nasty bump on the head. These incidents may sound as if I am a careless mother, but in every case I have been on the spot trying to keep a watchful protectiveness over her without being too fussy and interfering. Childish hands are so quick, and then it is sometimes embarrassing to deal with matters in which other people's children are involved. As there is a possibility that Pat may not be able to have any brothers and sisters of her own it is essential that she should be able to have lots of fun with playmates. I realize that small folks always adjust themselves to conditions as they grow older, but if there is anything I could do to prevent her acquiring the "pushing" and "taking" and other unpleasant habits, and yet at the same time be able to hold her own and not feel inferior in any way, I should be glad of a little helpful guidance along these lines.

A. Your little girl has been rather unusually unlucky in her first experiences These things often do happen in play with other little children; but it is the suddenness of them that is frightening to the child. Provided there are not too many such happenings the ordinary child soon appreciates that there is nothing very much to them. Certainly, in such a situation as climbing up and down the stone steps children of these ages need very careful supervision. I should stand very close to so young a child who was climbing stone steps. You must have done so to be able to catch her half way, of course, but I would be even closer in my supervision. A knock with a wooden spade on the head is another matter. It cannot hurt very much, and would not be so frightening as being pushed backwards down the steps. I should not worry if your little girl starts doing a few of these things to other people's children. If she is developing healthily, she is sure to do this. Professor Katherine Bridges, who has made very careful studies of the behaviour of little children with each other, is definitely of the opinion that an experimental hostility of this kind is a normal phase of the path of development from the self-centredness of the infant to the appreciation of other people as persons and true co-operative feeling. The child who is afraid ever to do such things as pushing and pulling other children would really have something wrong with her development. If, when these little actions happen, you yourself are undisturbed and good humoured, and do not treat them as major events, you will find that the child herself is able to bear them without more than a momentary unhappiness. In such a situation as the rubber ball being thrown in your little girl's face, I should help her to get up and to pick up the ball and throw it back again, saying good-humouredly that the boy "did not know it would make her fall. Perhaps if she throws it back to him and he throws it again, she can manage it without falling." She will not be able to do much with a ball yet, of course, but this attitude would help her to realize that the little boy was probably seeking her friendship rather than meaning to frighten and hurt her. It would be a mistake to try to prevent her from doing any of the natural pushing and taking which children normally do at her age. Good-humoured self-assertion is quite a desirable quality, and with a year or two's further development the children will discover that they can get the same pleasure of self-assertion in doing more constructive things together. Meanwhile, I certainly should keep a watchful eye over really serious situations such as the stone steps.

Q. I have a little girl of four years old, and I want to adopt a baby girl as young as possible, about April. I want your advice, please, as to how to tell and explain this to S. I must add that last May I had a baby boy who only lived ten days. S. knew all about it before he was born, for some months, and, although she was at times obviously jealous, was very interested and excited. She was very disappointed when he died—and from time to time, ever since, has talked about him, and wanted another— and once cried bitterly because "she hadn't got a sister", like some child she knows. So I think she will be quite pleased about it, but I want to explain it to her properly, and yet not in such a way that she may later on say things which might make the adopted one think it was different.

A. It is not altogether easy to know what would be the best to say to your own little girl in these circumstances. But it would seem wisest to be quite simple and say that you are going to take care of a little baby who has no mother of her own, and that you are doing this both because you want to do it yourself, and because you know that she, your little daughter, would like to have a sister to take care of. It would not be wise to try to pretend to the child that the adopted baby was really your own. That would be doing an injustice to her, since she would know it was untrue; and would be no help to the adopted one, since it would queer the pitch in your child's mind towards her. It would be better to be truthful—and to the adopted child herself, too, later on. Your own attitude will help your daughter to welcome the baby into the life of the family, without wanting to make her feel "different". It is the love and care she gets, and the friendly affection from her adopted sister, that will matter most to the little stranger. She will be able to bear the truth if there is love there too—but no mere pretence will comfort her, and it would only tempt your little girl to tease her. I don't mean that I should start telling the adopted child in very early days that she is not really your own—but that there should never be any lying or pretence about it when any questions are asked or comments made.

RELATIONSHIPS WITH PARENTS

Q. I have a small boy of two years, nine months, who objects very strongly to anybody except me doing anything for him. Until Brian was two years old I looked after him entirely. However, this year we were able to have a maid. I still continued to do all the essential things for Brian, but I wanted the girl to take him for his afternoon walk—so that I could have some freedom. We nearly always had a fuss on these occasions (it was about three times a week)—cries of, "Mummy!" and, "Don't want to go walk with Mary." It was only with great subterfuge that he ever got out without this fuss. I found that if I talked it over with him he seemed worse—not better. I made the change after our holiday, when for three weeks Brian had all my attention. We are now having great struggles. He's all right just playing with Mary. But he simply won't let her dress him, or take him to the w.c., etc. So I have had to give in and continue doing these things for him. As regards the afternoon walks—so far we have all gone out together, and then when his attention was distracted I slipped away. I did this in order to get him used to being with Mary on his own, and he hasn't made any real fuss, just kept on asking where I was, and when I would come back, etc. I should like to know the right way to go about this matter. Whenever I do go anywhere I keep on wondering if he is good, or if he is fretting for me.

A. Part of the trouble arises from the age of your boy. It is between two and three years of age that the child, whether boy or girl, is normally attached very strongly to one adult, usually, of course, the mother, but sometimes a nurse if the nurse has done more for him. This attitude changes very much after three years, provided the child has opportunities to play with other children, but up to three it is quite a normal thing for a child to resent losing the services of a loved mother or nurse, even for a short time. Not every child shows it, but the majority do. It would not, however, be wise to let him tyrannize over you in this respect. Where you have good reasons, connected with your husband's or your own social life, to leave the child, it would be best to do so, without feeling guilty about it. The fact that you yourself feel so anxious about him must influence his behaviour. Children are extraordinarily sensitive to the attitudes of adults, and you can be quite sure that your boy knows that you yourself are uneasy about leaving him, and that you perhaps even get some comfort from feeling that he will be fretting for you. Now if you are confident with the way your maid handles the boy, as you seem to be, and you know that your reasons for leaving him are good ones, then it would help the boy most if, when you do leave him, you would simply put the whole matter out of your mind and not worry about him, but come back to him cheerfully and joyfully. This would help the boy to become more independent. If he knows that you are so anxious he is more likely to fuss. If you go quietly and firmly about the whole matter, giving him plenty of companionship but not letting him interfere with your other legitimate interests in life, then you will find that he will grow out of this special difficulty as he matures emotionally according to his age.

Q. 1. *I have a baby girl of five months. She is a picture of content and good health, is entirely breast-fed, sleeps well, and is the right weight for her age according to her birth-weight. She was born eleven months after her father and I were married and of course last year we had no holiday together. We should so like to have one this year, of a week or a fortnight, and by the time it is due, the baby will be ten or eleven months old. I have asked my sister to look after her. She is devoted to babies and very successful with them. I look after G. entirely myself, but have a daily maid who will have more to do with her when she needs more watching. I thought of leaving them here, so that the baby's routine could be exactly as usual. Do you think this is likely to lead to trouble? I have thought very seriously since reading of the child who was upset by just a week-end's absence, and naturally I do not wish to take risks.*

Q. 2. Is it fair for parents who look after their children themselves usually, to go away for a fortnight's holiday and leave them? Will the children suffer any emotional ill-effects? We wish this summer to go for a holiday alone. By that time my little girls will be three years and one year old respectively. Their Grandma could come for a few days beforehand for the children to get to know her, and then she would be left in charge with the help of the maid, whom the children love, and whom I have never found behaving towards them in any way but that I should approve. The routine would go on for them as usual. I should be able to explain to N. that Mummy and Daddy were going for a holiday and would come back "another day". She remembers when the maid had her holiday last year, and when Daddy came back she said firmly, but not tearfully, "No Daddy go on a holiday again". The baby, I feel, will not be affected provided that she has a few days to get used to her new "nurse". N. is very sensible, and since we have always kept our word to her she trusts us utterly.

A. This is not an easy problem on which to give advice, since there certainly are some children who react very badly to such absences of the mother, and especially of *both* parents. Much, however, depends upon the way the arrangement is carried out, and after all, mothers and fathers have their needs and their rights as well as children. Not only so, but if mothers try to sacrifice themselves too much for their little children, this is bound to react upon their own health, and, therefore upon their tempers, and make it harder for them to deal with the difficulties that inevitably arise with all children. I do not, therefore, think that one would ever be justified in saying that mothers should *not* leave their children for a holiday, But one is justified in saying that every possible care should be taken to make the situation easy for the child. It sounds as if both the writers would be able to make such arrangements as would greatly reduce the sense of loss to the child.

In the first case the baby will probably hardly notice the change. In the second the children are older, and even the one-year-old can be aware of such important events. Since, however, both the maid and the grandmother are likely to care for the children in the way which the mother herself does, it seems reasonable and sensible for the parents to take this much needed holiday. It is not to be expected that the event will be free from difficulties for the child. The actual fact that parents have a life of their own and needs and interests of their own is a hard lesson for some little children, since they do really want to feel that parents want to live only for the satisfaction of *their* needs and desires. It is therefore likely that the elder child will be tearful and fretful. But she will get over this all right, since she has such reason for trusting her mother. It would be well to tell the three-year-old a day or two beforehand, or even longer than that if it seems likely that she could feel there was some impending change. I would not announce the holiday to her before the grandmother arrives, however. I would let her get to know her grandmother for two or three days, and only then tell the child that you are going away for two weeks. I would tell her just where you are going; if possible, show her a picture of the place, and send her daily postcards, so as to let her have a share in the experience. One of the difficulties the child has in bearing these situations arises from the fact that absence to the little child's mind, is hardly different from death. She cannot really feel sure that you are still there in the world, since the name of a strange place cannot seem very real to her. But every device by which you can make it real to her, and keep a constant cord of communication will help her to get over the worst of her anxieties. Will you be taking the child herself for a holiday later on? If so, it would be just as well to speak of this beforehand, when you are telling her about your own holiday. If you cannot arrange for her to get away to the sea later, then I would find some sort of special treat for her to have when you came back, for example, a week entirely devoted to herself in the way of excursions and visits, picnics, etc., of a kind that you know she would enjoy. With these precautions, I think no one could say you would not be justified in having your own holiday.

Q. *Father asks whether anything can be done to ensure that his children will not shirk responsibility when they are grown up.*

A. Such a question, from one who has the wisdom to look far ahead into his children's future, reminds us that the nursery world is but a part of the larger world of social life. In our ways of helping the development of our children we have to remember what the larger world will demand of them. Even in the nursery years we need to think of what children are to grow into as well as what they are at the moment. We don't nowadays, for instance, live in the sort of society where everything is built upon authority. It would be much simpler for parents if we did. But, in fact, we have to prepare our children for a social life based very largely upon the responsibility of the individual and upon mutual services. And so this particular question lies very near to the heart of our problem as educators.

But it has to be said at once that there are no certain recipes for ensuring that any particular child will be a leader rather than a follower, any more than there are sure and certain ways of making him into an artist or a musician. Such things depend in the last resort upon his native mental gifts and trends. But we certainly can do much to encourage the development of any social abilities our children may have, or to check and inhibit them.

To begin with, a little thought will remind us that the child can only learn to exercise responsibility by having it. He learns to walk by trying to walk; he learns to swim by swimming; to dance by dancing. He can't learn by mere teaching in words, nor by the power of our wishes, but only by his own efforts corrected by his own experience. Even the best teaching, in, for example, writing or playing cricket or talking French, can only come home to him through his own effort and actual experience. This is equally true of social behaviour. It is useless for us to say, "Be responsible, be a leader, not a follower", unless we translate this into real and concrete opportunity. We need to give him things to be responsible for. Even the young child can have the responsibility for the arrangement of his own toy cupboard, the spending of his own pocket-money (no matter how little that is), the choice of what to do in his playtime, of the playmates he will invite to tea, of what he will do with his own piece of garden, of the places he will go to on his afternoon walk. If we want him to learn to choose for himself we need to give him the chance to choose on as many real occasions as possible. And when we do give him the choice in this way it should be a genuinely free choice, and not a pretence of one. If, for example, we tell him to choose whom he will invite to tea, and then try hard to persuade him to invite a child he doesn't want, because perhaps *we* think, "So and so is such a nice little boy," or for any reason of our own, then it isn't really the child's choice, and it would be better not to pretend that it was. There are so many ways in which the child has to accept our views and our arrangements, that when we do give him choice and responsibility it should be a genuine gift. Such practical responsibility is a most valuable training.

Another thing is clear also. If we want our children to be

socially responsible, it is essential to give them plenty of the companionship of other children from their early years. The solitary child, or the child who only sees others at occasional tea-parties cannot learn either to lead or to follow well. He may try to get his own way by squabbling and fighting; but he can only become a real leader by understanding other people and by having learnt to co-operate with them. And this can only come about through the sharing of work and play with other children in everyday group life. For some part of every day young children between infancy and school age should enjoy a time of free play with other children, if possible not very much older or younger. And in that time of play they should be as free from adult interference as possible. Within the real limits of physical safety they should be left to play as they will. In this way they learn vividly from each other that other people's wishes are real also, and that if there are leaders there must be followers. They learn this from the real, concrete experience of the give and take of social life in a way that no words of ours can possibly teach.

The child's need for companionship is as great as his need for shelter and comfort. Without such real social experience he cannot grow into a responsible social being at any age.

II. OBEDIENCE, DISCIPLINE AND PUNISHMENT

I HAVE recently had a number of letters from parents about a problem as old as parenthood itself—that of how to get children to obey us. The ways of the nursery need to bear some relation to what will be asked of our children in later social life. It would clearly be a mistake to train our children in ways of behaviour that would unfit them for the demands of the larger world, no matter how easy that made life in the nursery itself. And yet, of course, they aren't *yet* responsible beings, and we can't treat them as if they were. What we ask of them has to be suited to their needs and powers at each stage as they grow. We should probably all agree about this in a general way; the problem is to see quite clearly what *is* the best thing at each stage.

Now, there can't really be any question as to whether or not the little child should be asked to obey us, in some things and for some purposes. The call for obedience, as and when it is needed, is part of the biological responsibility of the parent. It does not need to be justified. And it has its roots deep in the nature of the little child himself. Obedience comes quite naturally to him, if we ask for it in the right way. But it is not an end in itself. It is a *means* of education, not a final purpose. The problem really is one of *what* we shall ask children to do, or say they must not do; and of *how* we give our commands and prohibitions.

Many people's difficulties come from not being clear about these things beforehand. If we are muddled in our own minds about why we want obedience, and when and how we want it, we are very likely to ask for it when it isn't really valuable; or to demand it in such a way that we actually stir contrariness or obstinacy. Or else our own uncertainties get passed on to the children, and they never really know whether we mean what we say or not. And so we are liable to get into a vicious circle of scolding and nagging by nurse or parent, and of defiance and "answering back" (to use the words of one correspondent) by the children. When once this sort of mutual habit is set up, it is not easy to break. But sometimes it would help a little if we made a determined effort to get quite clear in our own minds what it is all about, and how and why and when we ask those things which the children have got into the way of disobeying.

In the first place, when we say that the child "should obey", we obviously don't mean that he should never do anything without being told, and never have any way of his own. Nor that we really want him to be docile to our mere whim and fancy. That would be sacrificing the whole of his future to our present convenience, and would make him a useless sort of person. What we surely imply when we say that he should obey us is that our particular demands are reasonable and just, and that obeying them will really be good for him. But are we sure that we are making no mistake about this?

Grown-ups very often *have* asked children to do what was bad for them, as, for instance, when we used to make tiny children "sew a fine seam" with fine thread. We believed that we were educating them; but later on we came to see that in fact we were just damaging their eyes, health and tempers.

Are we sure that as parents or nurses we are not making any mistakes of that kind? Do we ask our children to do *only* what is really suitable for them at their age and stage of development? That is the first thing to think about. The second is the *way* in which we ask for obedience.

Do we remember, for instance, when making our requests, how much less sense of past and future the young child has, and how much more he lives in the immediate present than we do? If we remember this, we shall also remember how much more urgent his desires are than ours, and how much sharper a disappointment or a denial is to him than to us.

And since he is necessarily given up more completely to anything in which he is interested, without thought of time and place, it means much more to him than to us when we have to interrupt what he is doing because we want him, for example, to come to dinner or to go out for a walk. If we remember this we shall not wantonly and suddenly cut across his interests, but shall give him a little notice, so that he has time to take in the request. If when he is in the middle of an absorbing game, and we have to call him to come to a meal, we can give him a few minutes' warning, "In ten minutes it will be dinner-time", he is much more likely to come cheerfully and readily than if we tell him only at the very moment we want him to come, and expect him to do it on the instant. We ourselves hate to be suddenly interrupted when we are reading or talking to a friend. The child hates it, too. And he appreciates our consideration very keenly. Such consideration can quite well go along with firmness about the request when it is actually made—and this, too, the child appreciates.

Again, having made sure that we are asking the right thing, do we take it for granted in a cheerful voice and friendly manner that he will do what we wish? If we ourselves are calm and friendly in our demands, he is more likely to agree, and to do what we want in the same friendly and cheerful way. But we *can* only be calm and confident when we really are sure that what we are asking is reasonable.

As I have suggested there are at least two important sides to the problem: (1) *What* we should tell the child to do, or say he must not do, and (2) *How* we tell him these things. I want to go a little further with the first point now.

The chief reason why it is so important to get this clear is because, if we do once make a definite demand, it is most desirable to keep to it firmly, and not to let ourselves be coaxed or stormed out of it. If we say too hastily, "You mustn't do that", or "You must do this", when we don't really mean it, and the child finds out that enough screaming or wheedling will make us give way, then there isn't much hope of being able to get obedience when it is really necessary. It is so easy to let a child slip into tyranny, and ourselves into helpless worry. And an intelligent child is extraordinarily quick to sense weakness and half-heartedness in our demands. Such half-heartedness is no help to the child but just muddles him. It would be far better to make no pretence of telling him what to do, but leave him honestly free to do as he likes.

No! If we do make demands and prohibitions, we must keep to them. The child readily accepts conditions when he is quite clear that they are steady and firm. An enterprising child may still sometimes try to rebel and get his own way; but he won't make a habit of doing it on every occasion, like the child who does not know where he is with our hasty do's and don'ts.

But if we are going to keep to our demands and prohibitions once they are made, how very careful we need to be that they are right and wise. If we don't exercise this care beforehand, we may find ourselves in the false position of having to carry through to the bitter end, for the sake of consistency, something that in our cooler moments we don't really think worth enforcing.

Q. I venture to ask your opinion on the question whether it is desirable, and if so by what methods, to aim at being able to secure "instant obedience" before a child is old enough to understand the principle underlying its necessity. My little girl, not quite two, is as obedient as a strong-willed child who is keenly interested in what she is doing at the moment can be expected to be, but she is quite capable of assuming complete deafness, or reiterating a determined "No", or just running away if told to come here, or to put something down. Relatives tell me that she is too young to be expected to obey, and advocate the—to my mind—lazy and useless method of distracting her attention. My own view is that while obtaining her obedience by distracting her attention is a useful resource when she is tired, or when there are special reasons for avoiding a scene, it does not teach her anything, and that suitable opportunities should frequently be taken for training her to obey as a conscious act. Surely life is too dangerous for a child who will not obey a sudden order without first having some interesting distraction provided. She might be electrocuted in the interval. I should be most interested to hear your views as to whether one should wait until a child is old enough for argument before attempting to teach it obedience. If you agree that the process can be begun as soon as the child unmistakably understands what is said to it, what steps do you recommend for securing obedience, in addition to the obvious one of limiting the frequency of one's "do's" and "don'ts"? Is a mild slap on the hand that persists in touching the forbidden object a very mistaken method? Sometimes I can see no other way of preventing the child from thinking: "Mother goes on saying 'Don't touch,' but nothing seems to happen if I do." Is it a psychological fact that at barely two a child may forget a repeated command within a few seconds? My little girl's persistence in picking flowers in the garden (though I always give her some for herself whenever she shows the slightest sign of wanting them) suggests that it must be so. Sometimes I wonder if it is just that the fascination is so great that she simply cannot desist, though she knows she must not pick. If that is so, how can I deal with it? Picking flowers for her and allowing her to pick for herself in certain places do not meet the case. It is not that I attach such overwhelming importance to the devastation of my garden, but that I feel the problem is probably typical of others that we shall have to face. In case it is relevant, I had better mention that the child has the very hopeful characteristic of being more obedient if I leave her for a moment or two than if I am present. She will remain glued to a chair if I tell her not to get down till I come back, though, of course, I never strain this virtue too far. Another small point: I have always been lavish with praise when it has been earned, and now K. is beginning to pat herself on the back in a way that is amusing, but might become intolerable in time. "Kitty's a kind girl to bring that flower to show Mother." "Good girl not to drop that parcel." "Brave Kitty not to cry." Such phrases as these are sometimes reiterated in tones of indescribable smugness, but provided it passes off, don't you think it is preferable to the sullen defensiveness of the child who imagines that people only comment on its behaviour in order to condemn? If you think I have been overdoing encouragement I should like to be told.

A. Instant obedience is only given by a child to a parent on the basis of trust and confidence, built up by experience. One can, of course, enforce it by fear. That is to say, one can stir up so much fear in many children that they will obey as long as the feared grown-up is present, although this has very little bearing upon what they will do when there is no risk of being found out. That, however, is not the situation which you desire. The instant obedience which is based upon love and trust cannot be secured by our mere willing it to happen, nor is it possible for many children to give during the first two or three years. It can be given by a child of four or five, who has learnt that his parents will not demand it without good reason. Two years of age is very rarely a period when a child can obey. Occasionally a child has such a naturally docile temperament that she will obey at any age, but this is not very usual, and not necessarily the most desirable attitude of mind. Any child who is going to be independent and resourceful in later life is certain to show a phase of obstinacy and contrariness in the second and third years, and your little girl is behaving quite typically when she resists your demands if you interfere with her pursuits of the moment. We cannot hope to train tiny children to the virtues of later childhood, and we shall only waste our time and exasperate ourselves and them if we try to do so. It needs real supervision by the adult and appropriate planning of the environment to keep the child of two years, or even three and four, safe. And it is quite useless to imagine that you can ensure this safety by mechanical obedience from the child. But surely you are exaggerating the dangers? In ordinary circumstances, how is a child of two to get electrocuted? If you are taking her by tube, for example, you are not going to rely upon any habit of instant obedience to keep her from running on to the line. You will surely rely upon your own arms and watchfulness to safeguard her, without putting upon her the tremendous burden of her own safety? The same applies to crossing the road, and to any of the risks that carelessness might bring in the way of a little child in the ordinary house; for example, dangerous knives, matches, etc. These are not the grounds for training obedience. The value of obedience is surely a social one, and the type of obedience that is socially valuable is one that rests upon experienced confidence and trust and love of the authority that demands obedience. As regards touching the ordinary objects, we have no right to have things about within reach of the child that are really dangerous to her. I would not take a two-year-old into a room where there were precious objects that I did not want broken. One can expect a child of four or five not to touch other people's belongings, but not a two-year-old. I would certainly never expect a child of two or under to be able to resist the charm and attraction of flowers in a garden. By the time she is three and a half or four, she can understand clearly enough that some things are for her and others for other people, although even then one should not expect too much in the way of being able to resist temptation. But at two years, it is really asking for the impossible to expect the child not to do what she sees her mother doing—reaching out for the lovely flowers and picking them. She cannot understand, and there is nothing in the child to enable her to check the impulse. Such a power is a matter of slow growth, and there is no use expecting it before the time is ripe.

It certainly sounds to me as if you had been overdoing the giving of praise. It is far better to take good behaviour for granted as the ordinary stuff of life—at any rate, to a greater extent that you seem to have been doing. However, you need not worry about her comments upon herself. They are natural enough, too, and are only part of the child's attempt to articulate the whole of her experience. However, I should be a little more sparing of the praise. A smile and a "Thank you" are usually enough reward for the child.

Q. Carol, aged three years nine months, has always been a child with a very decided personality, and a tremendously strong will. She has any amount of surplus energy, and a great desire to be independent. She walked alone at eleven months, fed herself as soon as she could hold a spoon; has used the high lavatory seat, and managed her own knickers, etc. for more than a year, undresses and dresses herself, in fact refuses to have anything done for her which she can do for herself. Added to which she is a very big child, and is often taken for five years old. Our present difficulty is over the vexed question of obedience, and as usual the situation has been aggravated by the fact that owing to illness we have been staying at my mother's for more than a month past, during most of which I have had to be in bed. Although Carol dearly loves the grandparents, and knows them very well and often stays a few days with them, she has missed her nursery, I think, and her toys and sandpit, and the freedom she has at home, as well as all the attention she is used to from me. There had, of course, been little difficulties at home because Carol seemed at times absolutely incapable of doing as she was told, but I haven't worried much about them, as I assumed that things would improve; but now there seem to be continual struggles. For instance, while I was writing this Granny was putting Carol to bed, and I heard her ask Carol to wait while she found some cold cream for her face. "No, no", Carol said, and began to go upstairs, so, as the light was out of her reach and the stairs in darkness Granny had to go after her. "Where's my cold cream?" she asked, and when she was told that as she hadn't been obedient Granny hadn't been able to get it there was a great outcry. This afternoon while she was out Carol refused to hold Granny's hand when told to do so, ran away across the road, which I have always tried to teach her never to do, and then fell in a puddle, which, of course, spoilt her coat. After this Granny refused to take her any further and brought her straight home. I think Carol was sorry—or at any rate sorry to miss her walk—she is not easily moved to tears, but she cried bitterly for some time. I suggested that as she was disobedient and gave Granny so much trouble we should have to get out the reins we used when she was smaller, but she was very upset at the idea. She is so anxious to be thought a big girl. Naturally my mother is very troubled about all this. She thinks that it is most important not to give in to Carol, and to make her learn to be obedient, and if she is disobedient she must be smacked. Of course, I have never (or very, very rarely) smacked Carol. I have never minded having to explain just why she must do anything that I ask, and I haven't ever expected what people call instant obedience. When Carol was very much younger she was a very obedient—or perhaps it would be more correct to say, a suggestible child, now she seems determined to have her own way. What ought one to expect of a child between three and four? I think much of the trouble may be due to excessively high spirits. Have I perhaps been too easy-going in not insisting on obedience directly I speak, and punishing promptly when it is not forthcoming?

A. It is surely a mistake to think of your little girl's development merely in terms of obedience. It is splendid that she is so independent and able to do so much for herself, especially as her independence takes such a positive form, and is not mere defiance. It is quite different from a child who merely lies down and screams and says she won't. There is such a positive drive towards skill and practical and social ability, which is obviously going to make her a splendid person in later life. It seems a pity to underestimate the great value of all these positive characteristics of the child, and it is clear that when you tend to do so the effect upon the child is wholly undesirable. She simply feels that you do not value all the good things in her and do not want her to grow skilful and independent. It is understandable that the child's grandmother should be nervous about such a degree of independence, and inclined to feel happier if the child leaves things more to her care. But such a policy is not going to help a child with these natural characteristics. I would suggest that whether or not you should give in to the child depends entirely upon the particular situation of the moment. Sometimes it would be better to let the child take the lead. For example, when Carol went upstairs instead of waiting for the cold cream, I cannot see why Granny should feel it necessary to go after her and put the light on. Why should the child not have been allowed to go up in the dark? If she was able to do this, it would not only do no harm but would be an excellent opportunity for developing courage and skill. The implication that she is too little to go upstairs alone in the dark was probably very unwelcome to the child, who was feeling herself a brave and clever person. Now if she were unwilling to go anywhere alone in the dark you might write to me and say: "What am I to do about my little girl, who is afraid of the dark?" Surely this was a situation where her independence was more valuable than her momentary impatience, and it would have been better for Granny to go and get the cream and leave the child to go upstairs by herself. The problem of running across the road is a much more difficult one, because there is real danger there. But if Granny did not make a fetish of obedience as such, but only demanded it where it was objectively necessary, the child would be far more likely to give it freely and happily, because she would then know that her spiritual independence was not at stake, but that Granny had a real reason, one concerning the genuine welfare of the child, for demanding this particular act of trust and obedience. Since she is so anxious to be thought a big girl, I would point out to her that *big* children are sensible enough to wait when crossing the road for the grown-up to go with them. I would not advise the reins, since this would not only be humiliating to the child, but would increase her compulsion to be defiant. I would say to her: "You are such a big and sensible person that I want you to show how clever you are by going across the roads with Granny. If you don't want to hold her hand, hold on to her coat or skirt." I would even say that Granny, too, feels happier in crossing the road if she is going together with someone else. And if they talk it over and say: "Now I think we might cross, don't you? the road seems clear", in a sensible and comradely way, instead of Granny treating it as a matter of authority and obedience, the child would be a hundred times safer. Her general development sounds so good that it would be a great pity to inhibit her constructive impulses and make her feel that these were not valued by turning the problem into one of authority and obedience.

Q. 1. Last night my elder boy of three years and two months had a temperature, so this morning, although better, I let him stay in his cot with plenty of toys to play with, and he was very happy. When he got bored with these toys, I gave him a pair of scissors to cut paper and cardboard. When I next came in, it was to find that he had cut pieces out of a new dressing gown. He knew as well as I did how wrong it was, and he had been given plenty of things he could cut. Now, if you suggest my taking him upon my lap for a good talk, it would never have helped nor impressed upon him the fact that it must never happen again; neither would taking away a favourite toy help, as I have tried all that. He either doesn't listen half the time, or it "goes out as soon as he takes it in". He is most independent of his toys and will not miss them. So what I do is, like to-day, take down his knickers and give him a good sharp slap on the correct place (it hurts me more than him, believe me), and leave him to himself for a while. I also put the scissors in his room and told him he could certainly have them there, but not to touch them. I am sure a child of his age is quite old enough to learn that some things that are about must not be touched. After all, you often suggest that little children should be given certain responsibilities, which they generally enjoy. This must surely apply in a negative form also? I know now if G. ever touches scissors without being allowed to, I need only say: "Darling, you remember what happened last time, don't you?" and he will put them back. Whereas in any other case of punishment I know him well enough to say he would not obey.

It is not a case of my losing my temper (though I sometimes feel very angry), but I really do believe it is putting less strain on a child of his type. What is your opinion? They know only Mummie can smack them, nobody else, and they always get it at once when the mischief is done, never have to wait or fear any coming unpleasantness; and once over, we are all happy together again and the incident is never unnecessarily referred to.

My smaller boy is twenty months, and the same applies to him, although, of course, I expect less of him. Please do not think after this that there is much smacking in our house; there are weeks and weeks without any, and it only occurs when a principle is involved. So I do not think "a smack out of love" can harm.

Q. 2. *I am writing on the vexed question of obedience! My little girl is only just two, but I want to start right. Of course, I started long ago, but now she is getting to be more of a little girl than a baby. Alison naturally is feeling her feet and seeing what she can do with me, and the old way of just saying, "No, baby", won't do any more!*

The more one reads "modern child" books one sees that discipline of the old-fashioned variety is quite out of date, but I am afraid I am one of the old-fashioned though young people who heartily believe in the "food sleep" methods—up to a point, of course. For instance, I think to resist correcting a child because of its turning squint-eyed if you do, etc., is all nonsense. I should hate to be a nagging mother always saying, "Don't", but what is one to do when the child won't do what you say, even though it's purely mischief? Alison is very mischievous, very intelligent and quick, and talks well though is not two till next week, and I could so easily do the wrong thing and make her into a disobedient, defiant child. She is generally very happy and sweet natured, but certainly has a very strong will of her own. I have no wish to crush this, but I don't want her to "get on top" of me. I know, too, that one should divert the attention to something constructive, instead of saying "Don't", but this is not always possible. Also it's not always a case of "Don't", but sometimes "Do". What do I do when, for instance, Alison knows quite well she is not allowed to stand up in Daddy's study chair (one of the dangerous tip-back variety with casters), yet out of mischief, I suppose, deliberately goes on it again and again and stands. I suppose the books would say, "Let her do it and fall backwards and see what it feels like", but I couldn't let her injure herself, as she would do, just to teach her. I repeatedly said "No, Alison", and diverted her attention a dozen times, but back she went and was up in a flash, full of giggles. Whereupon, I took her down and spanked her! She cried then and I felt awful. And when I want her to do something, such as "Come here and put your coat on for walk"—although she loves the idea of "walk and coaty"—she runs away or stays tight in a corner and will not come. I know it's only mischief at this age, but surely she should be obedient now, and having to go across the room and fetch her out of the corner is not helping her to learn obedience. She used to do things at once if I pretended to cry, but that doesn't work now. I do want her to grow up knowing that "When I say 'Yes' I mean it, and 'No', I mean 'No', and that's the end of that". But now is the most difficult time, when they begin to feel their own powers, and when they are too young for you to explain to them why you want a thing done. Character training is difficult, but once one is on the right track one feels quite happy about it. Do, please, put me right about this, "to smack or not to smack", etc.

A. First of all, let me say that I wish I could understand how it is possible for anyone seriously to claim that smacking a child hurts her more than it hurts the child. I confess that I feel that to be complete humbug. I have such vivid memories of being smacked when I was a child myself, and when I compare those feelings with my own as a grown woman when I have smacked children, it seems to me the sheerest nonsense to suggest that it hurts me now more to smack a child than it hurt me to be smacked when I was a child.

Secondly, what is the ground, rational or irrational, for speaking of the child's buttocks as the "correct" place for smacking? That part of the body has its function in the balance and poise of the body in sitting and standing, but why it should be considered the "right" place for smacking I do not know. My only surmise is that the people who dub it "the correct place" have an unconscious awareness of the fact that by whipping the child there, as compared, for example, with smacking the child on the hand, one adds indignity and a sense of helplessness to the child's feelings, as well as the actual pain of the slap. It is also true, of course, that it is possible to develop in a child a definite, though hardly desirable, pleasure in being smacked on the buttocks, and in the case of children who know that "only Mummy can smack them" this is very liable to happen.

Now I do not want to appear to exaggerate the meaning of smacking and being smacked to a little child, but if one is going to put forward a case for smacking, one must be aware of all its implications, and really be able to appreciate what the child's feelings are about it. My description of what they do feel is not mere surmise and speculation, but is based upon definite memories of actual people. Again, I would at once agree that smacking in the way that Q.1 describes, without any fuss and only occasionally, can undoubtedly do less harm than a constant moral nagging, a threatening without anything happening, or inconsistent and confusing standards of behaviour. These children at least know where they are. They know the worst the mother will do to them, and they learn the conditions under which she will do it. Nevertheless, my own personal experience and my study of the pooled experience of other people have not taught me that this is the *best* way. It is much better than some other ways, but it is not the best. To some extent again, that depends upon the children. It would have a far worse effect upon some than upon others. I can say with absolute certainty that in my own case no one ever did me the slightest good by smacking, but a great deal of harm; and I know how many other people there are of whom the same is true. But even with children who are average and normal, happy and healthy, and bear no grudge afterwards, it is nevertheless both unnecessary and far from being the most desirable way of educating them.

Q. 1. thinks that her boy was prevented from cutting pieces

out of his dressing-gown a second time by her smacking him; but if he is an average, normal, happy and healthy child, he would certainly not, in any case, have done it a second time. He must have been tempted by the feel of the scissors on the woollen stuff to cut it in an experimental mood, and if the mother, when she found it, had said, "Please do not cut your garments; that is extremely inconvenient—here is a piece of woollen material you can cut", he would not have done it again. If he had done it again after such quiet protest, it could only have been for neurotic reasons, and then he would not be an average, normal child. She adds, "He knew as well as I do how wrong it was". That again seems to me nonsense. A child of three years could not know as well as a grown-up how wrong it was, although he would be extremely quick, from the expression of face and tone of voice of his mother, to appreciate how wrong she thought it was and how angry it made her.

What those who advocate the smacking of little children do not realize is that by having recourse to this method they simply coarsen the child's responses and make him insensitive to other more normal and delicate modes of control. The worst is assumed from the start, instead of the best, and all the ordinary motives of doing and not doing things—to please other people, or because other people demand them, or because one wishes to co-operate with other people and takes pleasure in the mutual social relation—are all cut out from the start, and they cannot grow in that atmosphere. It is like riding a horse on a hard bit from the start and making it insensitive for ever after, except to the spur and the whip. I often reflect that those who have to teach children would learn a great deal from animal trainers.

As regards the little Alison, I cannot imagine which books would say, "Let the child fall out of the chair and see what it feels like". Of course one could not let the child injure herself. But I think one could demonstrate with a doll. One could do a good deal more than "Alison's Mummy" seems to have done to help the child to understand why there is the prohibition. Don't you think the child is particularly attracted to the chair in question just because it is Daddy's, and would it not be possible to stand it with its back against the wall so that it could not possibly fall over, and let her have the fun of climbing in and out of it? I cannot see why one should want to deny this pleasure to the child. You can be quite sure that the child thinks that is what you are wanting —simply to deny this pleasure—since she cannot understand the true care for her that goes into your prohibition.

I wonder whether there is not something in the way the commands are given: "Come here and put your coat on for a walk," that raises the spirit of contrariness in the child. In any case, of course, a great many children of her age have these fits of contrariness, which are part of their normal process of growing up. As "Alison's Mummy" says, the child is "feeling her feet and finding out what she can do". She has to be allowed a certain latitude, and in general the attempt has to be made to get her co-operation rather than her obedience. This involves quite a different attitude on the part of the mother. For example, with regard to the coat, it would be better to say, "We are going out for a walk. Here is your coat. If you can't put it on for yourself I will help you." And I should let her try to put it on herself. With a child of this degree of independence and such a spirit of enterprise, it is far better to help her to learn to do things for herself, and to treat the situation as a problem of mutual adjustment and one in which the mother helps the child to learn the requisite skills, than to treat it as a situation of command and obedience.

I really do not understand what you mean when you say, "I want her to grow up knowing that 'When I say "Yes" I mean it, and "No", I mean "No", and that's the end of it.' " Surely you want her to grow up able to say "Yes" and "No"

OBEDIENCE, DISCIPLINE

for herself—able to take her place in the social world as an independent moral being, not as someone whose simple guide is docility to her mother? Obedience is surely not the end and aim, but only a convenient instrument in some situations during the process of growing up.

Q. I wrote to you with regard to my only child and on your advice sent him to a kindergarten at four, which I have never regretted. At the age of six and a half he went to a preparatory school, which he likes very much. He will be seven in March and my difficulty now is his untidyness and forgetfulness. My boy has done extremely well during this first term and is described as a most satisfactory pupil. He is certainly not dreamy but most alert, and consequently I feel the fault with regard to untidiness must be mine. I feel I could help John if I knew how to do it. At present I seem to nag him. It amazes me that a normally active-brained, very quick child should never remember to raise his cap, never remember to close a door, never remember to put his shoes on a shelf where he has put them since he could put them away at all, never remember to hang his coat up. This may seem an exaggeration to impress it upon you, but it isn't—he never remembers, and every time I say as gently as I can, "Hang your coat up John", etc., etc. This is typical. He rushes into the house from school, flings his coat, hat, gloves, just anywhere they will perch (if lucky), dashes to his room, leaves door wide open, winds up train, tears down, shouts "Where's scissors?" "Where's scissors?" snips a newspaper to pieces, most of which remain on carpet, flings scissors anywhere, roars upstairs leaving doors yawning in his wake, crams bits of paper into a truck, sings at the top of his voice and either leaves me to clear up in sheer desperation or else it is "John, hang your coat and cap up." "Oh yes." "John, shut the door please." "Oh yes." Crash. "Where did you put the scissors?" "No idea."

"*Put all the bits on a tray dear.*" "*Oh yes.*" *And without any exaggeration this goes on all day long. He doesn't resent my continual reminders, but I do feel that some good ought to come of them. As for his writing and table manners! You just wouldn't believe that. Must I go on and on, and shall I ever make any impression? Can I ignore it? I should love to pick everything up and stop nagging, but would he ever be different then? What amazes me is that wearing a cap for the first time he simply loves raising it and showing off, but he loses all these lovely opportunities because it never occurs to him. My trouble is I never get any "forrader". There is no doubt that of all his friends who come to tea no one has such shattering table manners, and I feel then people must think we behave like pigs at home. He does. He is always in such a tearing hurry and enters into everything with such zest. Can I tidy him up? Also he won't wash! Quite normal, I believe.*

A. I don't think it is at all likely that your boy forgets to do these things. It is much more likely to be a form of rebellion, of actual defiance. He may say that he forgets, but even if he does, the forgetting is itself the expression of defiance and obstinacy. Now boys of this age normally go through a period of "turning the deaf ear" in this way, especially to people at home. Six to seven and a half is one of those ages when obstinacy and defiance are most characteristic, the other, of course, being the second year of life. But whereas in the second year the child gets into a violent tantrum, at six and seven years his mode of asserting himself against authority is to be forgetful or blind and deaf to their requests. I suspect that what your boy needs is greater firmness of treatment at home. You are being too gentle and deprecatory with him. He wants a rather more robust handling. He is not a delicate little child, but a big boy who doubtless *feels* himself to be a big boy at school, and he would probably be better if you were more definite and firm in your demands, treating him more as a big boy than as a child who must be handled very tactfully. I daresay you know, if you read my letters to other people, that I very often have to suggest a greater tactfulness and reasonableness; but one can err by extremes in that direction, as well as in the lack of it, and it does sound to me as if you were too timid and indirect in your demands. I should leave him to feel the consequences of some of his refusals to be tidy. I certainly should not run after him and put his gloves and hat and coat away, but should contrive to let him suffer the disadvantages of his untidiness, and should absolutely refuse to let him have newspapers to snip to pieces on the carpet if he would not clear them up himself. I would not nag him and say "Hang your coat up", but would warn him that you are not going to wait upon him, as he is now a big school boy, and that you know that he could do these things if he would take the responsibility, and that his belongings may get damaged if he does not put them away. As regards the table manners, I would take the same line. If they are really unpleasant, I would definitely say that if he could not be a little quieter and more orderly, so as to make the meal table pleasanter for everybody else, you would want him to have his meals alone. Meals are co-operative things which no one person has the right to make disagreeable for everybody else. I would not do all this in a censorious or disagreeable way, but with a quiet pleasant firmness that yet makes the boy realize that it is an ultimatum. He will probably feel that you are respecting him more by this method than by constantly running after him and imploring him to be tidy and considerate.

Q. 1. My little girl is four and a half years old, a very exceptionally healthy and vivacious child, and of a very happy disposition, but an "only" child who gets a lot of grown-up

admiration and company and not a great deal of other children's company, except for a dancing class once a week and an occasional child to tea, as I live in a district with very few children near. I am, and always have been, very firm with her, and when I tell her to do anything I will have it done. Lately she has become so stubborn I don't know what to do with her. If I tell her to do anything of any description, she will rather undergo any punishment than do it. In fact, I find it difficult to find anything that is a punishment, as she is so full of spirits she just doesn't worry about anything. I hate to think I am breaking her spirit, and perhaps I am doing her harm by keeping on at her, but she will be unbearable if I cannot get her to understand she must obey me. For example, at breakfast she has a glass of Ovaltine, which she likes really, but this morning she played about for so long that at last I told her she must drink it. She just sat and looked at the glass for an hour, knowing that she had only got to drink it to get down and play in the garden. I put her to bed with the glass of milk there, and she cried for a little and then started singing away without a care in the world. Then she decided, I suppose, she'd had enough of it, and said she'd drink it. She started drinking it, and then tipped some out on the bed and told me, "I did it on purpose". I have never spoilt her, and my principle has always been to tell her a thing and stick to it, and if she tells me anything or promises anything to stick to it. I have given you an instance to do with food, but it is just the same with anything else. She is a child with a great deal of character, but is not difficult in any other way, just a sweet, sunny temper.
Q. 2. Your advice has been so helpful in the past that I am writing to ask you for further help. M. is now just four and very intolerant of discipline. He will obey in his own good time, but refuses to be promptly obedient indoors. When he is out for a walk he is quite good and will obey quickly, but in the house he resents an order and takes his time in complying with a request, always wanting to know the reason why. Punishment of any sort makes him defiant—"If you punish me I will never do anything

for you at all," he said to-day. I have never given in to him and my word has always been law, but I have given the reason, and up till quite recently I had no trouble with him, though he was leisurely. We live among too many "grown-ups" who criticize his lack of obedience and my handling of the situation, considering that I should have him in subjection by punishment. This rather aggravates things. How can I best tackle him? If I carry on as before, giving the reason and being content with mere obedience, will this phase pass and prompt obedience gradually develop? The defiance is only when I insist on promptness. M. is a good and reasonable boy and easy to handle though highly strung.

A. There is much in common between these two problems, although there are many differences in detail. Both children seem to have developed a defensive attitude against their environment, which suggests that there is some general factor in their handling needing consideration. In the first place, it has to be said that some degree of obstinacy and self-assertiveness against the environment is a perfectly normal thing in this period of life. Somewhere between the end of the first year and the end of the fourth every child who is not too frightened or too inhibited to be able to develop normally has a phase of sheer obstinacy. With some children it comes earlier. I have often quoted letters which describe an extreme degree of obstinacy in the second and third years. Sometimes it comes later. The degree of it and the length of time it lasts vary very much from one child to another. In a milder degree it is part of the ordinary child's adjustment to the social world and his discovery of himself as an independent person. After all, how would he develop courage and independence later on in life if he never asserted himself against the grown-ups in the early years? It takes time for the child to discover that there are ways of real self-assertion which fit in with the family life and open new avenues of skill and pleasure to him, and that he need not be defiant all round in order to prevent himself from being overwhelmed by grown-up demands. The passage from the mere obstinacy of self-defence to a reasonable courage and independence of the kind that the happy child shows at four and five and six years of age cannot be made in a day. It is a matter of growth and learning and experience. But the way the grown-ups behave, the demands they make, the conditions they create, can certainly make it more difficult for a child to discover the satisfactory forms of asserting himself as an individual and to discard the unsatisfactory ones that make for unhappiness.

It seems that these letters illustrate different modes in which the environment of these children has made it harder for them to get over the contrariness that springs from the need to assert oneself anyhow and somehow, and to learn the useful co-operative, happy ways of independence. In the case of Q.1's little girl, the first thing that it would be as well to remember is that firmness and determination in the mother will very naturally result in firmness and determination in the child. We often talk about the influence of example, but we forget that we are giving the child an example all the time, not only just when we mean to, and when we ourselves say "I *will* have it done", we are, of course, setting that as a standard of behaviour to the child, who naturally herself says "*I* will have it done"—but her way, not ours. I cannot help feeling that in this case the stubbornness of the child partly reflects the unbending firmness of the mother When a child, however, gets into such a state of mind that she will rather undergo any punishment than do anything of any description which the mother asks her to, then there is something in the general handling of the child which has exaggerated in her the normal self-defensiveness of the ordinary child. Now it sounds, on the evidence of this letter, as if the mistake that Q.1 has been making is to demand obedience all round, even in situations where it is not appropriate. I fully agree that there are situations and occasions when one must demand it and it is right to do so, but to approach the whole problem of one's relation with a little child as if the sole key to it were command and obedience is not only undesirable but often disastrous. Q.1 seems to be turning every situation into one of obedience or disobedience. For example, why should drinking a glass of Ovaltine or not be treated as a matter of obedience? The appetite of grown-ups varies; why should not the appetite of children vary, without its being turned into an issue of mere naughtiness and disobedience? It is such a pity to take one's stand on the wrong things. It would have been far better to let her go without the Ovaltine if she did not want it, and let her understand that it would be taken away after a certain time if she did not drink it. When it is taken away, this should not be done as a punishment, but as a simple matter-of-fact recognition of the fact that the child does not want to drink it.

The source of the trouble with Q.2 seems to be rather different. As the writer suggests, there are too many grown-ups who criticize the child and his mother, and make contrary demands upon him. This situation is always a difficult one. There is a hint that this mother too, is too rigid in her demands. To take the attitude that one's word must be "law" creates an atmosphere that is not always helpful to the child. One should want things to be done for good objective reasons, rather than because one's own word has to be law. With regard to promptness, which is the special difficulty with Q.2, it is surely demanding a very great deal to ask the child that he should not simply do what one wants but do it in the instant, without giving the slightest expression to his contrary wishes! It is a great help to the child if we do allow him a few moments of unwillingness; even saying, when he asserts "I shan't", "Perhaps you will do it in a minute or two", or "Perhaps you will do it later".

Q. I have lately left my little charge of four years, after having been with her two-and-a-half years. We were devoted to one another, and, except for two holidays, were hardly ever away from each other. She was a very headstrong child, and had always been peculiarly resentful of the slightest change in routine or habits. A few days after I had left I heard that she was missing me badly, and being difficult, then I heard no more for three weeks, when her mother wrote to me. Her mother wrote that she was disappointed to find from "G's" remarks and behaviour in general that I had spoiled her badly, had allowed her to disobey me, and had altogether given in to her in many ways, presumably because she had been too difficult for me. It seems that "G" constantly cried that she did not love her new nurse, but wanted her own nursie, as her nursie let her do what she wanted! She even refused certain dishes at lunch, saying I had allowed her to leave them, and made such scenes over other details of routine that her mother was sure I must have allowed her to have her own way in everything. Of course I was distressed to hear this, as I know I never allowed her to do the things she mentioned. I am therefore anxious to know if you think, that "G's" behaviour can have been due to her being overwrought by the sudden loss of me, whom she had loved as long as she could remember? I have a perfectly clear conscience over the charge of having spoiled her. I always found her obedient and easily manageable, except when her parents or relatives were present. As we lived with the family a good deal, her "difficultness" was then very apparent. But when she was alone with me she was sweet-tempered, loving, and happy and obedient. So that it does seem to me that she was upset by the change, and consequently "playing-up" to her mother and new nurse to an alarming degree, even being led by her desire to have me back into averring that I let her do as she wanted. I am afraid I have not convinced her mother that I did not spoil her, but I should like to have your opinion as to whether a child would behave like this for the reason I have named? I may add that on the two occasions when

I was away on holiday her mother admitted that "G" gave them a terrible time, and was most disobedient, but now the mother puts her behaviour at those times down to the same reason, of having been spoiled by me, which all makes me very unhappy.

A. This, is in fact, a problem of quite general psychological interest, throwing much light on the naive behaviour of little children, and on certain aspects of the relation between nurse and parents. I am sure yours is by no means an isolated case, and many mothers and nurses will be interested in it and in the questions it raises.

I haven't any doubt that the little girl is "playing up" in the way you suggest, and that the reason for this will partly be her wish to get you back. But it won't be only that. Nor will the child's mind be as deliberate and clear as perhaps you feel. The loss of her nurse and the disturbance of her accustomed life will have aroused a general resentment in her mind, and much of her headstrong behaviour since you left will, as you suggest, be directly due to this resentment. Children do get very attached to their nurses, and may feel the loss very acutely—a fact which is often overlooked, and one which needs to be taken into account even when nurse is not altogether successful. That is one reason why it is so important to find a satisfactory nurse from the beginning. One cannot play fast and loose with little children's affections. If it seems that a change is really needed, mothers would still be wise to balance against the present ills those arising from the mere fact of change. But sometimes, of course, the change has to be made to everyone's interests, and sometimes nurse has her own reasons for leaving.

The special point of your little charge's behaviour since you left is not so much her general wilfulness, as her actually telling the new nurse that you had let her do what she wanted. Now I don't think that is to be taken as a deliberate cunning or conscious lie. It may very well be that it really seems to her now that she had her own way when you were there—because she feels she was happy then with someone she loved. And if (as I well believe) she was contented and obedient when you had her to yourself, her memory is not altogether distorted. It is easy even for a naturally headstrong child to be docile and contented with someone who, while handling her firmly and consistently, yet wins her love. She may remember the time when you were there as mainly a happy one. And in her memory that may well actually *seem* like "having my own way".

But I think that what is going on in the child's mind is even more complex than that. You point out how difficult she was to deal with when other people were present even when you were in charge—as has often been said of other children in letters from other people. She is evidently one of those children who always try to take advantage of several grown-ups being there to "divide and rule". And in saying these things about you to her new nurse and her mother, she is in part just using you as a stick to beat them with. There is a vast deal of common human nature in little children!

The new nurse will have a hard problem until she has succeeded in establishing herself as a friend, and gaining firm control over the child.

Both mothers and nurses would get a good deal of help in their mutual relation and in understanding their children if they could remember that a child who will not try to play one grown-up off against another is a very rare child indeed. And while you may not be able to convince your little charge's mother that the child's words are not to be taken at their face value, but are to be understood partly as an involuntary protest against losing you, and partly as a way of trying to get the upper hand in the present, perhaps what I have said will make you yourself feel a little less disturbed.

Q. There is one point in connexion with the upbringing of children that I have never been able to decide upon, and on which I should like your opinion. It is this: I always try and surround my children in their early years at least with an atmosphere of friendly co-operation. Somehow one is anxious that up till the very last moment they must feel the world to be a definitely pleasant place and that the people in it are pleasant people who will be always ready to, for example, laugh at silly little jokes, join in a pretence, cheerfully help to find a stone in a shoe, cut a tiresome hangnail or attend immediately though without fuss to any small ailment or symptom. I have always tried—and because I am hideously busy—hoped I succeeded in doing this in a fairly casual sort of way so as not to make the child fussy about himself. I have been rewarded by their truly marvellous health and appearance but—I cannot but see that when it comes to obedience, patience in a crisis, good manners at parties and a few other homely but necessary little signs of self-discipline, my children lag behind those of others who seem to have been simply and literally dragged up! For instance, in this place it is the fashion to send children out with any sort of a sniggering village girl whose sole idea of correction is a hasty shake or smack and whose conversation with her intimates must be often questionable from the child's point of view. If the poor little three-year-old gets a stone in his shoe he is shaken, dumped down by the side of the road, shaken again and made to hasten after the pram. His wants are not attended to, his little questions ignored—enough to break one's heart—and yet he turns out obedient, nice mannered, sober in a crisis and a generally suitable citizen. Another instance. A small girl comes to play in our garden. She has a rough and bullying elder sister who even gives her black eyes as well as teasing her unmercifully. She has also a rather questionable and not particularly affectionate mother, yet she is sweet! The point of these two cases can be multiplied over and over again. Can it really be that it is better for a child to learn while quite young that the world is a cold and unsympathetic place?

What is your answer? And what do you suggest should be a mother's ordinary attitude towards the child and his difficulties since mine quite obviously does not seem to supply enough discipline? I confess both boys are unusually strong and independent characters and physically enormous, which may complicate things a little in my case. My youngest is now four and a half. He would rejoice the eye of any child-lover, and his play and surroundings are really perfect. He grubs about with his little friends, and his hearty manly laugh can be heard quite a long way off. He never fights or quarrels and never has. He just placidly holds on! But....

A. I was very interested in your letter, but I don't think there is any doubt that you are generalizing too much on the basis of what is a rather accidental set of experiences. If one takes a wider range of experiences, for example, that of all the workers in child guidance clinics of every complexion, all the biographical studies of children brought up on different methods, all the published facts as to the general development of children, without considering any particular theory as to how things ought to go, but simply weighing up recorded experience, then your conclusion that it is the people who have had the hardest time in childhood who turn out the most responsible and pleasant adults would certainly not be supported. Everything depends upon what you mean by the "hardest time" in childhood. For example, it is quite certain that illegitimate children, or children with quarrelling parents, or a broken home, children who are severely treated in the early years by brutality or deprivation or too stern punishments, all *tend* to become not merely unhappy and unsatisfactory, but delinquent and anti-social. It is equally true that children who have always had everything done for them and have never been trained to independence, or to face the realities of life, are equally unsatisfactory as adults. And it is also true that there are people who weather every kind of educational mistake, and still come out as useful and happy grown-ups! In most people there is an amazing degree of elasticity which will carry them through a great many adverse circumstances. Only the other day, I was told of a young woman who had had a surprising series of bad circumstances in the home and the family all through her life, and yet had turned out a normal and charming person in the end. But that is very unusual and only means that as far as human affairs are concerned there is always a margin of difference.

Another point is that it does not in the least follow that the children who have developed the accepted standards of table manners and self-control in the early years of childhood will be the most friendly and co-operative and independent people when they are grown up. This is sometimes true, but by no means always. The facts you quote, therefore, would on a larger scale of experience have to be a good deal modified before they represented the full truth. Now, as regards the problem of your own children, it does sound to me as if you had worked with a rather extreme desire to make things pleasant for them, and that your opposite suggestion that they should learn that the world is a cold and unsympathetic place is equally extreme in the other direction. It is not true, is it, in that absolute way, that the world is a cold and unsympathetic place? It is true that there are a great number of people in it who are cold and unsympathetic, and indeed worse than that, full of hatred and cruelty and wild passions, as the general state of the world at the moment shows only too vividly. But it is also true that there *are* people in it of genuine good-will, friendly and warm-hearted and co-operative. To destroy the child's belief in the possibility of meeting such people, to let him think there were no such people in the world would be either to drive him into despair or to make him in turn cold and unsympathetic, as the only means of self-defence. The ordinary life of any little child, however, provides plenty of opportunities for learning that there are hard and bitter experiences which each of us has to endure—physical pain, people who do not like us, tasks that have to be carried through for the sake of something that is valued, for example, all the cleaning and drudgery of domestic life. It is obviously very undesirable to try to keep the child altogether from the knowledge of such things and to try to act as an air cushion sheltering him from any rude shocks. I would not try to do that, but I would try not to let these things overwhelm the child in the early years, before he was ready to deal with them. It does sound to me as if you had tried to make things rather too soft for the children. And yet I cannot quite see from your own picture of your children what faults of development they show, that cannot be dealt with by encouraging them to recognize that other people have their rights, and that things run more smoothly if one follows the accepted standards of manners. But in general it sounds to me as if your youngest boy was an admirable person, and that you would be seeking after an impossible perfection if you felt unhappy about his development. The picture of the little girl whose elder sister gives her black eyes sounds to me a little unnatural. Surely what one wants to aim at is a reasonable standard of independence and friendliness. Your boy is sure to find when he goes to school and has to settle down to all the tasks of learning and of adapting himself to the society of older boys that there are plenty of disagreeable things which have to be accepted.

III. LACK OF SELF-CONTROL AND CRYING

Q. *I have taken a new post with two little boys of five and three. They are very sweet little boys and I have grown very fond of them in a month, but this is where I need your help. D., aged five, is highly strung and sensitive, and C., aged three, not quite so highly strung as D., but both of them cry for the least thing and cannot bear to be corrected in any way. I have only to say to either of them, "Now don't do this or that, dear", and at once there is a cry. "I didn't nurse," or "I don't. You are naughty to say that, nurse." If either of them hurt or knock themselves they cry and grunt for half an hour or more, no matter what I say or do to comfort them. They keep on crying, "I am hurt badly, nurse, you must kiss it better". I do not mind doing this, but I feel that as D. is five he ought not to be such a baby and want the hurt kissed better. Also D. seems to delight in, "keeping on", as I call it, and if I say, "Now that is quite enough, stop at once", he will shout out louder, "I am stopping it", and will stamp his feet and get very red and cross. Then I put him in the night nursery and tell him he can come out as soon as he stops that horrible noise. He will then shout, "It is not a horrible noise, you mustn't say that, nurse". Both boys cry if I am not pleased with one of them. C. acts very much in the same way as D. but gets over it sooner and does not need to be shut up quite so often.*

A. I agree with you that it is a little unnatural for boys of five and three to make quite such a fuss about small hurts and want them kissed better. I should be inclined to lessen the attention you give them in this respect, not by getting cross about it, but by saying, "Come, be sensible. The little hurt will soon feel less. Come and do", this or that or the other—some activity they enjoy. Again, I would avoid any unnecessary occasions for saying, "Now, *don't* do" this or that, and would give them the reasons why you make such a prohibition when you have to. I would do it, not appealingly, by the use of endearing phrases, but in a quiet, firm, matter-of-fact way, which assumes that there won't be any fuss about it. You will find that during the next year they will grow out of this fussy way if you can keep your own attitude rather more matter-of-fact and good-humoured, and use a more positive approach, putting useful activities in their way, rather than endearments such as, "sweet", and, "dear".

Q. My little girl is now eight, and once more I should very much appreciate your guidance. I want to know how you would advise me to treat her frequent bouts of hysterical crying. She begins to cry for very little reasons—refusal to grant an unreasonable request, such as allowing her to play in the garden without a coat, etc. She works herself up into a hysterical state, when it is very difficult indeed to calm her. I do want to know how I ought to act on these occasions. I'm sure I am wrong somewhere. I feel very impatient with her when she starts to cry for trivial reasons, but try to take no notice of her, except to repeat my request, whatever it may be, at intervals. I think she is too big a girl for me, for instance, to give in good-humouredly to her rudeness at table. Don't you think so? On the other hand, it would possibly prevent the dreadful crying, which must be so bad for her, unless she found some other reason later on. Am I right in comforting her when she gets to the uncontrollable stage? Or should I try to compromise with her sooner? I know the reason for her frequent tears is partly due to her state of health. She is always very tired at the end of term. Although she is very happy at school, I know it is a strain for her. She sleeps badly, but has a fairly good appetite. I know these attacks will be less frequent as she is more rested, but I do want to know what my attitude should be at the time. *We always have a little talk together at bedtime, and I wondered if I could do any good by mentioning it to her then, though we usually talk about happy things.*

A. Such frequent hysterical crying for slight reasons is nearly always a sign of some emotional conflict, but you mention one thing in your letter which may be increasing your little girl's difficulties. You say that her frequent tears are partly due to her state of health, and that you know school is a strain for her. Is her physical health delicate? And is the school perhaps pressing her too hard in the way of formal lessons and scholastic achievements? If the child is over-tired, that would very largely account for the behaviour which you describe; and if she is physically delicate she needs an easy, free, school life. You do not give me enough information to judge the situation, but I would suggest that you think the matter over, and if you consider she is being pressed too hard at school, try to find another school—a happy, free place where her all-round interests and activities would be provided for and where things would be easier for her. With regard to the actual fits of crying, I would try as far as possible to prevent their occurring, but if a situation of difficulty occurs, be as matter-of-fact as possible. For instance, I would not reproach or scold her for lack of politeness at the meal table, but would remain quite unmoved by it. She probably feels a temporary defiance, and then gets so upset because she has defied you and her father and does not know how to put it right. If, at the meal table, she is the only child among adults, she may feel little and insignificant, and then want to assert herself by means of rudeness. I would let meals be an occasion for happy, free, friendly discussion between yourselves and the child, not making it a situation where she has to be on her best behaviour. Then I would pass things to her politely as you would do to another adult, and always be polite in your requests to her. Politeness in the child should spring from affection and from the wish to be like a loved person who is polite to her. If it is "taught" it will be likely to remain an external veneer. I think you will find this impoliteness a phase which she will outgrow if you follow the lines I have suggested. When you are talking to the child at bed-time you might possibly, in a careful and tactful way, ask her if anything is worrying her and encourage her to talk it over with you. There might possibly be some specific worry, but it is very likely that the child herself does not know what she cries about. As I have suggested, however, I would look into the general conditions of her life and of the school, and if anything seems unsatisfactory I would try to alter it. But if external conditions seem to be satisfactory, then I would trust to her further emotional development to bring her through this present phase of difficulty.

Q. Will you give me your advice about my elder child, the boy, who is five and a half years (the girl being just three years). He is so absolutely lacking in self-control and is such a cry-baby. I have tried all means of getting him to control his tears, but I feel at times hopeless about it. I think he is perhaps slightly better since going to school for two hours every morning. This is his second term, but he still yells the moment he is hurt, and I feel unless he learns to be braver he will have a terrible time when he goes to a proper boys' school. He is very strong and healthy, except for a tendency to acidosis, of which he had quite a bad attack at the age of about two years. He has always been a difficult child ever since this attack.

He was always very impatient even as a tiny baby. Eventually between two and three he got very much worse, having screaming fits in his sleep, and he lost all his colour and his appetite, and was very difficult. It was diagnosed as acidosis, and with diet, etc., he recovered, but he has always been nervous of the dark, is very self-conscious, though that is rather better since being at school; till then he would refuse to come and say, "How do you do", to a visitor, and would scowl at anyone who spoke to him. If you tried to draw him forward he would as a rule start to scream and cry; that is, I'm glad to say, much better, but he still shrieks and cries the moment he hurts himself, and doesn't seem the least ashamed. I think I am far more ashamed than he is, as he will let out yells and tears wherever he is, no matter how many people are about. He is terribly stubborn and self-willed.

If he is told to do anything he doesn't wish to do, he will invariably start to whine and cry. I do feel by now he should obey an order or request, such as bedtime, without question and without a scene. I don't say there is always a scene, but one never knows, and if there are strangers there he invariably will make a scene. Many people have told me I should give him a good smacking, but I do not feel this is the right method. I have on a few occasions smacked him, and I can't say I have felt it has done much good. I don't punish much, but the most effective one is, I find, to send him to his room or to bed, where he can scream until he recovers, and leave him there. One never knows with him, one day he will do something he is told perfectly pleasantly, and the next he will start to yell and scream. And I always feel if I have once asked him to do it and he has refused I must not give in and fetch it myself or let him off what I have asked. I admit, if there is going to be a scene, it's better not to ask him to fetch something. But then again I feel it's not good to fetch everything for him, and also some days he would do it with no trouble. I know I do get exasperated with him at times when he won't do as I tell him at once, but starts to whine and make excuses.

When he was tiny, if he hurt himself he always ran to me to be kissed and would stop crying as soon as I kissed the place, but as he got bigger I felt he must learn to be less babyish. So I took to being less sympathetic, and tried a sort of bracing attitude, and then rather ignored it or paid very little attention. Then I tried telling him he mustn't let people see him cry, and it was dreadful, and I was ashamed of him, etc. but nothing seems to make him any better.

He is jealous to a certain extent of his sister; he is very fond of her although they quarrel a good bit, and although he likes her to have any treat he is having, he can't bear her to have anything and he not have it, or to feel she is with me and he isn't. He is very sensible in many ways, can cross roads, etc., alone, and will look most carefully first. He is very athletic, and has taught himself to bicycle and roller-skate.

A. It seems to me that the acute emotional trouble which upset his digestion so seriously between two and three years of age must have been his conflict of feeling about the birth of his sister. In its turn the acidosis would increase his emotional difficulties. It is very likely that the uncertainty of the boy's behaviour, being pleasant one day and disagreeable the next, expresses this deep conflict. Also I have the impression that you never made quite enough allowance for the effect of this physiological disturbance upon the child's emotional life. Children who are suffering from such digestive difficulties need a great deal of cheerful patience in handling, and one cannot reasonably expect the same degree of self-control as from a healthy child. I emphasize this because other mothers may be having the same problem to deal with now, and, although the advice is too late for your little boy, it may be useful to other people.

What I feel is that if, perhaps, you could have realized more definitely that a child suffering from acidosis is bound to be fretful and nervous, and therefore needs more patience, you would not then have felt so acutely ashamed of him as you seem to have done. Now I think that your own feeling of great shame when the boy made a scene in the presence of others must have been a factor in the building up of this very habit of making a scene. Children are very quick to realize when they have this sort of power over us, and naturally enjoy exercising it. But after all, the presence of strangers does not really make the temper and the stubbornness and the screaming *more* shameful, does it? All parents, of course, like to be able to be proud of the behaviour of their children, and that too is natural. But if we are over-sensitive to what other people may think of our children, so that we get more worried about bad behaviour when other people are there than we do when we are alone with the child, this really makes things worse, because the child then knows that he will probably get his own way if he makes a scene when strangers are present. Sometimes parents do not bother about certain sorts of behaviour except when other people are there, and that has a very bad effect. I don't suggest that you have been so inconsistent, but your letter does rather give me the impression that the child has been able to sense how very ashamed and sensitive you felt when other people saw him making a scene. If one can avoid that, and keep one's standards and ways of dealing with the child quite consistent, whether other people are there or not, it is a very great help.

I need scarcely say that I should not advise smacking him. We can hardly encourage self-control in our children unless we are able to show it ourselves, and to the child smacking always seems to be loss of self-control on the part of the parent. It would be better to send the child to his room, as you have actually found.

You are certainly on wise lines when you feel that it would not be good to wait upon the child and fetch everything for him just in order to avoid a scene. I think what is needed is a careful judgment in deciding *what* to ask him to do. I should at present definitely avoid asking him the sort of thing that is known to make him contrary, unless there were a very good reason for it. Of course I agree that once he has been asked to do it it would be a mistake to let him off. But as regards training him to wait upon himself, that surely can be done chiefly through appeals to his independence and pride, and by positive suggestion rather than by command. And when there was something he wanted but refused to fetch for himself the best training would be to let him go without it. As regards going to bed, so much depends upon the way this situation is handled. If, for example, we suddenly say to the child without any warning "Now it's bedtime, you must come at once", that is not very considerate on our part, and not very wise. If we were to tell the child a little while beforehand that it would soon be bedtime and that he would then have to put his toys away and come, and we were then quite firm about it at the actual time, yet without getting cross or worried, we should soon find that he would come cheerfully and willingly. With a child who is so affectionate and tender-hearted, it should really be quite easy to train him, by firm, consistent methods, once his digestive troubles were fully cured.

The good sense of your little boy in crossing roads, teaching himself to cycle, etc., should make you feel more hopeful that, as he gets out into the larger world of the school, he will grow out of his babyish ways. It may very well be that his tearfulness and stubbornness are bound up in his mind with the nursery and nursery ways, and the fact that he has improved already since he began school suggests that this is so. I should be inclined to increase the time he has in school, and to let him make friends outside the home, both with children and grown-ups.

Q. My little girl of four and three-quarter years of age has always been a difficult child, and needed more care and attention than our other little friends do. She had a difficult birth, and owing to instruments the specialist said she would not recover.

However, he managed to pull her round, and after three weeks put her in charge of the doctor. How can I deal with disappointments? Some are unavoidable, she cries heartbrokenly and gets so depressed. She cannot stop crying once she starts, and says, "I do want to be a good girl, smile at me mummy—you don't cry. I don't want to cry", and this goes on until she is completely upset and it upsets her sleep. Comforting her does not help. She has had a slap on her hands when I have had a very trying day with her and lost my patience, but it has done more harm than good, and although my friend says, "I should not be able to be so patient with her", I know I have to be. She has a heart which troubles her sometimes, and after crying, her face is a mass of red blotches, which go down after an hour or so. We are always having the doctor to her, and he says we must work with her, as nerves are her trouble (they have always been mine). We try to arrange for friends to play with her and go to friends, but she is worse with other children than alone—she doesn't want to do this or that, only wants it her way. She gets these days occasionally—can be sweet and good when alone with me. We try to get out a lot, and she is most happy if out. She would like to be out with me all day, but does not want to play alone. She has a sand pit, but there is no interest unless I am in the garden with her. Her biggest disappointment, or the one which has lasted the longest, is not getting a tricycle from Father Christmas (last Christmas). Her friend has one, and last Christmas the girl opposite our house had one. She says Father Christmas does not love her, or he would have brought her one. It may help her to play alone, but I cannot get one for her, they are too expensive. She is pleased and excited when friends are coming, but cries dreadfully when they go, and no amount of reasoning seems to make any difference. She has just begun to sleep without me staying in the room, she has no fear of anything, and is very, very *independent, yet so jumpy at a sudden noise, a knock at the door, or a spoon dropping I would like to help her. I do not seem to be making things much easier for her, the crying is so upsetting both for herself and everyone else. We had to give in to her over the scenes for some time owing to her heart, but the doctor says that it is now very nearly normal, and next year she can start swimming—she likes water. She is quite good at doing things for me, she has a toy mop and sweeper, brush and tray, and loves to help in the garden—weeding and planting seedlings, does not destroy anything, in fact, fears other children may destroy her toys—is rather selfish with them, as she has always had them to herself, is obedient and very kind to animals. She can use scissors and cuts pictures very well; has a very good memory and recites poems very well, having had a few lessons in elocution. She is if anything too independent. After an upsetting day at my friend's, we have decided to leave visiting alone, and see if she improves. She has had two weeks at school and I have asked the teacher how she behaves. She says she is very good, does not cry, plays in the percussion band, drinks all her milk, and altogether is quite happy and wants to go. Yet when she is at home with one or more children she is not herself at all. When out to tea last week, and contrary to everything, she was asked to help with the little concert—she did not want to, but after hearing the others she seemed to leave her cranky self and was a dear little girl for five mintues while she gave her recitation, and she got top marks. I mentioned she was obedient, but only when with me or other grown-ups. When she has the moods, no amount of reasoning has the least effect. I would like your opinion about Santa Claus, as she will probably be expecting the tricycle this Christmas, and I do want to give her the best answer in the circumstances.*

A. You certainly have a very difficult problem with this little child, owing to the very severe experience she had at birth. She is obviously more than usually sensitive to shocks or disappointment. A child who has been so delicate physically, and has had so much extra consideration because of the physical handicap, is bound to find it more difficult to accept the ordinary disappointments of life. And yet time is on your side. It will take her longer than it takes most ordinary children to get over the period of most acute emotional difficulty, and she will necessarily require greater patience and consideration from those around her. In many respects her development is obviously very satisfactory, and there is no doubt she will get less sensitive as she grows more mature emotionally and more robust physically. It is very fortunate that she enjoys her new school experience and is happy to be joining in the social life with the other children. With regard to the specific problem of Father Christmas, I believe you would be wiser to tell her beforehand that Father Christmas will not be bringing her a tricycle, since you cannot buy one. It would be a mistake to let her go right up to Christmas Day in the belief and hope that she would be getting one, and it would be far more help to the child to dissipate the too literal belief in Santa Claus, and to let her know that her parents are the real Father Christmas. I should tell her that you certainly would buy her a tricycle if you had enough money. But as you have not enough money for that, you will get her the best thing you possibly can. I can remember myself how terrible the tragedy of disappointment following on a simple-hearted belief can be. It would be really cruel to your child to bolster up the Santa Claus phantasy and let her suffer such a disappointment. She is sure to cry when she hears that you have not enough money to buy the tricycle. But she will not feel such absolute loss and distress in this way, since you can give her real proof of your solid affection and goodwill. I think you will find that she has a better idea than you imagine who Father Christmas is. It is bound to be a difficult moment. But each year of her development will help her to get more stable and robust, and she has so many excellent qualities for her age that I do not feel you need worry unduly about present difficulties.

IV. TANTRUMS AND STUBBORNNESS

Q. My little boy, now three and a half, is naturally excitable, in spite of the fact that he and his little sister, just a year older, live pretty quietly and are kept to a most regular routine; but he gets frequent fits of excitement, quite often for no apparent reason, when he seems almost beside himself. He is a very sturdy child, and has greater strength than his sister. Consequently in these moods he is not only excessively rough, but sometimes almost dangerous. Apart from that, it is extremely worrying to one's temper when he keeps hitting, or nearly hitting, with frequent accidents that do actually hurt. He is never intentionally cruel, but in these excitable moods he just sets his teeth and "goes for" anything handy. No amount of reasoning seems any use.

He is a difficult child to reason with at any time, quite unlike the girl in that respect, as he just waits for a break in the conversation and adroitly changes the subject! At present when he gets unbearable I have to shut him in the nursery by himself, where he yells and kicks in a tantrum for a while. When he is quiet I fetch him, and he is quite penitent, but these fits still occur just as frequently. He is usually at his worst when I have visitors, and he comes into the drawing room rolling about, fighting and shouting, and generally being a nuisance. As I am just about to discharge my nurse-help owing to the present hard times and run this fairly big house and, I hope, look after the kiddies and keep their routine as usual with just a morning help, I am more anxious than I should have been otherwise. The children are used to a well-ordered nursery existence, walks twice daily, etc. so that I shall have my work well cut out to manage, and my chief dread is the way Ian behaves when visitors come. This will happen but infrequently, I hope, for a while, but a certain amount is unavoidable. When we all go out his behaviour is splendid.

My other difficulty arises partly out of the previous one. When he gets into these fits of excitement he shouts out all sorts of ridiculous things. Some of them are just nonsense, but he has got into the habit of shouting a few really objectionable remarks, always with reference to his daily motion or his "botty". It sounds quite horrible when he goes round shouting, "You're a dirty botty", and, "I'll sniff your botty". In common with, I believe, quite a number of little children, the whole subject has always fascinated him, and in his own private conversations with his sister he frequently talks about these things in a very amused way. I am sure he has never heard any coarse remarks, and, as far as I can tell, I do not think anyone has ever shown amusement when he says these things. I have always been quite frank about it all with the kiddies, explaining why we close the w.c. door and hurry to empty chambers, etc. and when they have seemed interested I have told them a little of how their bodies work. On the other hand, I have told Ian he must not say these things for fun, but although I occasionally see evidences that he tries to remember, when he gets excited he is incapable of remembering anything. He appears to have no control at all. I am afraid he does not sound a very nice child, but really he is a very attractive one, a real boy, and most headstrong, but generous and unselfish almost to a fault, and full of personality. He and his sister are general favourites everywhere. We give him as much outlet for his energies as we can. They are often on the beach, and we have a good garden where, whenever we can, we play "cricket" and "football" with him. They have plenty of toys, and he and his little sister are wonderful companions, fitting in splendidly together. They are almost equal in capabilities, except perhaps mental, and both get an equal amount of attention from outsiders, so I feel the trouble is not to be found there, although the boy will do all his sister does, even if he is afraid, like climbing heights, etc. where her greater age is an advantage. Can I do anything further to stop this excitability, and how should I deal with the other subject?

A. It is very trying when a vigorous child has these attacks of excitement and aggression. But it is, as you find, most difficult to deal with when other people are present. I think I should try to avoid having him about when visitors are there, as far as you possibly can, during the next year or so. Perhaps you could arrange for your morning help to take him out for a walk when your friends come, or for him to visit other people. What I feel is that with firm, sensible handling he is sure to grow out of these unpleasant moods during the next year or two, and that if you avoid the most trying situations of having to cope with his excitability when visitors are there, this will save you a great deal of nervous wear and tear and won't do anything to retard his development. Since he behaves well and is happy when visiting other people, it is obviously not a question of general unsociability, but something rather special in your having visitors that makes him so wild and difficult.

When you can't avoid having the boy present with visitors, then I should talk to him about it beforehand, and try to give him a sense of personal interest in the visitors and the occasion, both by getting him to help you prepare the tea and carry a plate of cake or biscuits to the visitors, and by giving him a chance to show them his toys or something he has made. I think it is pretty certain that his wildness on these occasions comes from feeling left out and jealous and not knowing how to put himself in the centre of the picture in an agreeable way. If you can find some way of giving him a real part in the proceedings, he may then be more pleasant and happy. I should try this line for two or three occasions, and if it did not succeed, I would then definitely tell him that you like him to be there and see your friends if he will be sensible and pleasant, but that if he shouts and gets wild he will have to stay somewhere by himself. I think this may help to develop control, but as it is making rather a big demand on a child of three and a half, I would keep such occasions rather few and far between until you saw that he was managing things more easily.

In the ordinary way, when he is rough and wild with his sister, I should certainly tell him very firmly that you wouldn't have him hitting or hurting, and I should shut him in the nursery by himself, but without speaking too severely or reproachfully. I should just let him know in a quiet, sensible way that he can't be with you and his sister when he has these tantrums. But you must not expect that one or two months of firm treatment will reform a child who is subject to such fits of uncontrol. It will take time, but he is pretty sure to grow out of it during the next year or two. I wonder whether there is a nursery school or any group of little children with whom he could play away from home for an hour or so a day, or even two or three mornings a week? It is very often a great help to such a child to get away from the nursery and to build up fresh social contacts.

With regard to the talk about the motions and lavatories, you are perfectly right in believing that amusement at these things is extremely common amongst little children, and it is not in the least abnormal at his age. One therefore need not scold the child too severely or feel horrified. It means, in part, that he is expressing in bodily terms his guilt and distress about his naughtiness, but denying this at the same time by being amused and accusing other people. I should definitely make the child understand that whilst you are willing to answer any questions and give him any knowledge of digestive or excretory processes that he wants to have, yet in consideration for you he must recognize the ordinary social conventions as regards jokes and discussion at inappropriate moments. It is not at all an easy thing to deal with, because we don't want to shut down the child's legitimate curiosity, nor to create too great a sensitivity and reticence. On the other hand, it is not fair to a child to let him feel that he is at liberty to disregard the feelings of other people entirely about such matters, and particularly to let him put you into a situation of embarrassment with other people. What, I am sure, one needs above everything else in dealing with this problem is a sense of proportion.

Q. My small daughter, who will be two next week, is most difficult. She has a very strong will of her own, and when she is with my Nannie, who is devoted and most kind to her, she cries and whines constantly at such things as eating her dinner, or when she is lifted at ten o'clock at night. She cries herself into a heat. It is positive yelling. She will not sit on her "pot", and sometimes will not go back to bed, but when she is with me she is perfectly good, though she always chooses Nannie to go to if hurt or cut, etc. Nannie was away this week-end, and a better child you could not wish to have, and the minute she came home R. would not eat her dinner, after eating it perfectly for me the last three days. She has never been smacked (though lots of people advised me to) as I feel it would not do her any good, and might in fact turn her against me. She has a five-year-old brother M., to whom she is devoted, but they are jealous of each other's toys and fight, and cry, especially R. over them. M. had exactly the same upbringing, and the same Nannie as R. has, and we never had one hour's trouble with him.

A. Evidently your little girl of two and her five-year-old brother are of very different temperaments, and respond to the same upbringing in different ways. As you have had your Nanny so long, and she has brought the older child up satisfactorily, it is clear that her general methods cannot be blamed. It seems that the little girl is one of those children who behave better when only one adult is in charge than when there are two. The fact that she is so good when Nanny is away and she has you to herself seems to suggest this,

TANTRUMS AND STUBBORNNESS 71

especially as she goes to Nanny for comfort when she is hurt or cut. I suppose you both treat the child on the same lines, and don't let her get her own way by playing one of you off against the other? It is rather important to be careful about this. Another possibility is that the little girl feels that Nanny belongs specially to her brother than to her, and is jealous of them together. I don't feel I can judge the exact cause of the difficulty, and it may be any one of these situations which disturbs her. In any case I can only suggest very firm, steady handling, with constant affection and cheerful suggestion.

One thing definitely I should be most careful to avoid, and that is, any indirect suggestion that she is naughtier than her brother. It is extremely easy for this sort of tradition to grow up in people's attitude towards a particular child, so that the child knows that they more than half expect her to be naughty. To say such things as "Look how good your brother is, can't you be like him?" is, of course, quite fatal to a good relation between them. But even short of saying this, it is possible to convey such a suggestion in one's manner and voice and general behaviour. And then, of course, the child gets naughtier than ever, and it is very difficult for her to get out of this circle. If you and Nanny can let her realize that you believe in her affection and willingness, if you can assume her cheerful docility, she is more likely to be able to give it to you.

Q. My little boy of just three has been so used to doing the same thing at the same time that when asked to dress to go out for a walk at what seems to him not the right time there is trouble. Perhaps his will is beginning to develop, but it is difficult to know what to do when he simply will not do what is wanted of him. When he is naughty he says he wants to be left all alone and

Nanny and I do leave him alone if it is possible, and in about five or ten minutes he cheers up and says he is a good boy again. I admit I have smacked him on his hand sharply to make him realize what happens when he is disobedient, but I do not want to build up a resistance. Then could you tell me how much a little boy of this age should be able to do in the way of undressing; he cannot button or unbutton either on a buttoning frame or his teddy's waistcoat or on himself, he can take off cardigans if unbuttoned, how can I help him to overcome this difficulty? He can put on and take off his bedroom slippers and his shoes, but has no idea how to put on his socks and nobody seems to have invented easy clothes for a little boy. When I dust and sweep every morning the child plays on his bike, playing at doing messages, but if I do not join in he gets unhappy, and yet it cannot be good for him to get so much attention. When I have finished I give him my duster to wash, but he has very little idea how to do it; the same applies to when he washes up his plate and cup after tea in his little bowl, which is at a height he can reach in the bathroom. Do little boys develop in these things later than little girls, and does it worry and strain them to try and do things for themselves or should we persevere?

My last question is, should he be taught to say "good morning" nicely and "good-bye" and shake hands, etc., the many times it is needed, or is it worrying, when he comes in to see his Daddy on his bike? He often comes in the character of a message boy. You can see by the look on his face and the tone of his voice who he thinks he is; is it fair to break in and get him to say "Good morning, Daddy", because if you do break in he gets uncontrolled, stamps his feet and says, "Don't want to, I'm a baker's boy". Then should I start little lessons at this age, or should from three to four be a play year? We often have flour and water and mix it and roll it out and then wash it up. Is this good? He has little companions to play with and is quite good with them, but does not like to be left alone, and do you think that he is too young to join a Dalcroze Eurhythmics Class or a

TANTRUMS AND STUBBORNNESS

dancing class? The one thing he is terribly keen on is cars. When out for a walk he knows many makes, and just glances at the back of a car and knows it immediately. He is very observant. I feel that now is the time and the years that are in front of us to prepare for a preparatory school, because I feel that little boys who have not learned how to obey and control themselves will suffer terribly when among other children.

A. It is very sensible to leave the little boy alone when he has a tantrum until he regains a cheerful control of himself. That is a much better way than smacking his hand. He knows himself that he only needs time to get over his temper and obstinacy, and it is far more helpful to give him this time than to humiliate him by smacking. Children of three vary very much in the amount of independent care of themselves that they can achieve. You can only help him by giving him opportunity and time. He cannot learn these complicated actions in a hurry, but he can learn them if he is given time, and if his failures are treated good-humouredly it will not do any harm to join in his games of messages while you are busy about your housework. If he has no children to play with, then he quite definitely needs your companionship. It is a mistake to think that to give that degree of attention can do any harm. You would hardly expect a child of three to have any idea how to wash a duster, but you could show him and let him do his best. I think it is true that boys are slower in learning these things than girls, but there are very big individual differences. I should certainly persevere in giving him a chance to do things for himself, but I should not press or urge him, or be ashamed of him if he cannot manage them just yet.

It would surely be a pity to spoil the child's make-believe play of being a messenger boy by compelling him to behave in a conventional manner at that moment. *We* should not like it if he interfered with our pursuits in the same way!

Why should we feel we have a right to do it to him? It is hardly teaching a child politeness if one cuts so rudely across his deep interest of the moment. One has to show some sense of proportion and appropriateness of situation in teaching a child "good manners".

Your little boy is not too young to join a dancing class that is run on lines suitable for his age. Such classes differ very much, but if you could find one which has other children of his age learning happily, then it would certainly be quite useful to let him join in. It would be better not to start any formal lessons yet, but to answer his questions as intelligibly as you can and follow his own natural activities. He is obviously learning a great deal about the things he sees in life, and his development seems to be going satisfactorily.

Q. I have charge of a little girl of four years and two months and until recently she has been very good, but at the moment, and I think I can say for the past six months, we get unearthly tempers or scenes from her, chiefly when her Mummy and Daddy are present. When on her own with me, we rarely have a scene, and if on her own with them, but with three together it is getting worse than ever. To-night for instance, on leaving the beach she discovered a loose piece of skin by her nail. I cut it even twice, and then she screamed and threw herself down, asking for the scissors again in less than two minutes. Later we were walking off on our own, and she sang songs all the way home, and during bath time went to sleep quite happily. These scenes upset all three of us, and are quite spoiling our holiday. Last week she went out to tea and enjoyed it with her parents. I took her the other day and she was happy, yet as soon as we arrived back a scene commenced.

A. It is very common for children of about this age to get

into the way of being specially difficult when both nurse and parents are present, although remaining docile and happy when with either alone. It is a very exasperating type of behaviour, but nevertheless one that you need not worry about in itself. She will grow through it all right. I wonder whether you could not discover by reflecting upon recent events, some possible cause for her excessive tempers? As a rule there is some source of difficulty that gives rise to these violent tantrums, but I cannot discover from your letter what this might be in her case. Her screaming about the loose piece of skin was undoubtedly an expression of anxiety. It would not be the piece of skin itself, but what it meant to her, that disturbed her. Loose bits, things coming to pieces, things out of order are often signified to a child by a little bit of loose skin of this kind. What she really wanted when she asked you to cut it again, was to make her tidy and orderly all through in her inside and her feelings. I wonder whether she has enough opportunity for active learning: building, modelling, dancing, singing? Sometimes these tantrums arise from a lack of that sort in her environment. However, it may be a temporary phase which will pass away if you go on handling her with even, steady affection.

Q. I should very much like to hear what you consider is the best way to deal with a small boy of four who has a very strong spirit of contrariness. He is a very clever child and can read almost anything. This is the kind of thing which occurs. When out for a walk he saw on a gate leading to the front of a hotel, IN, and on the next gate, OUT; and remarked, "It says IN and OUT on these gates, I will go in where it says OUT and out where it says IN." He never missed an opportunity to do so whenever he passed the gates, almost being run over on one occasion. Explanations and punishments are never of any use, only tend to make matters worse. He also has a great love of power and will do horrid kind of things, like upsetting other children's games to gain it or attract attention to himself.

The attitude of contrariness may be for the sake of bringing attention down to himself. It sometimes seems to point that way. He is a difficult little lad and as sharp as can be in every way, and requires very careful handling—but a darling all the same.

A. Your problem is certainly a most interesting one. Children as intelligent as your little nephew can be such delightful companions, and are so much more promising than the duller ones, even though these may not make so many demands on our own quick understanding and adaptability.

In his contrariness, such as the IN and OUT game, the boy is clearly setting himself a problem to solve. His mind is actively reaching out for something to do that is a little harder than the straightforward going in where it says IN and out where it says OUT. I have known the same sort of thing in other intelligent children. One boy, e.g., loved to arrange the Montessori colour grading tablets in the wrong order; and a little girl made a great game of putting the names of pictures of common objects on the wrong pictures. But in doing this deliberately, they both got as much practice in reading and sorting as if they had arranged them correctly! And if they got real fun out of it, why shouldn't they? There is of course, a trace of self-assertion in it, but of a quite healthy kind. I should have thought that the only thing to trouble about in your nephew's game (which shows a delightful inventiveness) was the risk of getting in the way of the motors. Now cannot that be dealt with separately? Can you get him to make a compact to keep on the side-walk, or close against the railings if there is no pavement? If you enter into this game with him, and share its fun, only demanding

TANTRUMS AND STUBBORNNESS

his attention to the real point, won't that help towards managing him in other matters?

In the general way, it is clear that the child needs plenty of active occupation for his head and his hands—things that really give his mind something to bite on. Then his love of power might be satisfied, and his need for attention would be met in your sharing his games and providing constructive occupations for him. And regular companionship with other children in play would be a help.

Q. My wee daughter is one year old, her brother is two years eight months (he is of a sweet-tempered disposition). Just lately she has become very bad tempered. Throws her food away when she has licked the butter off, and so on. Screams when put on the chamber very often, and always wants to be picked up. She has only two bottom teeth, and is cutting four at the top, I think. She is remarkably strong, plump and fit, and as brown as a berry. She has always had a temper from her earliest days, and she does not care for strangers. She is full of determination, and is obviously "able to take care of herself", even at this age. She always wants to come to me as soon as I enter the room. She is, on the other hand, a very happy child, quite fearless in her bath, and splashes and kicks, not caring if she falls over or gets her eyes wet. How am I to treat her so that she grows out of this temper? I will add an important point. It is inherited. I have, and did have as a child, a terribly hot temper (soon over). My father also has it. It has been my one great sin in life, my one and only trouble. It has caused many regrets in my life, and I do not want my little baby to have such a curse in her life. I was spoilt, for peace' sake, because my mother's heart was not strong. When the children scream and are very naughty I get very irritable and very often lose my temper. I know how wrong this is, but I am anything but a perfect mother. I have only a smallish home and one maid, who is far more patient than I am. They are good kiddies really, but as I can see this trait in my baby I do most earnestly want to guide it rightly.

A. I sympathize very much with your difficulty, as it is never easy to handle a child who has such a ready temper, especially if one feels guilty oneself over the same sort of thing. I agree too with the importance of trying to train your little girl so as to curb her temper. There is, however, only one general piece of advice to be given—that is, to be perfectly firm in not allowing the child to tyrannize over you or other people because you are afraid of her hot temper. If she finds that she gains advantage by her outbursts she will naturally go on indulging in them. If, however, she finds that they bring her no gain, and she does not get any privilege or consolation through her temper, she is much more likely to control it. In your own case this policy of firm control could not easily be followed because of your mother's delicacy, but I gather there is not the same reason in your case for indulging your little girl for the sake of peace. I know that the problem is more difficult for you because you find it hard to be both firm and patient, and children screaming can be extraordinarily trying when they are vigorous and strong. But there really is only the one way to train a child of this kind, and that is a calm, steady firmness. If one can possibly attain this it does gradually make the child more sensible and controlled. I am sure you know this quite as well as I do. What I wonder is whether you are not worrying too much about your own temper and striving after an impossible perfection. I sometimes feel that my remarks in these columns do suggest a standard of perfection that cannot possibly be attained by anybody. But, after all, all I can do here is to point out the *direction* in which wiser handling of children lies. I don't imagine that children need perfect parents, or that they have a right to reproach us if we are im-

TANTRUMS AND STUBBORNNESS

perfect and sometimes lose our tempers and get impatient. I think you probably get a feeling of hopelessness when you see the child screaming in temper because of your own difficulties, and that makes you less able to cope with her than you would be otherwise. But there is no need to give way to your little girl for peace' sake, and so you should be able to train her gradually to greater sense and self-control.

Q. I am quite at a loss to know how to deal with my little charge, aged three years. He has the most violent temper and is terribly stubborn; simply will not do anything he does not want to do. I coax him, change the subject and try all manner of means to get him to do things, but all to no purpose. He will sit at the meal table, continually repeating, "I'm hungry; but I won't eat!" until I am heartily sick of hearing him speak. I have tried just ignoring him but if I do he just yells, "Nanny I want you to take some notice of me", until I am forced to do so. I have appealed to him, treated him as a big boy, let him do things for himself, thinking that might help; but in no way can I break down his terrible stubbornness. Every day in everything he wants to go in opposition, and I really find it very tiring. I might add that he has a brother, aged four, who is very sweet and good. Timothy often bites, kicks and pushes him down for no reason at all. I have honestly never lost my patience with him, but I do feel I can't go on for ever, especially as we are expecting a third baby in October, and I shall need all my energy to cope with the three single-handed.

A. Your little charge is *quite* unusually stubborn. As you probably know, a fair amount of obstinacy is quite common and normal at his age, but this boy is remarkably determined to assert his power over you. Now there must be some reason for such a marked attitude of stubbornness. I cannot tell from your letter what that reason may be, but there always is some general cause for such a situation. One thing seems extremely probable, namely, that he feels a tremendous sense of rivalry with the brother who is older but so close to him in age, and who has such a fortunate temperament. This rivalry must have been there from a very early age, and it must partly be because the elder boy is so successfully good that the younger one feels he can only assert himself by being difficult and stubborn. You say that you let him do things for himself, but I wonder very much whether you go far enough in that direction, whether you give him enough independence of choice? It is very important with such a child to avoid situations that give rise to the obstinacy, by never asking the child to do anything that isn't important enough to insist upon even in spite of his defiance. Wherever you can possibly give the child his head, I should do so; and do it not merely in form but in reality, not minding what he chooses to do. But where there is something that has to be done, then I should insist upon it in spite of his shouts and storms. For example, with regard to his saying, "I am hungry, but I won't eat", I certainly would leave him to be hungry. That is quite a different problem from the child who doesn't feel hungry. I should leave him perfectly free to eat or not and take the food away if he doesn't. You need not fear that he would starve himself. I would, of course, assume that at the next mealtime he would want to eat, and I would not show any reproach or contempt for his not eating, but be entirely matter-of-fact and good-humoured about it.

I think his demand that you should take notice of him comes from his feeling that your "ignoring" him is a reproach. There are so many different ways in which one can apparently "ignore" another person. It can be done in a way that implies the utmost contempt and anger! I do not ever believe in ignoring *the child*, but only in taking no particular notice of the specific piece of behaviour—which

TANTRUMS AND STUBBORNNESS

is quite a different matter. I would let him feel that I was still perfectly friendly, and ready to talk about interesting things. If he feels that you are ignoring him in a hostile way, he is sure to get more angry and stubborn. I have the feeling that you might appeal more than you do to his sense and reason, not by way of trying to persuade him to do something that you think is right except where this is really necessary), but more by way of letting him choose what is reasonable, and letting him carry it out himself. If you could give him opportunities for really free choice, and at other times let him feel that you have not merely a negative patience towards him, but a real friendliness, I think you would find the stubbornness would grow less. It is in any case sure to lessen within the next year. But you could help it along in the ways I have suggested.

Q. My little girl is two years and three months, and is a very strong, healthy, bright and affectionate child, but recently she has become very wilful and has fits of temper. For example, she simply hates being dressed in the morning, having her hair brushed and face and hands washed. She fights and kicks and screams and bites. I've tried reasoning with her and letting her put on some of her clothes herself, but unless they go on properly at once she becomes more furious than ever. She is most independent, and likes to do everything herself, and won't be helped.

Another thing that really worries me about her is this: For the last nine months I have had a young girl to take her out in her pram for a couple of hours each day. As soon as the girl arrives in the morning, baby begins to cry, "No go with Eileen", and won't leave me. I always tell her she is going a very nice walk with Eileen, and suggest little games and different places they could go to, but baby nearly always cries while being dressed, whether I am in the room or not. The girl says she is very good while they are out, excepting that she never wants to get back in her pram, and she always cries and kicks when the girl brings her into the house again. She will play with the girl after a time quite happily till I come in, and then she runs and tries to bite her if we start speaking to each other.

She is quite fond of my one maid, too, when left alone with her, but if I come into the room she will shout, "No Hilda", and bite her if she can; and she does the same whenever the girl enters the dining-room at meal times, which is most uncomfortable for me. Baby is very disobedient to me, and if I try and insist she cries and bites and says, "No love mum-mum". She is always good and obedient with her father, whom she only sees for a short time in the morning and evening, and he never has to scold her; but she treats me rather like an enemy if I ask her to do anything of which she does not approve if he is there.

I'm afraid she tries my patience sorely at times, but I never smack her and only try coaxing and reasoning with her, but it very seldom has any effect.

A. Your little girl obviously has a very difficult temperament, and your task of training her will not be an easy one yet her behaviour in itself is not unusual at her age. With regard to such things as dressing and undressing, I would suggest that you make a very definite attempt to train her gradually to do these things for herself. This won't be easy, with her temperament, but I think that it would be better for your own patience to be spent in this direction rather than in trying to make her let you dress and wash her quickly. I should let her do everything for herself that she possibly can, no matter how long it takes in the beginning. When she gets furious because her clothes won't go on properly, I should try to be quite good-humoured about her temper and encourage her to try again, and gently suggest the best way of doing it. But I should not force her to accept your way of doing it, nor scold her for her impatience. As regards her jealous anger when you talk to her nurse, I should say plainly to her, *not* in a coaxing or pleading way, that you so often talk to her, and so does Nurse, but just now you and Nurse need to talk to each other. And I would be quite firm about this. On the other hand, I would reduce the number of occasions when you had to talk in her presence and make the occasions as short as possible; and then afterwards talk to her or play with her for a short time.

Q. My trouble at the moment may seem to you a small one, but to me it seems unnecessary, and I wonder if any other readers have had to go through it. Ann, aged twelve months, simply fights and screams when she has to be either undressed or dressed. We have a hundred and one things to play with to try and keep her occupied, but all to no use. As soon as I sit down to take her nightie off she starts, and arches her back and throws her head back, which of course makes it very hard work. At the moment she is very irritable with her teeth. She cut six in a month at eleven months, which certainly has pulled her down, and she is at the moment having trouble with some more teeth and is off her food, but I really can see no reason why we should have such trouble with dressing her, can you?

A. Your little girl is not alone in her objection to being either dressed or undressed, although she obviously feels it unusually strongly. I have sometimes referred in these columns to a very interesting study of anger in young children which was made in America two or three years ago by a group of mothers acting under a trained psychologist. They made records of all the different occasions which gave rise to temper tantrums in children under five years, and the frequency and severity of these outbursts. They concluded what I had myself already observed—that the second year of life is the time when such tantrums occur most often and with the greatest severity, and they found that the processes of dressing and undressing were amongst the most frequent causes. There are other occasions, too, which cause many children to fly into a temper or an attack of obstinacy——washing, feeding, changes of plans, interference with routine, and so on. But there are some little children who cannot tolerate the dressing and undressing business. Now it is not always easy to say what has brought this about. Sometimes it begins in a rather uncomfortable garment, perhaps one that had shrunk in the wash, being pulled over the limbs or over the head. Some children are more than ordinarily sensitive to such things, so that the garments cannot really be blamed. Sometimes it seems to be some wholly irrational feeling in the child herself. In your little girl's case, it is clear that the anxiety caused by the teething process must have a good deal to do with this special irritability as well. It is indeed difficult to deal with while the child's anxiety is at its height, but there are one or two things that can be borne in mind. One is, never to start the process of dressing or undressing suddenly, so as to take the child unawares. Let her see clearly that you are going to do it, and approach the whole thing as calmly, quietly and cheerfully as you can, and as early as possible let her help in the process. She is, of course, very young yet to be able to do anything towards the dressing or undressing, but soon, if you encourage her, she might be able to help by the way she holds her hands or feet. You might be able to get her to make a game of pulling off her socks. I should try to turn the whole thing into not merely a pleasant game, but an opportunity for her activity and her learning and skill. This does, of course, take longer than if she sat perfectly still and let you do it all, but not longer than trying to undress a fighting, screaming child; and it is the only way to lessen her anxiety about it. Let her feel that it is something that *she* can do, that you are not expecting her to be perfectly passive and simply submit to something she fears and hates, but one that can be a pleasant and interesting activity of her own. Whilst she is cutting these teeth so rapidly, however, I think you are bound to have an unusual degree of sensitivity about this situation. It will pass away within this next year if you can handle it upon the lines I have suggested.

Q. My little boy, aged nine and a half years, has fine health, but often he gets spasms of uncontrollable temper—when he must just shout or bang. Apart from that, he is terribly slow in everything. He will not remember a thing, and must even be told to undress himself and undo this and take that off. I have to send him each day to the lavatory. If I send him on an errand he sometimes is gone an hour or perhaps two. He is always very late from school. He has rather a great trouble in making friends. I have not believed in caning him, but just once or twice I have smacked his knees very hard (he is a big boy). Apart from that I treat him like a real pal, and talk to him a lot. I sometimes, or rather it seems I am always, grumbling at him, and yet he'll just walk off and whistle as though nothing had happened. The only thing that makes him get a "move on" is the thought of being late for school, and then he will get quite frantic and gobble his food. Yet I know he could be such a good boy. We are so fond of one another. I have a little girl of two and a half years and a baby of ten months.

A. I feel there must be something seriously wrong with your general way of handling the boy of nine and a half. Whenever a child gets such general contrariness or spasms of violent temper it always means that some far reaching change in the way the grown-ups treat him needs to be made. He is obviously on the defensive all the time against the grown-ups, attitude. I cannot, however, tell from your letter what the mistake is, unless it be that you treat him too much like a little child. You call him a "little" boy, although he is nine and a half, and I do wonder very much whether the key to the difficulty does not lie in the fact that you still in your mind consider him to be a little boy and will not treat him as a big responsible person. I know it is very hard to avoid nagging a child who is slow and contrary, especially when you have two so much younger children to deal with. Yet I feel sure that if you could give up nagging and leave him much more often to suffer the consequences of his own slowness and mistakes, and in general treat him as a more responsible person, you would find the difficulty getting less. For example, with regard to his going to the lavatory, I think it would be wiser not to send him there or even remind him, but let him take charge of those processes entirely for himself. I would leave him alone about dressing and undressing. I would provide him with a little alarm clock which he could wind up for himself and set going at the time when it is necessary for him to get up and go to school; and I would let him be really responsible for all this, bearing the consequences himself if he did arrive late. I would have his school friends to visit occasionally, again letting him choose whom he should invite and how he should entertain them. In general, I would try to make the friendship between you and him far more real and far more like a friendship between two responsible people.

Q. My son Michael, aged two years three months, is being extremely difficult to manage and I shall certainly be greyheaded soon. Nine weeks ago he suddenly got sick and for three weeks lay quite still in bed puzzling the doctors completely and worrying us considerably. All the time I was with him, night and day, so it was only natural that he took my presence rather for granted in the end. At the end of the three weeks he produced a boil in the outer ear and recovered immediately, though, of course, it left him extremely weak. Now, his very regular routine is completely upset and he's perfectly awful. I have battles every morning over his rest, so have tried putting him down later, after a lot of exercise in the fresh air, and then reading or telling him a story or else letting him play with one of his animals which he always takes to bed or with a quiet game of some other sort. As soon as I attempt to leave him he screams and continues to say "Michael wants Mummy" until I appear again, in terror that such awful screaming will cause a rupture or make him ill again some other way. His nursemaid, is powerless with him when he's worked up like this. Also in the early mornings, sometimes as early as 1 a.m. he'll wake up and cry for me and eventually scream unless the nursemaid calls me. He tried to come into one or other of our beds for some time, but now doesn't, but wants the nursemaid, J. to dress herself and him and play. I have a baby of six months of whom I can't think he's jealous, as I see much more of him than her, and for months before her arrival he had to be almost entirely in the hands of J. He is liable to get worked up at any time during the day and I'm really frightened about it.

A. Your little boy is of an age when difficulties connected with emotional development are most acute, in many children these find expression in such fits of violent screaming and anxiety as Michael is suffering from at present. It is possible too, that his recent illness, when he lay quite still in bed for three weeks, was also connected with these emotional difficulties. On the other hand, the infection and physical illness would increase his anxiety. I would not worry about this present problem, but would rely on time to bring him through. It will perhaps make it easier if you realize that these emotional troubles are inevitable in the child's development. He is struggling with his primitive impulses, and this is part of learning the difficult art of growing up. You can help him best by showing him constant friendliness and affection, while being as calm and matter-of-fact as possible in your general attitude. With regard to the difficulty of the day-time rest, you were quite right in feeling that it would be very unwise to leave the boy to scream. I would without hesitation stay with him at this period until he falls asleep, for the present; and even if he does not sleep, let him rest and amuse himself quietly, as you have been doing. It is best not to urge or to try to force the child to go to sleep; none of us can sleep to order. But if the child is not afraid of your leaving him, you may find that he will fall alseep after a time. I would go on as you have been doing, letting him have his toys, reading to him or talking to him quietly, making this a time of pleasant companionship for you both. If you are busy, you could have your sewing or some quiet occupation of your own for this time. Similarly with the night-time waking: if he wakens screaming I would go to him and would sit beside him for a little while, talking quietly and soothingly to him or singing, until he goes to sleep; for the boy is in real trouble and needs the comfort of your presence. I would make arrangements to keep yourself quite warm and comfortable, of course. If you give him this help, lovingly and ungrudgingly, I think you will find, as has been found so often by other mothers who have tried this method, that the boy will soon begin to need you for a shorter period, although it may be some time before he grows through this phase of difficulty. Let him have some toys and playthings beside his bed, and then if he wakens early in the morning his nursemaid could suggest that he should amuse himself with them. You say that you cannot think he is jealous of the baby. Nevertheless, although he does not show open jealousy, I think this feeling is bound to enter into his present troubles. The best thing you can do to help him in this is to show your love for him in your behaviour; you should show him that

TANTRUMS AND STUBBORNNESS

you love him now just as much as you did before the baby came. It would not help Michael, however, to err on the side of showing the baby too little attention, the thing to aim at is to try to show equal affection for both. If or when he shows any curiosity about the origin of babies, I would tell him as simply as you can how the baby came. With regard to the fits of screaming or anxiety during the day, I would try to avoid as far as possible anything which would be likely to produce such an attack. Try to avoid making any unreasonable demands on him, but if you have to make a demand for practical reasons, I would insist on it quite firmly. And again, do not leave the boy alone to scream if a situation of difficulty arises.

Q. Our son, who is two and a half years old is troublesome in getting ready to go out. It does not matter whether it is just for a walk, or visiting, or in the car. He is so much trouble, he kicks and screams and struggles until I feel I could weep at him. I have tried sending the person away who was to take him out, but it makes no difference. If I am taking him myself he is so glad until it is time to get ready. He is very excited when Daddy brings the car round. He really loves motoring. Once he fussed so much that Daddy put him to bed, then he got ready, but he sobbed and it spoilt our evening. My husband and I get very little time together and so we like to take the children with us when we go out. Everyone seems to think I should smack him, and I have done, but I do not think I should. I was ill for a long time after he was born and he has had such a lot of different people to mind him. Unfortunately he got chicken-pox just before the new baby was born, and as baby was expected any time he had to go to his Granny. Anyhow, baby did not arrive, and so he came back five days before baby came. He was rather odd and quiet and would not leave me. Then the day baby arrived

Granny took him again, but only for one night, because I wanted him home. I did not think it was wise to make *him go, not even for one night. Granny is a very big person and she holds him down firmly to do anything for him. She smacked him rather a lot whilst he was there. He certainly seems to give in to smacks, but he is very dare-devil, and if I smacked him for all he did it would be dreadful. I am not too keen on smacks. Do you think he is old enough to be made to sit at the table until the others have finished a meal? He has started to eat and behave badly at mealtimes. I have not made too much fuss about this but Daddy objects. I find that if I am alone with him and his brother and baby I have no fuss. I have not got strong yet and I could not manage everything single-handed, although it makes one feel like trying to. Baby is only two months old and so Robert has had very little of him yet. I suppose some of the trouble is just because of baby. I do think Daddy expects a lot of the boy, yet his elder brother is very quiet and sensible, so it makes the younger child appear worse than he is.*

A. Your little boy, has had very difficult experiences, first in having so many changes in his environment in early infancy, then in being sent back and forth between his own home and his Granny's, at just the time of this special difficulty of the new baby, then the apparent lack of understanding on the part of his Granny, who, from what you say, treats him rather like a manikin, to be washed and dressed by force and smacking. Again, would it not be extremely surprising if such a series of experiences did not arouse great anxiety in the child? It seems to me most likely that he cannot bear to be dressed to go out because to him it always means he is going to be sent away from you to his hardhearted grandmother. At this age a child's feelings are so much stronger than his knowledge and reason, and to him, being dressed to go out simply means these frightening and disturbing experiences. I confess your letter troubles me a good deal, since your question as to whether a child of this age, who has already had such troubles, should be forced to sit still at the table until the grown-ups have finished seems to suggest that you yourself do not realize how difficult things are for him. Two and a half years is in any case much too young to compel a child to sit quietly at the table while older people finish the meal. It would be far better to let him have his own meal separately beforehand on a low table and chair. But this is especially true in the case of a child who has already been frightened by such severe and un-understanding treatment. I would strongly urge that you should try to see the whole situation of the child from his point of view, and reduce the element of force and give him a good deal more affection. I do not think there is any need for you to feel that you ought to be always the one who goes out for walks with him, but I think it is very important that you should find someone to take him out who is really sympathetic and friendly. Perhaps a change is needed there, if you could find a young woman who really enjoyed being with children and would not just force the child to go but would make it a pleasant excursion sharing his interests and pleasures on the walk. And it would be a help to the child if you explained to him that you quite understood that he was afraid he was going to be sent away from you, but that that was not so, and you would be very pleased to see him when he came back from his walk. In short, what this child seems to need is greater affection and greater appreciation of his point of view, and helping him to see that you do understand his feelings.

V. SHYNESS

Q. My little girl is aged two and a half. Up till about four months ago she was such a friendly baby, adored other children, and would talk to any stranger. Now she is the shyest child I have ever seen! She is accustomed to seeing many people and many children, as we move about a lot, and in India all the children meet every evening, either at the club or elsewhere, and she has never met with anything but the greatest love and affection. It has come to the stage now when she won't play with the other children at all, she won't even speak to them; in fact she will spend the whole evening without speaking when she's out, yet in her own house her tongue is never still. Even with people she sees every day, if they speak to her she will hang her head, and shut her mouth tight, and look as cross as she possibly can. She never laughs, or joins in with the play, keeps entirely by herself, looking frightfully sad and miserable and disagreeable. A dog rushed at her, barking, once and frightened her badly, and ever since then she has been terrified of dogs, and I think perhaps the beginning of her shyness dated from about the same time, but I don't know whether the two are connected in any way. She is better with dogs now, but not by any means right. In order to get her over her fear, we kept one for several months, the quietest and most gentle animal, but even with him she would suddenly show great fear. She will ride and pet horses, elephants and camels, but she often cries if a cat or a dog goes near her.

I know you often say that placid children in their third year begin to be difficult, and I am noticing that with my little girl. Whereas formerly she would go to bed and to sleep without a sound, and without caring if anyone were near, now she keeps up a cry of "Don't go, Mummy", or " Don't go, Ayah", and will sometimes burst into tears and make a frightful fuss. One night when I came home and found she had got all the servants round trying to pacify her, I did—what I know you don't approve of—give her a good spanking, and for many nights afterwards she went to sleep without any shouting out. In fact, she has never made any attempt to scream since, though sometimes calls out "Don't go, Ayah", for about ten minutes on end.

She sleeps for two hours every morning, and plays in her cot for an hour in the afternoon. I keep her in her cot because then she can be under a fan and cool. I don't let Ayah play with her then, as I think it is good for her to amuse herself, but whatever I give her to play with she now puts into her mouth. She will eat up a whole book in an hour. She doesn't swallow the paper, but chews it up and spits it out, and what she doesn't chew she will wilfully tear up. So, although she loves picture-books, I can't let her have them. She will take her hair ribbon off and chew that, or pull a button off her coat and chew that. Yet she doesn't do it at other times. If I give her a doll or a woolly animal to play with she will throw it out of bed, so, although she probably chews out of boredom, it is difficult to keep her from being bored. The refusal to talk and play with other children really worries me, as it is such a handicap to her own happiness, and I do think a shy child is a very obnoxious thing.

A. It is difficult to say, on the basis of your letter, what the change in your little girl's attitude to other children and strangers might be due to. Evidently you don't yourself know of any frightening thing that has happened except the incident of the dog's rushing at her. As you describe it that hardly sounds enough to cause so general a change. I suppose it is not altogether impossible that there has been some other frightening experience of which you are unaware. At any rate, it is certain that she will need the greatest patience and encouragement to help her get over this phase of shyness and timidity when not in her own house. I do think that if you could feel less worried by her shyness you would be more able to help her get over it. You don't tell me what sort of thing you say to her about it, whether you scold her or urge her to talk to other children; and I wonder, since you call shyness by such a strong term as "very obnoxious" whether perhaps you had let yourself reproach her in some direct or indirect way. Now, I am sure that such reproach is never the least help to the child. It only adds another fear to the one that is already there, fear of your displeasure and the loss of your love. If you could altogether avoid any reproach, or scolding, and let her feel free to talk or not to talk, to play or not play with the others as she wishes, whilst continuing, of course, to give her the opportunities and to be yourself friendly with the other children, it is quite likely she will grow through this phase.

With regard to her boredom in her cot leading to her chewing up books, etc. I should have thought that it would be more sensible to play with her, talk to her, read to her, or tell her stories. The forced inaction in the cot evidently makes her unable to amuse herself in the way she could if she were up and about and doing things. If she is so bored when lying alone in the cot (not needing any sleep after her two hours in the morning), then would it not be better to make a really good use of that time, in the way of pleasant talk or play with her Ayah, or, better still, with yourself? This would not only develop her gifts of language, but also help towards maintaining the happiest social relations with you, wouldn't it?

Q. I would like to know how to deal with my very sensitive and shy child for his future benefit. I would like him to overcome these two failings, so that in later life he may not have so many uncomfortable moments as I have had, nor be hurt so much. In order to be more explicit I feel I must talk about myself for a time. As a baby I was showered with over-indulgent love, and I grew up to feel that if my mother was not always demonstrative that she was ceasing to love me. I was always asking "Do you love me?" I was adored by all friends and relatives largely because of this shyness, which was considered winsome. When asked a question I would cuddle up to my mother and answer in a quaint and hesitating manner, and if I did not know I would just smile, which my mother assured me was even more captivating. Yet if she happened to leave the room I was dissolved in tears. My mother, realizing my weakness, sent me to a dancing class when I was five, and I continued classes for years, and enjoyed them. In my teens she made me join a tennis club, where I was very happy. When I was twenty-one I married, and now some of my old shyness seems to have returned. Strangely enough, people who know me well think there is nothing self-conscious about me whatever, but I know what it has cost me even to try and maintain this attitude in public. My son is just like me, and it will be worse for him when he is a man. He is now two years old. In the family circle, or with anyone he knows, he is an imp of mischief, yet if a stranger speaks to him outside he will laughingly disappear under the pram covers. Someone once said to me, "Michael can't talk yet, then?" "Goodness!" said I, "he seems to have been talking ever since he was born." In order to help him I have deliberately refrained from a lot of demonstrative affection, although I'm dying to give it to him. He will stand any amount of smacking if I'm not cross, but if I'm serious the wee-est touch will dissolve him into tears, and if I refuse to kiss him he is heartbroken. He hates being left alone in the nursery with his brother, who is three and a direct opposite. He has formed a habit of crying if a ball is taken away from him, or almost any little thing, just calling, "I want to come downstairs, Mummie". One day, I suppose, he will have to go away to school, and how can he be happy if he is so self-conscious? His father is intolerant of this crying of an apparently healthy child, and just smacks him and demands that he stops at once. Whereupon Michael will refrain, with many gulps, and it seems to be all over; but I think it is wrong. It is quite easy for me to quieten him by saying, "I will fetch Daddy"; but he is so afraid that I don't mention him any more."

A. This is not at all an easy problem to deal with. I should almost be inclined to say that it is all the harder for a mother who has herself the same temperament to deal with such a child successfully, just because she knows so well what it feels like from the inside, and can realize so vividly what the child is feeling. It would be easier for someone who, whilst sympathetic and loving, had herself less of the same way of feeling, and so could be cooler with the child. Mother and child act upon each other so very subtly in such a situation, and it is very hard for the mother to be as undisturbed and steady as it would be wise to be. Yet perhaps your knowing how very painful such a way of reacting to social life can be will help to stiffen your resolution to encourage the child to more independence and hardihood. I am sure that you are right in not indulging in demonstrative affection except to a very limited degree. However much you may want to express your love in words and caresses, the fact cannot be got over that it will help him more not to do so, except as an occasional thing: certainly not to do so as a way of comfort against small physical hurts or tempers and tantrums. It would be a pity to try to quieten him by saying, "I'll fetch Daddy", partly because it would increase the child's fear of his father, and partly because it would really be shifting the responsibility on to the father, the responsibility which you can reasonably be expected to bear yourself. Moreover, if the mother uses the frightening father in this way it means that *she* becomes more than ever a simply indulgent person to him, and so his way of wheedling and trying to win her indulgence will go on all the more. If you can bring yourself to be perfectly firm and cool with the boy and undisturbed by his shyness or his tempers, that will be the best help you can give him. But, of course, another most valuable help would be plenty of the companionship of other children, away from you. This would be the best possible preparation for his going away to school in a few years' time. I don't think that anything one can do will alter his temperament fundamentally, but if he is handled sensibly and calmly all through these early years the worst difficulties arising from such a temperament can probably be avoided. It should be possible for you to convey the constancy and the warmth of your love to the child through the sharing of activities, joining in his play, talking freely about things he is interested in, and generally making an atmosphere of steady affection that does not need frequent reassurances.

Q. Christine, aged three and a half years, is a terribly nervous child. She is a healthy child—eats and sleeps well (she has always slept in a room alone and with no light), is normal in weight and height, and looks fit except for being rather pale, in spite of loads of fresh air, but is very frightened of noises, and trembles like a leaf and clings to me, and jumps at any noise or weather storm. Another thing that worries me is that, although she has always had playmates, when she goes to a party she won't join in with any little game, nor pull a cracker, nor have her photograph taken. We try gentle persuasion, and then, I'm afraid, become angry with her and tell her "She's a silly girl", etc., and then there are tears. She loves the idea of a party, but when the time arrives all she likes to do is stand and stare or cling to some grown-up. She goes very white, too. She is naturally quite a bright, intelligent and sensible child, though lacking in any power of concentration. I let her play alone (in bed, for instance, in the early morning), but then also she plays every morning with another girl who lives in the same bungalow as we do, and each evening she meets other children. On knowing she was going to a party where races for toddlers would be held, I ran preliminary races with her to show her, but when the time came she refused to run. After much persuasion she lined up with three or four children of her own age, but after running a few yards she burst into tears (she is a tearful child). It appears to me as though she doesn't like any competition, because if she is dancing, and another child in the bungalow comes in and dances too, she stops and looks a bit sulky, and sometimes says, "I can't do it". I don't want her to grow up "not a sport", nor with an inferiority complex. She has never been spoilt, but my husband complains that she takes no notice of what I say and that she whines. Sometimes I feel rather depressed over having such a nervous child, and do want her to be happy and able to stand the rough and tumble of school life later on.

A. As regards general treatment, I think you will just have to give your little girl plenty of time to grow out of her unsocial ways. Lots of little girls of three and half are shy and frightened at parties, and although we naturally want them to be happy and enjoy themselves, we can't alter their temperaments by scolding or even by persuasion. And when a child is also very nervous, as your little girl must be if she goes so white and clings so closely to a grown-up, it is much the best to leave her alone and let her find her feet gradually. As a rule, the more we try to persuade or urge or scold such children into joining in with the games or races, the more they fight shy of it. After all, if one is shy, to have one's shyness taken notice of is bound to increase it, for it brings one into the worst possible place, the very centre of attention! I would always suggest leaving a shy child quite alone, letting her get what pleasure she can out of watching the other children run and romp. I would be ready to welcome any movement she did make to join in, but without the least suggestion of force or of disapproval. She is far more likely to grow up "not a sport" if we continually remind her how different she is from the others, than if we leave her to be drawn into the general fun by seeing how other children enjoy it.

If no fuss is made about her fear of noises and general nervousness, and the general way of her life is wholesome and happy, she will very probably grow out of these troubles. Such fears and shynesses are very common in the years between one and seven, but are usually left behind in development. It does not follow that she will not be quite happy at school later on, although it is quite possible that she will shine more at other things than at competitive games. But, after all, games are not the only important thing, are they? And in any case lots of children who are shy at three and a half are bold and jolly at eight or ten. Even the strong feeling of rivalry that makes her unable to dance with the other child there will get less acute as she grows a little older. I should do my best to give her quiet, calm encouragement, without any over-persuasion or special attention.

Q. My little girl of one year and five months is terribly shy of all strangers and will cry if anyone looks or speaks to her, and makes quite a face, turns her eyes upwards, etc. She is splendid at home, sleeps well, and leads a well-regulated life; she never cries and is as good as gold all day, except when out. Can you tell me the best way to help her?

A. I think you can best help your little girl by leaving her quite alone about the shyness. A very great many children of her age are extremely shy with strangers, although from your description it would appear that she is perhaps unusually so. But it is the sort of difficulty that is quite certain to pass away by natural growth, provided that the child doesn't have any specially unhappy experiences. If you comment upon it, or reproach her, or try to over-persuade her, you are likely to increase the shyness rather than lessen it. If, however, you leave her alone about it, and choose (as far as this is practicable) grown-up friends for her who are pleasant and gentle, she will get used to meeting people and lose this excessive fear of strangers. I should not try to *avoid* her meeting people, but should let this happen quite naturally, yet at the same time, whenever possible, making sure that she doesn't come much in contact with people who make rude remarks about her shyness, or try to force her to smile or talk to them. If you follow these general lines you will find the difficulty pass away.

Q. My little girl of two years and eight months is really quite a sociable and friendly little girl, who very much enjoys the company of others, but always makes me feel awkward when I take her out or have people to see us. When you ask her to say "Good morning" or "Good-bye", she will look very solemn and say nothing but "No". If she is left alone, after five minutes or so she becomes very friendly and playful, but this cannot always be done. She will not even say "Good morning" to her daddy or to me, and to most questions she answers "No" in a very cross way. I feel I can never take her to see anyone that I do not know well, as she appears so cross, and unfriendly, which is not really the case. Sometimes after having a very nice afternoon somewhere she will not say "Good-bye" when leaving. I should mention that she has been late in talking, and it is only about the last three months that she has said very much. I daresay she will grow out of this, but I wondered which way is the best to treat this matter, as I am afraid of making things worse.

A. It is a very interesting psychological problem how so many tiny children, who are quite sociable and friendly after the first greeting of strangers has been safely got over, will yet show this negative feeling in the first moment or two, and particularly will not respond to the formal greeting. It seems clear that the first moment of contact with strangers or people who are not very familiar causes a certain amount of fear in the child, and the child has to defend herself in this way by having nothing to do with them. But if the strangers do not press themselves upon the child, but remain quietly friendly and take no particular notice, the child has time to get over her defensive mood. She then discovers that after all they are not going to eat her up, and will herself make advances. It is much the best to let her discover this for herself. She is much more likely to learn to respond immediately with a happy greeting if no notice is taken of the sullenness and no attempt made to force conventional behaviour. It is really only a matter of waiting, perhaps a year or two, perhaps less, and any little child who does not have unfortunate experiences of rough or unkind grown-ups will learn to trust even strangers enough to greet them pleasantly at once. Your little girl's behaviour is most common between two and four years of age. It is comparatively rare after that age, except in children who have been frightened or cowed. As your little girl is generally backward in talking, it is particularly important not to increase her self-consciousness by making any fuss about these greetings. When, however, you and she are leaving someone with whom she has had a nice afternoon, I would not hesitate to make a cheerful suggestion that she should say "Good-bye", and to tell her that people rather like to have a cheerful parting of that kind when they have all enjoyed themselves. But I should not go further than such a comment. And if I were taking her to see strangers, I would try to let them know beforehand that she was rather shy just yet, but really quite friendly, as they would find if they wouldn't mind leaving her alone for the first few minutes. But I would not trouble unduly about the matter in any way.

Q. How can I prevent my little girl of five and a half years from being self-conscious and shy? As a child and also later I suffered with shyness. I have had to force myself out of it. I was one of a family of five, not any of my sisters were self-conscious or shy and we were all brought up on the same methods. My little daughter—she is an only one—is not shy at home, but anyone she only slightly knows she will not speak to except in a self-conscious and shy way. I feel these uncomfortable feelings will only persist if not dealt with and should like to know the best method of doing so. She attends a good morning school, her mistress considers her an intelligent little pupil, she goes out a fair amount with me and meets people, she has other little friends to tea; she is not shy with children, but as soon as a grown-up speaks to her the uncomfortable feeling comes over her and she is shy and speechless. I feel it as a problem as I know to what extent I suffered.

A. There is no direct way of helping the child over her self-consciousness. To pay attention to it directly will only increase the trouble. But since your little daughter is happy with other children and getting on well at school you can be sure she will gradually grow out of this shyness with grown-ups. I wonder what your position was in your own family—whether, for example, you were the youngest child? Although you say you were all brought up on the same general methods, every child has individual experiences in the family, and, of course, the family situation is very different according to whether one is the eldest, the middle or the youngest child. Sometimes a dominating or unpleasant grown-up may speak to a very little child in a way that frightens her permanently about strangers. I don't know whether anything of this kind can have happened with your little daughter. But shyness with grown-ups is not half so serious a difficulty as being inhibited with other children.

Q. I am at a loss to know what attitude to adopt with my son, now five and a half years. Will you help me? Until recently he has been a most sociable child—never shy and willing to go and stay anywhere. Now he has become a proper "stay-at-home". On reflection I feel perhaps two occurrences may have some bearing upon his case. He had a baby brother, now six months old. Until baby came R. had been an only grandchild and received a lot of attention from everyone—also soon after baby arrived his friend, a girl, had three illnesses consecutively—which meant isolating R. for some months. When this period elapsed, he did not renew this friendship as I had always felt that she was much too old for him and not an altogether suitable playmate—he did not make any fuss. But I do think he missed her. She is unfortunately the only child around here, consequently he has had very little children's company. He has not started school yet as we live rather out of the town and we've had difficulty in fixing a school. However, he starts after Christmas holidays. He hates the idea of school, and begs us not to send him—he gets really upset. Last week he was invited to a party of this friend previously mentioned. He went, but only stayed for an hour, then came home and said he didn't like it, "he wouldn't stay to tea"; he said, "I want to go to the party and I want to stay at home". I must add he adores his Daddy, to the exclusion of everyone else. He appears to be highly strung and sensitive in some ways, yet he has no fear of the dentist or the dark, etc. Again, since baby came, he keeps saying to me, "Are you cross with me?" I could add lots more, but do hope I have said enough.

A. As you suggest, it seems clear that this phase of shyness in your little boy has arisen chiefly as a result of his conflict of feeling about the birth of the baby. And if, as you say, he is actually getting less attention from relatives and friends since the baby came, it is quite understandable that this would increase his loss of confidence in himself, since he probably feels that he is unimportant, unwanted now. His saying, "Are you cross with me?" shows that he is afraid that you do not love him so much now you have the baby. He is bound to have feelings of anger and jealousy against his little brother, and he is probably afraid that you are angry with him because of these impulses. I would make quite clear to him by your behaviour that you love him just as much as you did before the baby came, and I would tell him so explicitly. You might say to R. that you "think perhaps he is afraid that you don't love him so much now you have the baby; but this is not so. You love the baby, and you love R. too. The baby is little and cannot do anything for himself, so you have to do a great many things for him; but you have also done all those things for R. and are going on doing things for him." I would try to keep a special period each day for R. alone, which you can spend in play and talk and happy occupations. Since R. is so fond of his Daddy, it would be a help if Daddy joined in "big boys" games and pursuits with R. so that the boy could find that there are other pleasures, connected with growing up, to compensate for the loss of more babyish satisfactions. Perhaps R. could also join in some of his father's interests, for instance, gardening, if Daddy has a garden. You might get your relatives and friends to co-operate also, by not making too much fuss of the baby. I would answer any questions the boy asked about the origin of babies, simply and frankly.

With regard to the shyness itself, I would not urge R. directly to try to overcome this, and I would not press him to go to parties if he does not feel happy about them. I expect that by now he has started school, and although he did not like the idea of going, provided you have chosen the school well, you may find that after a time, when he has got used to the change and has settled down a bit, he will be happy there. If he wants to do so, let him have one or two school friends to tea or to play with him, but I would not press him to any social activity at present if he does not feel inclined. One can sympathize with the boy when he said, "I want to go to the party and I want to stay at home". His shyness on this particular occasion was certain to have been increased by the break in his contact with the older girl. But if you do not press him socially, and let him make his own friends at school just as he likes, perhaps you will find that by next Christmas he will enjoy his parties as much as he used to do.

Q. My little girl, aged five and a quarter years, has always been terribly shy, so shy that she hides when strangers come, and if spoken to runs away or is rude. I had hoped she would grow out of this and of course in a tiny child it was excused; although I feel she is better left alone, it makes her disliked and unpopular, and I get a lot of criticism from older people. With people she knows she is extremely sweet and kind and very thoughtful. We never have any trouble over the daily routine, she plays happily, without worrying anyone, and goes to bed cheerfully at six. She is rather temperamental and excitable, which causes occasional scenes when she is misunderstood. I have a nurse who is capable of teaching her to read and write, but I cannot imagine what I should do if the school problem arose, as I am sure she would make herself ill with shyness and misery. When I was in a nursing home for a fortnight last winter, she would not eat and ran a temperature; the nurse, who had only been with us a week or two, sent for the doctor, who was mystified. On my return she quickly recovered. If I tell her now when I am going away for a day or two, and explain where, and when I am returning, she is much better, but if I was away for any length of time I am afraid she would be terribly unhappy.

I do feel I ought to make her better able to face life. I suppose she is too sensitive, because when punished her feelings are so hurt she will cry for hours. This makes another difficulty, and I am so afraid of spoiling her. Please do advise me how I can make her more normal, as I feel she will have such an unhappy time later, and even now difficulties are always cropping up over impoliteness, through shyness. If I say I will not take her unless she is polite, she only says she is much happier at home, but there are some places she has to go to. She hates parties, so I have given up taking her, she dislikes any noise so intensely. Should I try and make her face things or avoid as much as possible?

A. It is very wise of you not to bother your little girl about her shyness and not to try to compel her to be sociable if she does not feel like it. She may grow out of the difficulty, quite satisfactorily within the next year or two, and may, in fact, be very much happier when school life begins. I should choose her school very carefully. Let her go to understanding people and a place where there are not too many children in proportion to the staff. I would also try to avoid suggesting in any possible way by your own manner that you take pleasure in her clinging to you, and preferring your company to that of anyone else. Sometimes this is true with the parents of shy children. The child is extraordinarily quick in sensing our own attitudes, even if we ourselves are not quite fully aware of them, and it is very easy to feel flattered because one's child prefers one's company to anyone else's. I am not suggesting that this is so in your case, but only that it would be worth your while thinking over this and making quite sure that you have not sheltered her too much because of the pleasure that it gives you. One cannot force a robust sociability upon a child, but one should avoid any tendency in the other direction. I should certainly invite little playmates to stay with you in your home, and make very sure that you left the children free to be fond of each other, so that your little girl gradually becomes aware that she can give you real pleasure by having a life of her own and real friends of her own.

Q. I do not know whether my baby aged nine months is too young for your notice, but I am most anxious not to ruin her nervous system in any way. My problem is her dreadful shyness. She does not mind strangers in her own home and will go to anyone. But when I take her to her grandmother's house she seems to look worried. Then after about ten minutes she starts to cry and will sob her heart out until I bring her home. She is not spoilt—though she is the only child—and is such a good and sweet baby in her own home. It is simply pathetic the way she cries in a strange house. I am wondering whether it is better not to take her out for a while or whether she will get over it better if I take her out more often. I have not taken her out very much in her babyhood and now, of course, I do not like to take her anywhere except to her grandmother's, as she cries so much. My sisters and I were dreadfully shy as children, and I am most anxious that my baby should not be the same.

A. Your little girl is going through the normal phase of shyness which most children show in the middle period of their first year. A great many observers have recorded that there is a period centring in the middle of the first year, in which the great majority of babies are shy of strangers. A very interesting study was made of the smiling and laughing of a large number of babies by Washburne some years ago, and she found that whereas up to about the twenty-sixth week, anybody who handled the child pleasantly could win a smile from the baby; there was a period after that when the infant would not smile at any stranger, no matter how kind or loving she was. Children first begin to be aware of strangers as such from about the eighteenth to twentieth week, and this intense shyness of them sets in about the middle of the year and lasts until roughly the fortieth week. After the fortieth week most children will then show a discrimination amongst strangers, and smile at those who are really pleasant and gentle and who do not move too suddenly or make too many demands upon the infant. There is commonly a further period of shyness later on in the second year of life. The timidity that your little girl is showing, whilst more marked than with many children, is, nevertheless, a normal phase that has been observed in the great majority of babies. How far she is able to grow out of this marked degree of shyness will really depend upon the handling she receives. If people are gentle and rather passive with her, she will soon begin to trust them again. But if they pick her up ungently, move suddenly, talk loudly, or try to *make* her respond to them, she will only get more frightened and confirmed in her distrust of them. You would be wise for the next month or two not to take her into strange houses, but to content yourself with walks out of doors and letting her see people at a distance. It seems very likely that she has had some experience that she felt to be frightening when she visited her grandmother's house, since her reaction there is so very marked. You may be able to remember, perhaps, whether someone there has treated her in an ungentle though well-intentioned way—has perhaps talked and laughed too loudly or done something that made her feel distressed. If so, she will need time to get over it, but you can feel sure that she will grow out of the difficulty if she is wisely and understandingly treated. If grown-ups *deserve* the trust and friendliness of little children, they will get it; but not if they try to *demand* it from the child.

SHYNESS

Q. I have two boys, K., aged six and a half, and N., aged five. K. has always been highly-strung and is a stammerer, but is very healthy, jolly and reasonable; even when he becomes excited he does not become unmanageable and he is very quick to appreciate that other people have rights, largely because we have always scrupulously regarded his rights. I cannot claim that he is quickly obedient, but he is obedient and it is an unknown thing for us to have a flat refusal to any command or request. My reasons are often asked for, but I think that reasonable and a healthy sign. So it is no problem of discipline which troubles me but a vague, but very real lack of confidence in himself which is, I believe, at the back of his troubles. The stammering is one distressing sign of this, and another which will give him much trouble in school life is a painful tendency to "show off". At present both boys go to an excellent school, where they are very happy. N. is clever and advanced for his age, and is a child of character and calm confidence. He was born like that, and is a great contrast to his brother, who feared many things as a baby. K. is not clever and seems afraid of learning to read, but eager to learn from me at home, but he loves his school and is eager and bright, though not clever. At school there is no competition, so at present there is no reason to think K. is conscious that he is much slower than N., and we are all on our guard to give K. credit for all his achievements. He is quite good with his hands, and does a lot of carpentering at home, and has a full, happy home life. But if any visitors come, gone is our sensible K. and in his place a rather silly little boy, who shows off and is noisy and stupid. At school, when any visitors come, his teacher tells me it is the same. Instead of carrying on happily with his work, he becomes conspicuous and silly. It is just the same when I visit the school or if his teacher comes to tea with me here. On those occasions he loves to dress up and come in, singing and talking in a forced voice. Is this very abnormal at this age? As a toddler he was very shy, but has lost all trace of that, but I realize that this "showing off" is perhaps his method of dealing with the feelings that previously made him appear shy. What attitude should I take up when visitors are present? Should I ignore the silliness or stop it?

A. You will probably find that this tendency gets much less during the next year or two. The boy's general development is obviously so satisfactory that I am sure you have only to wait patiently, strengthening all the sources of confidence in him, and he will outgrow this particular neurotic symptom. I think the boy's age has something to do with it. This period between six and seven is often an age of special nervous strain due to the emotional and general disturbances connected with the second teething. It is after the eighth year that boys so commonly settle down into a much greater stability and solid sense. You are certainly right in feeling that the "showing off" is his way of dealing with his shyness. I should be inclined to say a quiet word to the boy when visitors come and he starts being silly. I would not altogether ignore it. I would try to give him some responsibility, for example, if it is tea-time, let him serve or hand things, and I would try to get him talking about something he is doing or is interested in. Let him show off something that is really useful, if you can; and shorten the period, too, when he is actually with the visitors. Give him some attention in the early part of their visit, and then turn him out into his workshop or nursery or garden, and relieve him from the strain of trying to adjust to strangers. But it is very probable that you will find the tendency getting much less after this next year.

VI. JEALOUSY

Q. I have a little girl of three and twin boys of thirteen months. On the whole, until fairly recently, there have not been any undue signs of jealousy, especially considering that the babies were delicate at first and took up a great deal of my attention. Of course, we all made a point of not neglecting the older child more than was absolutely necessary, and from very early stages we let her help to do little things for the babies which she liked very much. During the last few months, however, her attitude to them has been changing. She is devoted to the elder one, who is on the whole rather placid and not very advanced—he does not stand and scarcely crawls—but is horrid to the other one and constantly tries to hurt him, so much so that it is impossible to leave her alone with him. When reproved she says that she does not like him at all. I can quite understand her differentiating between them, as they are quite different in character. The younger one, whom she dislikes, is rather more advanced in some ways, very energetic and lively and rather bad-tempered. Since earliest infancy he has had a quite peculiarly loud and trying scream, which I think may unconsciously be at the root of her antipathy. He is also rather difficult to manage in some ways and much more attached to me than the older one, who is equally happy with any member of the household. The moment I come into the room the younger one starts to crawl as fast as possible towards me, which of course she may have noticed and resented, though I try to make a point of always greeting her first when I come into the nursery. Another small detail is that the disliked one is still very bald, while the other has fairly thick curls. Once when I asked her if she could explain her antipathy, she said she did not like his hair. Putting everything together I think I can understand how it is that she dislikes the younger twin. My difficulty is how to treat the matter. We tried once or twice hurting her in the same way as she had hurt him—which seemed quite unsuccessful. One day when she had deliberately hurt him just at tea-time, I made her have her tea in a room alone, which she did not much like. After that she was better for a week or two, but now it has started again. We were quite frightened the other day when she tried to push him downstairs. I may add that we often play and do things with her quite away from the twins, and except when we are away for our holidays she sees plenty of children of her own age. She has a room to herself and is quite sensible and independent. Except that she does a good deal of screaming I do not consider her a particularly naughty or difficult child, but naturally we do not want this attitude towards the twins to continue. One last small point I might mention is that as soon as she has done anything naughty, in particular after maltreating her brother, she says at once, "Mummy, do you like me? I want you to kiss me". In regard to my treatment for other offences it is usually enough to say that we do not like her or do not want to be with her. She occasionally has a good smack for persistent disobedience or prolonged and deliberate tiresomeness. I have found this the most satisfactory punishment. She never becomes sulky or bears malice. But I have never smacked her for hurting her brother.

A. You seem to be right in the reasons you suggest for your little girl's dislike of the younger twin. Such things as the loud scream and the bald head are so much more important to little children's feelings than to ours; and doubtless his great attachment to you makes her feel more jealous of him. I do not think it is helpful, however, to hurt her in the way she has hurt him. You found yourself it was unsuccessful, and I have never known this method to lead to any satisfactory results. Putting her alone in a room if she does hurt the child is a much more logical and humane method of dealing with her aggression, but you cannot expect that such strong impulses in a child of this age will be improved in a very short time. She is little more than a baby herself. It will take a period of growth and readjustment for her to learn to tolerate the little boy who arouses so much dislike, and you will need to show a good deal of patience, and constant supervision, until she has achieved sufficient control and understanding. The fact that you play with her apart from the twins and that she has friends of her own age is extremely helpful. I would suggest that you make up your minds to recognize that you cannot change such an emotional attitude in the little girl all in a hurry, and that it will take time and patience. It would be advisable to try to avoid any situations of temptation, not to leave her with the younger one unless there is an adult close enough to prevent any serious harm. If she did really hurt him such as by pushing him downstairs, she would only be the more wretched about it and hate him all the more for it. Careful supervision, constant affection and patience, will help her to grow out of this attitude. Meanwhile the baby's bald head will improve naturally, and he will become a more interesting person to her as he leaves babyhood behind and becomes more of a boy.

Q. I would be glad if you could help me once more over my little girl. She is five and a half years old. I have now got a son of six months. Other mothers have written to you about jealousy before, but in those cases the child seems to have suppressed it to a certain extent. There is nothing suppressed about A.'s jealousy. A. is quite ready to say that J. is a nuisance if she feels he is, and that if only he had not been born I would have more time to give to her, etc. She once said, "I don't like J." "Why?" I asked. "Because you love him more than me." I said, "I don't. It may seem to you that I spend more time on him, but that is because he is a baby and quite helpless. You must help me to teach him to do things for himself and then there will be more time for everyone." I also told her that when she was his age, I spent more time on her than I ever have on him, which is the case, as she was a very delicate baby and I had no one to help me. They have an excellent young nurse who is very good with both of them, but A. grudges every moment she spends on J. A. herself is charming with J. She takes him on her knee and is never anything but gentle. She is also a real help with him on nurse's day out. She has half an hour with me every day after he has gone to bed when I do whatever she wants. It is quite impossible to send her to school, as the nearest is twelve miles away. But I take her in once a week to do dancing and ballet dancing. The nearest children are two and a half miles off, and they come over once a week to a rhythm class and percussion band we have here. I try to arrange for them to come to tea at other times, but I am very busy and their parents are too, so it is difficult to arrange often. She does easy lessons with me every morning. She likes them and is really quite clever, I think and loves everything except all kinds of handwork. As a matter of fact, with lessons and everything, she takes up quite as much of my time as J. does. She plays alone very happily in our big garden. She is very imaginative and highly-strung, and since this trouble has begun to look pale and tired. She has always been bad about her food, but now the amount she eats is almost nonexistent. She has become very rude and dictatorial in her manners. To give an instance: to-day I went into the nursery and she said, "Go away at once, I'm playing". I said I had not come to disturb her but to speak to her nurse. When I had spoken for one minute, she said, "Now go". I said I must wait till she could be kinder, at which she began to scream so loudly that I said that I would smack her if she did not stop. I know that you will not approve of this, but I never do smack her. When she is beyond all reason, a very rare occurrence, I threaten to, and I have never known the threat to fail. When she is wound up, it is *the only thing that does work. I may say that no one ever speaks to her as she sometimes speaks to other people! You will understand that this letter is only about her faults. Most people who meet her tell me she is entirely unspoilt and quite charming. She is the kind of child who always does attract strangers, so that is the other side of the picture. She seems more advanced than most children a great deal older than she, in the books she likes, and in her interests. I take great care not to make a fuss of J. in her presence, and so does my husband, but of course visitors always make a bee line for a baby. Is there anything I can do to help her to get the better of her jealousy? She seems to me so very ready to admit it that I sometimes wonder if she does make an effort to get over it? But I thought I must write to you before talking to her about it. She often says, "I shall like J. better when he's older. He's no use now."*

A. You seem to be dealing wisely with your little girl's jealousy, and all that is needed is time for the child to adjust herself to this very real situation of rivalry with the little brother. It is a pity that there is no school or group of children nearer to you, since that would be such a great help to the child in easing the tension of rivalry between herself and the baby brother. But as this is not practicable, I think you are doing all you can to help her grow out of the difficulty the only possibility being that rather firmer handling, before she gets to the point where she needs to be threatened with smacking, might help her more. I wonder, too, whether you could let her actually do more for the baby herself than at present? You say she does help you on nurse's day out, and that she is very gentle with the child. All this is to the good, and it is certainly very much better that the child should feel able to be frank about her jealousy than if she had to hide it altogether within herself. She will learn to control it and temper it with time, without getting such undue guilt about it as if you scolded her and said that it was a shocking, unnatural thing for her to feel any jealousy. It sounds to me as if she were making an effort to get over it, and if you speak to her about it I should certainly say that you realize she is trying not to be jealous, or trying not to let her feelings affect her behaviour to the baby. It is quite true that the boy will be of more interest to her when he is able to do more, although the age difference between them will prevent his being a companion for her in childhood years. But she will be able to play with him more when he begins to walk. I should take the line that you know that she feels jealous and is trying to be sensible about it, and that you are sure as she gets older she will be able to take more pleasure in him. But otherwise it seems that you are dealing with the problem quite satisfactorily.

Q. My two little boys, are aged six years and two months and three years and ten months, and were quarrelling rather a lot. That, however, has improved a little, since the elder recommenced school (mornings) and they have agreed very well while out in the afternoons. But the elder teases the younger, who does not seem able to stand it. Do you think I should interfere? I do so now, and am wondering does the little one make a fuss to draw my attention? They are rather rough, and I am always correcting them. Do you think this is necessary? I have often smacked them, but have decided not to do so any more, and already they seem to be better for it. Do you agree with me in this? I think the elder boy is sometimes jealous of the younger, as he is rather peevish and irritable with him. I do not make any distinction between them, so am wondering could you suggest something to make him less peevish? Also, he is very rarely asleep before 8.30, although he is nearly always in bed before 7.15. Whatever I do he remains the same, and always has been. The elder always wakens first between 7 and 7.30. He is very

JEALOUSY

quick at school, his teacher says unusually so, and I wonder is his brain too active to allow him to go to sleep? Between tea and bath time they play with bricks, trains, and all that type of toy, as Daddy is at home just then and he won't allow them to be noisy while he is in as he himself really needs a rest; so they don't get over excited before bed-time. Whatever the cause, it is something that doesn't affect the younger. But he is the stolid type and the elder the excitable. I feel sure that ten and a half hours sleep is not enough for a six-year-old.

A. Aren't you worrying unduly about your elder boy's sleep? Children differ as much as grown ups do in the amount of sleep that they need or can take, and whilst I should certainly do everything to help him to sleep, I don't think you need be so anxious about it. Doubtless the elder boy is jealous of the younger one, and has been so from the time of the latter's arrival. You are certainly wise in not smacking the boys, since that is not a helpful way of dealing with their difficulties. How does your elder boy spend his afternoon? Does he get out for open-air exercise? If they have an enforced quiet time between tea and bed, he certainly needs to spend every moment of the afternoon interval in outdoor exercise. This should be of a free kind, not just soberly walking, but running and jumping and ball games, or digging and playing on the beach. If his school has out-door sports in the afternoon, as some schools do, it might be a very good thing to let him join with these. But I am sure it is very important that that afternoon time should be one of free outdoor activity, so that he is thoroughly satisfied and healthily fatigued when bed time comes. The quarrelling of the two brothers, as you have seen from your experience, is most easily helped by giving the elder one a life of his own with boys of his own age. He will be more easily able to be friendly to the younger brother when he is with him if he has plenty of opportunities for games and exercise and friendship away from him. The two problems you put to me seem to be interconnected, and whatever you do to help the child's relation with his brother is also likely to relieve the difficulty in sleeping.

Q. I should be much obliged if you would suggest a treatment for my daughter, aged three and a half years. She is troublesome with her brother, aged five months—she is liable to slap him, hug him too hard or poke him, shout at him till he cries, etc., and I am afraid that she may really hurt him. This happens most frequently when I am responsible for the two children, and nurse is away or out of the room. It appears to me to be partly jealousy (I am suckling the infant), and partly interested but misplaced experiment. She is a healthy, happy and capable girl —full of energy, but has unfortunately lacked much companionship of her own age, as we live right in the country. In an endeavour to combat the jealousy I have allowed her to come into my bed for half an hour in the morning and when she has been rough with him I usually put her straight out of the room. Often after she has hurt him she appears sorry for it, and at times she is very charming with him. I have let her help as much as she can with bathing him, etc., and she seems to enjoy that— also she holds him sometimes, but once, probably deliberately, she dropped him! What do you suggest? She is inclined to be rather rough with other children, particularly if they flinch from her at all. If they stand up for themselves she does not tease them so much.

A. I don't doubt that you are right in saying that your little girl's unkindness to her baby brother arises partly from jealousy and partly from a sort of experiment. The jealousy motive will be the important one, since a child of her age does not need to be told that she is hurting a baby when she does this to him. It sounds to me as if you were handling the situation on good lines, letting her feel that she has a part in the baby's life, and that you will allow her to share so long as she is friendly and helpful. I should, I think, be chary about letting her hold him unless you are close by to prevent his being dropped. After all, she is only a tiny child herself, and it is a very big responsibility. To be actually dropped would be very frightening to the baby himself. I should let her hold him, but only when you are quite close, because it is just as important for her to feel that you can protect the baby against her jealousy as that you are friendly and helpful to her, too. Apart from this, you have only to go on the lines you are following, and to remember that *time* is always an important factor in getting over these difficulties. Even adults take time to get over crises in their lives of one sort or another, and there is never any situation in adult life which is as difficult as this one is for a little child of three. Feelings and wishes and phantasies are all so intense at that age, and the powers of control grow quite slowly. So that one needs to be patient with the child and to realize that the solution is a question of time and growth, not of a recipe which can be applied in a moment.

Q. My little girl Hazel, aged one year and ten months, has become very difficult to manage, owing, I expect, to jealousy, as she has a little brother, five months. At first she would hit him and start whining whenever I picked him up. I have not taken any notice of these fits, and never asked her to do anything for him, as I realized it only made her more angry. I am pleased to say this has been very effective, as she now asks to tuck him in and mind him for me. She also offers him her toys, although she does not like parting with them. The real trouble now is that she absolutely refuses to have anything to do with strangers. If anyone says "Good morning," or speaks to her at all, her reply is nearly always a very definite, "No, don't", or "No, won't". She screams if they touch her or try to pick her up.

"This has been going on for some months now; it started before baby was born. If I refer to it and tell her it is rude she is much worse. I have tried ignoring it for some time now, but she still carries on.

I have tried having other children to play with her, but find she screams as soon as they go near her or touch her. She is quite all right so long as they don't speak to her. If strangers ignore her she will immediately start talking to them, but few do ignore her; and it always means a scene, besides making people think she is spoilt. Her Daddy makes a great fuss of her and is really very patient, and very rarely gets angry. She worships him, and is really very upset if he is cross, but often whines and carries on when he is there. Hazel knows that she is being naughty, as she often comes in from a walk and tells me a doggie said, "No, don't", and he is rude. It is very difficult to explain everything, but perhaps I have made it clear that she is continually having scenes when other people are near, and is quite capable of being exceedingly sweet and lovable.

A. It is clear that the little girl's first reaction to her brother was of open jealousy and direct hostility. These feelings, however, would be naturally frightening to the little girl herself, because she would at the same time have impulses of love and tenderness to him, and because she would be afraid of losing her mother's love if she showed her jealousy so openly. What, then, happened was that she turned her jealousy on to strangers, other grown-ups or children, and so freed her relation to her baby brother from this distressing emotion, and became wholly maternal towards him, tucking him up and taking care of him like a little mother.

Now, the problem is, what should be done about her attitude of fear and hostility to strangers? Well, what I should do in such a situation is to leave her largely alone about it, trusting her natural affection and her proved ablity to get over her less desirable impulses to carry her out of this difficulty too. I would leave *her* alone, but I would very definitely ask the grown-ups not to touch her or take any marked notice of her, telling them that if they would be just quiet and responsive she would be sure then to talk to them and to be friendly. She is quite certain to grow out of this difficulty within a year or two if her experiences with grown-ups are happy.

To ask adults to accommodate themselves to the emotional crises of little children is surely not difficult or unreasonable. What is the use of *our* superior self-control and politeness and reasonableness if we cannot exercise them to help little children over a stile? If we were talking to a grown-up friend who was in a temporary emotional difficulty of some sort—the loss of a loved one, or some other trying circumstance—we should surely give them special consideration. We should not expect them to do and say exactly what we wanted them to. It is only with little children that we let ourselves be offended so readily when they cannot immediately respond to our advances. And, after all, what right have we to demand, any of us, that a child who doesn't know us should immediately like us and be friendly? If we want the friendship of a child we surely have to earn it, and we don't deserve it if we insist upon picking him up and talking to him the very moment we meet him. If, however, we can be just quiet and friendly in his presence he will very soon come and make the first advance.

Whenever Hazel is going to meet quite new people it would be worth while just telling the strangers beforehand that if they leave her alone for a time she will be sure to make friends. She will then grow out of the particular shyness and fear which make this difficulty as she becomes assured that grown-ups are friendly and understanding people. With other children, of course, it is not so easy, as one cannot very well explain to them as one could to grown-ups. But one could very often say, "Hazel will soon come and play with you if you leave her quiet for a time".

The way Hazel puts her naughtiness on to the doggie, saying it was the doggie who "was rude and said, 'No, don't'," shows how hard she is struggling with these impulses of fear and hostility. It is a not uncommon way of dealing with a feeling of naughtiness—quite ordinary in small children. I am sure you are right in feeling that she becomes worse if you tell her that she is rude not to be friendly with people, and I think you can rest quite secure that she will grow out of the difficulty with the sort of help I have suggested.

Q. I should so much like to have your advice on a small boy of nearly five. Peter is and always has been a difficult child. He is a nice child, as he is kind and can be very sweet and adores his two-year-old brother and cannot bear him to be punished in any way. The trouble with Peter is a general spasmodic naughtiness. He will suddenly hurl a cushion at the ready-laid tea table and spill everything, or even break everything. He will suddenly lie on the floor and kick the door till all paint is removed, or he will put his tie deliberately into the gravy. He frequently throws books out of the windows or he will go and unmake all the nursery beds. I have tried rather ignoring his naughtiness as his mother seemed to think this was the best way of treating him, and his previous nurse had lost her temper with him a good deal, and had smacked him and shut him up in cupboards. This ignoring him seems to have done a certain amount of good, as his parents say there are less scenes than there were. However, he really is very very naughty and I would so like to know what is at the root of his trouble. I have been firm with him and seen that direct orders were obeyed, though this has meant several fits of most alarming screaming. I have never yet lost my temper with him, nor I think, shown that his tantrums were inconvenient or worried me. I have laid stress on his good deeds and ignored the bad where I could. I should add that if he is so naughty that I am compelled to put him in his room (as I am when he starts wrecking things) he screams for about five minutes and later returns smiling cheerfully as though nothing had happened. I have been most careful to treat both children alike in case jealousy were the cause, but I do not think it is, as he does not seem at all jealous of his brother. He likes to boast of his naughtiness rather, and if I praise him for anything, generally adds, "but I shall be naughty again to-morrow". He incites his small brother to annoy, saying such things as "Leon, stand upon your chair to eat your dinner". Actually it seems as though his sole wish is to annoy, as these difficulties are never when he is thwarted, nor when he has any kind of provocation. I thought, perhaps, he had been rather thwarted, where physical activities are concerned, and have given scope for these and as great a freedom as possible. I have also tried to avoid many "don'ts". He is a bit better, I know, but it is a very little bit, and I somehow feel I have not quite got to the root of the matter, and would so like to be able to. In one way I feel all this is not terribly serious, because underneath it all he has a really nice character, only it is very trying for the whole household as there is very little peace.

A. It seems to me likely that this small boy seeks these dramatic situations of sudden and extreme destructiveness, mainly because he has not enough satisfaction in other directions. When these spasmodic outbreaks occur I would try to understand them by considering what has gone before. You can be sure they are not uncaused, although it may not be easy to trace the course of events which has led to them. I notice that you say that he adores the two-year-old brother, and I have been remarking in a number of letters recently how often difficult or naughty children are said to "adore" the younger ones or to be passionately fond of them, and so on and so forth. Experience would suggest that excessive fondness for the younger child, without any open signs of natural rivalry, nearly always means that the jealousy is being expressed in some other indirect way, such as these outbreaks of your little charge. In this boy's case, however, the previous severity of punishment and lack of understanding must have increased his difficulties, and since the boy's mother is so sure that his tantrums are lessening and he is less difficult than he was, it seems clear that you have only to go on in the way you have been doing. You are quite right to put him alone in his room when he starts smashing things up, since he appreciates just as well as you do that you have the right to protect yourself and other people and their possessions from his naughtiness. When the child says, "But I shall be naughty again to-morrow", this is not a simple boasting so much as an expression of despair. He is afraid lest you should imagine, when you praise him, that he can go on *always* being good: but he knows how urgent the naughty feelings are sometimes, and he wants to make sure that you understand this and will not withdraw your love altogether because he cannot be perfect. I would therefore not overpraise the boy. He himself knows what strong feelings of rivalry and anger he has against his little brother, and is afraid that if *you* knew this and how bad he felt inside, you would not love him. Then he has to be naughty in order to show you how bad he feels inside. Whilst, therefore, you want to go on showing your belief in him and your affection for him, it is very important not to overdo the praise and approval, but to be rather more matter-of-fact, and to take it for granted that he will be good and sensible, and at the same time to let him know that you understand that he is jealous of his little brother. I often think we fail to realize what an enormous strain we put upon little children when

JEALOUSY

we show that we expect them *never* to express a sign of jealousy or hatred. We can do this, of course, not only by disapproving if they do show it, but by an excess of approval when they are loving and affectionate to the younger child. They then become terrified of losing our good opinion about them, and can really suffer great distress about their own hidden knowledge of their less satisfactory feelings. In general, therefore, I would go on treating this child quite firmly and sensibly and quietly, in the way you have done, but avoid over-valuing his sweetness with his younger brother and over-praising the good qualities that he does show.

Q. My small charge is nearly three years old, and has a sister of four and a brother twenty months. But J. is the problem. She screams if the slightest thing upsets her, or if either of the other children touch anything of hers, and sulks when corrected in any way. The difficulty is she will not give in, but will keep it up for an hour or more. Putting her in a room by herself seems to be the best method of dealing with her, though she screams all the time, which is most wearing, and refuses to say she will be good unless we threaten to go out without her. But however long she is left alone it has no effect on her. The next time anything goes wrong she will go through the whole proceeding again. Sometimes J. will go without her food if corrected during a meal, or she will sulk and refuse to eat for no apparent reason.

A. It seems very likely that jealousy of the other two children is the essence of J.'s difficulty, as she cannot bear them to touch anything of hers, and is so intolerant of any thwarting. Such continual sulks and screams are extremely wearing and unpleasant, and yet you must know from the letters that appear in these columns how very common this sort of difficulty is amongst little children of two to five years of age. I should try to make quite sure that J. has no real basis for her sense of injustice, and that she is not interfered with in any arbitrary way or on occasions that could be avoided with a little care and thought. But with the utmost care you will not be able to avoid thwarting her and upsetting her altogether, nor would it be a good thing to save her altogether from interference by the other two children. If, however, you do avoid any arbitrary or unjust dealing with her and use every possible opportunity to encourage friendly play and a steady sense of affection and understanding, I think you will find that the tantrums and selfishness will gradually get less as she grows older. Putting her in a room by herself when she actually has the screaming fit may be one of the most useful things, as it is not too severe to be frightening, and even a little child can understand that other people don't want to hear screams. But I should not try to make the child say in so many words that she "will be good". I remember as a small child myself how people tried to force me to say I was sorry and that I "would be good", and how impossible it felt to frame one's mouth to say those words! If, however, someone came to me with a smile and said cheerfully, "Now come along and be sensible, let's all be friendly together", I could respond to that quite happily, and did, in fact, whenever I was treated in this way. But the formal acknowledgment of naughtiness is often very hard for little children to make, and promises to be good are not much use when one is very small, as they are often so hard to keep. And when they are again broken they make one feel defeated and miserable. If you can go on treating J. gently and cheerfully, not letting her gain any advantage by her screams, nor, on the other hand, making too much of them yourself, you will find that they get less frequent and less marked as she grows and discovers the delights of co-operative play. With regard to her response to the other children's touching anything of hers, I should try to deal with that by scrupulous fairness in judging between them, and by trying to encourage mutual lending and borrowing of treasured possessions.

Q. I am a young nanny, and have complete charge of three boys, ages nine years, five years, and twelve months. The eldest is a real bully and will do anything to cause tears in the nursery. He is, of course, at school, but comes home mid-day for lunch. The moment he is in, the nursery is in an uproar. I have tried treating him as a grown-up, and we always have a chat when the little ones have gone to bed. I never mention any misdeeds that he has done during the day, and during this time I see some of the very nice ways that he seems to be hiding. I see the bad result this is having on my next charge. When we are alone he is most affectionate to me and his baby brother, but when his elder brother is in he is entirely different, and will even make the baby cry. He is also growing very nervy. I have several times caught him nail-biting. I have not scolded him for this, but just told him that big boys never put their fingers in their mouths. He is also rather backward, and extremely slow in all his movements. I have been forced sometimes to separate the two, and make them play apart; but this I do not like doing, as my aim is to bring them together. The baby is very good-tempered as a rule, but is given, like the older boys, to having sudden bursts of temper about a very little thing, mostly when having been hurt. During these I can do nothing with him, but just let him get over it in his own time. After these outbursts he is just his own sweet self again.

A. This is a very difficult problem. It seems to me that you are going on the right lines in being friendly to the eldest boy and not mentioning his misdeeds when you talk with him after the others have gone to bed. On the other hand, I think that it is necessary to be very firm with him at the actual time when he bullies and disturbs the younger children. A boy of nine does want very firm handling, and real strictness is not out of place at such an age and in such circumstances as you describe.

The distance in age between the three children must, I think, cause part of the trouble, as the ordinary companionship in play and the mutual advantage that boys of the same age can be to each other are lacking here. If, of course, the elder boy had more protective fatherly impulses towards the younger children, it would be easier. Perhaps this will come a little later, but at present there doesn't seem to be much of it from what you say. If you could appeal to that side of the boy, to the idea of his helping and protecting the younger ones just because he is a big boy, that might possibly have some effect; but otherwise you will just have to be very firm in actually preventing and forbidding his bullying ways.

You are doing quite wisely in not scolding the second boy for his nail-biting. With him I should use every sort of encouragement in his play and practical achievements of his own. He may be happier when he, too, goes to school.

Q. I am a trained nurse and have charge of two children— David just four years, and Peter, twenty-two months. David is the problem, as he is so intensely jealous of Peter. He openly says that he hates P. and it is impossible to leave the two of them together as D. instantly attacks P. in some way or other, often really hurting him. It is very difficult to know how to deal with the situation. I may add that it is not a case of Peter coming in for a lot of attention and David being left out; it is rather the other way about. We live right out in the country and D. has absolutely no other companions. We tried him at a Nursery School a short while ago, but the excitement proved too much for him, although he loved going. I have been with D. since he was a month old—he is of a very lovable nature, but very determined and extremely wilful. Another thing that rather worries me is his dependence on me. It is very difficult to get him to do anything for himself, such as dressing, etc.: he always insists that he can't. What is the best line to take—leave him to it or go on hoping?

A. I wonder how long you left the elder boy at the nursery school. It sounds from your letter as if you only tried it for a very short time, and the problem you put does rather suggest that a good nursery school would be a very great help to the elder boy. Many children find a nursery school rather exciting to begin with, but settle down to it very happily and contentedly after a time. I would recommend trying it again, not necessarily leaving the child there the whole morning, but say for a couple of hours to begin with. At home I would be just as careful not to give David more attention than Peter, as I would not stir David's jealousy, by giving the younger child too much. If you give David more attention and affection than Peter, that will make him feel guilty and anxious. It might really help him if there were a more just balance. I would certainly not put temptation in the elder boy's way and risk hurt to the younger one by leaving them together. I would say to David that you know that he feels very jealous of Peter, but that when he is older he will probably not feel like that but will enjoy having a brother to play with. Do not say this with any reproach or scolding, but in a quiet, matter-of-fact way. Very often brothers who have been acutely jealous of each other and constantly quarrelling when they were small become splendid friends when they are older. You do not need, therefore, to fear that there will be no change, and it will help the boy if you yourself are confident that this phase of acute feeling will pass. The nursery school, of course, would be the best help towards encouraging the boy's independence, and he would then be less jealous of the younger boy. I would not urge him too much to do things for himself, but would try to make a compromise: "You do this, then I will do so-and-so" or, "Let's do it together to-day, and then perhaps to-morrow you may feel like doing it yourself". It is often more helpful to graduate one's demands upon the child than to insist that he should be independent all at once.

Q. I have two sons, one aged three and three-quarters and the other one year. The latter now stands up a lot with the aid of support and shows signs of beginning to walk. His brother is very fond of him, but is also rather jealous of him, I think. He plays with him a lot very nicely, but seems to get fits of "bullying" when he often hurts him, sometimes intentionally, or so it appears. We have tried to explain to him that baby is little and he must be more careful, but it seems to have no effect. He seems to resent the idea that he may not do as he likes with his baby brother. On a few occasions we have spoken sharply to him, but he does not seem to realize the cause of it, and we have tried to avoid this and have not attempted to punish him in any way. Could you let me know what line one should take over this "bullying"? I have been obliged to do a great deal for the younger boy, as I have only had a young and untrained nannie to help me, and my husband has been in India for the past year, so though I have tried to prevent the elder boy from being jealous, it has been very difficult, and I am afraid I have not succeeded. We both have him with us a great deal now.

A. You are very wise in not punishing the elder boy for his bullying of the baby; but on the other hand I would quite firmly interfere to prevent him if he attempts to hurt him. I would do this without scolding or reproach, but in a matter-of-fact way ask him not to do it. When a child behaves in this way, however, one has to supervise the children carefully when they are together. It is a phase of development which he will grow out of with kind and sensible handling. And you may find it easier if you realize that children are always jealous of other members of the family, and that though we may aggravate their jealousy by unwise behaviour, we cannot altogether prevent them, however wise we are, from feeling anger and jealousy against the baby who to them is a rival for their parents' love. Now that your husband is back and you and he are able to give the elder boy more attention, this will be a help to him. I would show the boy clearly by your attitude that you love him just as much now you have the baby as you did before. You might say to him, "I know you sometimes feel angry and jealous of the baby, though at other times you love him. Perhaps you are afraid that we don't love you so much now; but that is not so, we love you and the baby."

But you will remember, won't you, that it is bound to take the boy time to get over his trouble and to feel again fully sure of your love—and that you love him *in spite of* his jealousy.

Q. I should be most grateful for your advice concerning the behaviour of my little boy, Michael, aged two and nine months, towards his baby brother of eleven months. Michael is a nervous and sensitive but very affectionate child—he is most intelligent, full of life and joy and has a sweet disposition. Although in many ways Michael shows affection for his little brother and plays with him very sweetly, he will suddenly smack him in the face or shake him violently, or strike him with a hard toy, and if we cannot stop him in time he often really hurts and upsets the poor infant who is truly beginning to fear him. We stop Michael in a most matter-of-fact way, and then take his mind right off the baby, but he soon begins again. He has never been smacked himself and has never seen it. He gets a lot of love and perhaps too much attention, but he has plenty of occupations and interests and leads a very healthy outdoor life. He certainly has not had any children to play with him lately because the few children we know of his own age have been ill. I am not really worried because I feel certain that when baby grows and becomes more independent and can play better with Michael the situation is bound to adjust itself.

A. You are very wise in not being worried about the matter, and in feeling that the situation will improve later on, when the baby is able to play more with Michael. With regard to your present handling of Michael in the matter, I don't think you can do much more than you are already doing, that is, preventing him in a matter-of-fact way when he does attempt to hurt the baby. I would also ask him quite firmly if he will "please not do that to the baby", for you do not want the boy to think that he can get away with this bullying. On the other hand, I would not speak to him in a reproachful way about it, but be as matter-of-fact as possible. As I have suggested before, children who show this kind of aggressive behaviour do need very careful supervision. You could show the boy that you understand his feelings by saying to him something like this, if he has shown aggression to the baby: "I know that sometimes you feel angry with the baby and want to hit him, although you love him as well and want to play with him. But I am not going to let you hurt baby, and perhaps if you feel you want to hit him you will hit something else (perhaps a cushion) instead." I would provide him with some of the hammering toys that are now made, to allow him to work off his desire to hit in some way that will not matter! When he is able to play with his little friends again, that will be all to the good in helping him to

JEALOUSY

overcome this difficulty. But your general treatment of the boy seems to be very sensible, and the general conditions of his life satisfactory, so that I am sure you can have every confidence in the boy's growing out of this difficulty, with further development.

Q.1. My little girl of four simply will not behave herself at table. Before her baby sister came a year ago she was perfect, sat nicely and needed no correction. If I have visitors she is much worse, talks the whole time and throws her arms about and is thoroughly naughty and will not do as she is told. How can I get her to eat and behave well at meal times? She has always been so good until the last year, and so sweet-tempered and happy, but now she seems quite the reverse, and is always whining and crying. At one time she would play for hours and be contented all day. She is kept to a certain time in everything, but now she seems not to know what to do with herself. I know she is older and perhaps needs something different to do, as before she would amuse herself with almost anything. What toys, etc. should she need? She is really still a very lovable child, as when she is tiresome and naughty, she always says, "I never mean to be naughty", and "I'll never do it again". But she seems to forget. She is nervous and highly strung and gets easily tired. She has always been difficult to feed, never wanting anything much, and I have never fussed about it, but just taken the food away. Also, how do you advise me to act in the case of a baby of one year who gets in a temper?

Q.2. Will you kindly give me your help with my four-year-old daughter, who, up to the age of three years, was a perfect child and such a good baby, no trouble, was most contented, cheerful and obedient and was always happy. At three years she had a baby sister and was not at the time at all jealous; she was told about the baby before its birth and was most happy at her arrival.

But now she has completely changed, will not do a thing she is told without a lot of fuss, and is continually naughty, and I seem to be always correcting her. She has always gone to bed splendidly at 6 p.m. without a light, up to the age of three and a half years, but now she is frightened of the dark and is always calling me, and wakes once or twice during the night. She is rather a nervous child and highly strung. I do hope you will be able to help me, as we should so love to see her again the obedient and happy-natured child she was. Could you also tell me the kind of toys a child of this age requires? She has always played happily by herself up to now, but at present seems to need other things to amuse her.

A. It is clear that each of these little girls is suffering from very acute conflict about the birth of the baby sister, and is quite unable to deal with her feelings of rivalry and inferiority. Neither of these mothers tell me just how the elder child was prepared for the birth of the baby, and dealt with at the time. Q.2 says her little girl was told about the baby before its birth, but, as so much of my correspondence on this problem has shown, it is not so much the mere telling that helps the child, as the way in which the whole situation is handled. The knowledge that a baby is coming will not help her very much if, when it arrives, she has plenty of reason for feeling shut out of things and lost and neglected. I do not say that either Q.1 or Q.2 have done this with the child, but both letters do strongly suggest that the natural and inevitable jealousy of the elder child has not been sufficiently allowed for, and ways of getting her to feel she has a part in the new baby have not been found. It would be a great help to both children if the mother could give a definite period of each day entirely to the child for play and talk and mutual concern. And it would be very helpful if ways could be found of letting the child feel that she can share in the baby sister, help with its bathing and dressing and feeding, and be allowed to ask questions. The right sort of toys and play material would also help her, but just what would be the most valuable for her can only be found out by experiment. It is possible, for example, that a baby doll of her own of a good size, with clothes that would take on and off, and a pram to take her out in, would be a great help. It is so to many little girls. Others are more helped by having a puppy or kitten of their very own. Others, again, by being shown how to make something that baby sister could use; for example, to sew some beads on a coloured coverlet, or to wash one or two of the baby's garments in a bowl with soap-suds on a low stool, where splashing would do no harm. All the ordinary child's toys, dolls and dolls' house and pram, etc., are a help in a crisis of this kind, but especially so if for one period of each day, the mother will share in the child's play with her doll baby, and allow the little girl to play the part of mother and hostess.

The difficulty about the child's naughtiness when visitors come could be helped if, occasionally, the child were allowed to give a tea-party, all of her own, and receive visitors and act as the hostess; sometimes a real one with little girl friends, or even pleasant-mannered grown-ups, who would for the occasion adapt themselves to the little girl's needs and allow themselves to be her guests; sometimes with a toy tea-set, and mother and an aunt or two or three dolls to be her guests. There are endless ways in which we can meet the need of the child to get rid of the feeling that she is unimportant and shut out—neither a baby nor a mother. Entering into the child's play and letting her not merely assume important parts in play, but have occasional real responsibility, for example, as a hostess, would help to adjust the balance that has been upset. These little girls are rather young for sewing material, but they could use large darning needles, threaded with bright wool, to sew soft material and make doll garments or real aprons and coverlets, etc. They love threading coloured beads, and washing real things in soap suds and water, ironing with a play iron and doing all the things that help them to identify themselves with mother and nurse.

With regard to the fit of temper of a baby of one year, there is only one thing to do—to remain quiet and calm until the temper has passed. All healthy babies of this age get into occasional tempers. One needs to find out what has caused it, whether the situation can be avoided, but, above all, to realize that in itself it is a normal thing, part of the child's normal growth. There is no need to do anything but remain quiet and pleasant until the fit passes and then just go on with whatever has to be done, never letting the child feel that she has committed a serious crime.

Q.1. I would like your advice regarding my little charge now three years eight months old, with what seems a deep-rooted jealousy of his baby brother. P.'s jealousy takes the form of spite on the baby, and always has done since baby first came to the nursery. When the maternity nurse left, P. was told that little baby brother was coming to the nursery and that we would now look after him, and he said, "No, not yet". This was a year ago, and the trouble still persists, in fact it gets worse, as baby is now at the crawling stage and very much resents being kept in the pen for long at a time. I quite understand P.'s feelings in the matter. The baby is nothing but a nuisance to him, gets in his way and generally interferes with whatever he is doing. As soon as baby is put on the floor P. rushes at him and either holds or lies on him to stop him from going along, pulls his hair or treads on his fingers or pushes him over, which results in several bumps on the head. Baby is really very long-suffering with him until he goes too far. We try to keep him away from all P.'s most treasured possessions. I have suggested that he should take his things into the pen whilst baby is out on the floor, getting in and out as he likes, but I think he feels too restricted if he does that. I must say that before baby was born or talked about P. always showed signs of jealousy when other children came to tea, treating them in the same way as he now does the baby, especially if his mother came into the room. Baby was breast-fed up to six months, and Mummy would never allow P. to know anything about the feeding, thinking it would make him more jealous. I never agreed about this, and thought it a great pity, as he used very much to resent baby going to Mummy so many times a day and not himself, although of course he had his own special time of being with her, and still has. I only take baby to the drawing room about ten minutes before his bedtime purposely, so that P. can play without any interference. P. has an intense love of play, especially with other children, of which he has plenty of opportunity, as he plays in the garden nearly every morning, with at least half a dozen children to play with. If not, I take him out a little while on his tricycle while baby is sleeping. They all have hoops and bats and balls and dolls' prams, and P. is allowed to dig in his own little part, and has tools and his own bulbs, etc., and seems perfectly happy otherwise. We try not to restrict him in any way. He is allowed to put lights on and off, play with water, put coal on the fire, with supervision, of course, controls his own gramophone, is allowed the step ladder to climb on, to dust, sweep or scrub just as he wishes, but obviously we cannot allow him to hurt baby as he does, and would be very pleased to know how to deal with this trouble. Baby sleeps alone, and I sleep with P. We tried the other way round, but P. always seems to have a reason for waking up some time during the night, and got distressed on finding himself alone. This trouble also started since the advent of the baby, as before he was a perfect sleeper; also he bites his nails, but this he has always done. I try to amuse P. as much as possible when baby is out of the pen, with books or games, but it is so trying at times and a great strain.

Q.2. *We have three boys: Major, four years; Minor, three*

years, and Minimus, one year. Our trouble is this. Major is terribly jealous of Minor, to such an extent that it spoils our family life a good deal. If Minor has, or does, anything different from Major, there are tears or unhappiness on the part of Major, who is always on the look-out for any slight advantage Minor may gain. I try to treat them alike and to be fair, but little things crop up all day to upset Major. For instance, if I dress Minor first or help him before Major at meals, or take Minor out to tea with his friends of three years' old, it causes unhappiness, grumbling and jealousy. It is difficult to say how all the little troubles crop up, but it is constant troubles of this sort in Major's life which are making him a grumbling, bad-tempered little boy. It is a pity, as he is really such a bright, happy child, and I feel it needs understanding and expert treatment. I looked after Major entirely for fifteen months, then he had an excellent girl to look after him, of whom he was very fond, and to whom he was well accustomed before Minor arrived. I took entire charge of Minor for four months while the girl looked after Major. Of course I was with Major a great deal and tried to make him feel he was wanted, etc., but I may not have stressed this sufficiently, as it seems from then that things have been difficult for Major. The arrival of Minimus has been a help if anything. Major adores him and has no difficulty in keeping ahead of his tiny brother. Is it the strain of keeping ahead which may be the cause of jealousy? Minor is very large for his age, and this is commented on by a great many people who say in front of the children how much of a size the two are. Major also shows off a lot, trying to compensate for his feeling of inferiority I imagine and has, from time to time, nervous habits, like screwing up his nose or pulling his mouth awry. He is a great deal the more intelligent of the two and very popular among little boys of his own age. It has shown so clearly lately that the complex is caused by Minor's presence in the family as for a week Minor has been ill in bed, and we have had Major himself again happy, easy and very peaceful. I may add the two fight a good *deal, which is unavoidable in a family, I suppose. I have tried reasoning with Major and giving him extra attentions and privileges, etc., but I do not seem to have eased the situation very much. Please advise me.*

A. It certainly *is* a strain to have to try to deal patiently and reasonably with so acute and persistent a jealousy as Q.1's charge shows. But, of course, the biggest strain of all is felt by the child himself. Anyone with a memory of situations in childhood or adult life which caused even slight pangs of jealousy knows that it is one of the most miserable and painful feelings we can experience—and how much worse for a small child, who has so little to set against it! In this boy, however, it is specially strong, although the reason for this does not seem at all clear. It may be an inherent temperamental difference—undoubtedly children differ very much in the readiness with which these feelings are stimulated.

The first thing to remember is that P. is at an age when all the child's feelings are most intense and unmanageable. The course of the next year or eighteen months is bound to bring a considerable alleviation, simply by natural development. And especially will this be so when the child is so well handled as in this case. It seems to me that Q.1 and the child's mother are treating the problem most wisely and helpfully. All it needs is this continued patience and good sense, to help the boy out of his worst trouble. Time itself is a great healer of these difficulties. It would certainly be a help to the child to tell him that you fully understand how annoying it is for him when the baby gets in his way and interferes with what he is doing; but that this will only last a few months, whilst baby is learning to walk and learning how to make things for himself, and that later on P. is sure to find him even a help in his play. Such talks with the elder child will not remove his jealousy, and will not have much immediate effect; but in the long run they are a help to an intelligent child, especially because they show that the grown-ups understand his side of it. But along with this should go a clear statement that you will not let him hurt or torment the baby—and a careful supervision (without reproach or nagging) to prevent his doing this. However, time and the boy's natural growth under such sensible treatment are your chief allies.

In the case of the eldest boy of Q.2, it seems a little easier to find the cause of the intensity of feelings—since it must have been a great loss to Major to have his mother hand him over entirely to the nursemaid when Minor arrived, even though he already knew her well. Moreover, as Q.2 herself feels, the greater size of Minor for his age must be an important element in Major's problem—he has not even the compensation of feeling himself naturally the bigger and stronger. The fact that he gains psychological help from the presence of the youngest baby shows this very clearly. Again, I would remind Q.2 how important the age factor is in these early emotional problems—every month or two of development at this age brings the child nearer to a period of greater control and stability. Patience and understanding on the part of the grown-ups are a deep need of the child in these situations between two and five years. The fact that Major and Minor fight occasionally is perfectly natural—they may become excellent friends in later childhood, all the same. I would try to provide Major with plenty of friends of his own age, outside his home, and if there were a really good nursery school or Kindergarten available, I would certainly let him enjoy it.

Q.1. My little charge is four and a half years old, and now we have just added two little cousins to our nursery while their parents are in India. The visitors are aged two years and seven months. I feel that the three years they are to be with us should be happy for all of us, but so far—two months—H. has been so miserable, I am at a loss to know how to deal with him. I've had him from a month old, and we've always been more or less alone, so I realize he must be jealous, but I think he ought to be used to things now. True, he has to take a very back seat, as naturally I can't do everything for and with him as I used to, and he is left a great deal to the nurserymaid. She is good at playing with and talking to him, and seems really keen. Of course I am with him whenever possible, and once a week I manage to take him for a walk alone; but he is always whining and crying, and gets so furiously angry when I ask him to do things for the babies. I do want him to love them, and really to enjoy their being here. Another annoying way he has is of walking round and round the room and fidgeting from one foot to the other whenever we stop or have to stand still for a minute. He has lots of books, chalks, bricks, puzzles, trains and lines, carts, a farmyard, soldiers, a beautiful ark, scooter, car bicycle, in fact everything I can think of to amuse and interest him, but he doesn't play, but just sits about and fidgets, or walks round and round. Do help me to deal with this, and if you could suggest any toys he ought to have. I have taught him to write, and he can spell and form words of one syllable from letters I painted on plain postcards. I may add that he is very sweet with A., the two-year-old, and will play with her as long as she keeps away from me, but he won't come near the baby. I don't try to make him, and he gets into awful rages when I bath A. or feed her occasionally. I'm afraid this is a very long letter, but I am absolutely at a blank.

Q.2. A month ago two little two-year-olds came to live with us as companions for my son of the same age. They looked so sweet together—but, unfortunately, they hated each other. I was in despair. I'd no idea babies could be so horrid to each other. We daren't leave them alone for a moment—such shrieks and yells would come from the nursery! They would pull each other's hair out by the handful—scratch, bite, push each other down—tread on each other. It was heartbreaking. I've seen chickens perse-

cuting a lame fowl—almost pecking it to death. These babies were just little animals. If one fell and cried because of the bump, the other two rushed over to pull hair and increase the yells. "Pip" loved to bang the others on the head with a brick. Nurse said she was sure the experiment was a failure and very bad for our "David", as they all seemed to be getting so bad-tempered and irritable. My problem was particularly difficult too because I was so anxious to make the "visitors" feel that I loved them as much as David, and in so doing I think I hurt him and made him feel miserably jealous. However I couldn't back out of a job I had undertaken, and I kept telling myself and nurse that they would get used to the new conditions and learn to be social beings. To add to our troubles they are all cutting their double teeth, and they all caught colds. Now, happily, they seem to be getting really fond of one another. They play together, and we can leave them in the nursery alone for as long as a quarter of an hour without hearing any yells. They still take things away from each other, and are little egoists in most ways—and they still fling themselves flat on the floor if thwarted in any way, but I do feel so much more happy about them. Do you think two years old is a little young for this kind of thing? It is the most difficult age, I believe. Please tell your readers some general things about this age of "unreason", when wills and tempers develop, and power of expression is so infuriatingly limited. We are such a happy family now. I dread the moment when Pip and Lynette leave us. I shall have to find someone else to fill the gap or David will be miserably lonely.

A. The problem of jealousy is, of course, always more acute when children of about the same age as the one already in the nursery are introduced than when a new baby is born in the actual family. That is because children of about the same age are, to begin with, *merely* rivals; the first child cannot mother them or feel "like a big boy" to them as he or she can to a tiny infant. Tenderness and protectiveness cannot easily provide a way out of the jealousy, as they do when the intruder is a new-born baby. On the other hand, once the most acute phase of rivalry to the stranger has been lived through, the playmates of the same age are better playmates than the new-born baby. For this reason we can afford to be patient through even such storms as the writer of the second letter had to put up with for the first two or three weeks after the arrival of the little visitors. Many people would, of course, have given up if they had had such acute difficulties as she describes, but it was evidently worth it after all. I have known other cases very like this, and companionship does always seem to be worth while in the end, both from the point of view of the children themselves and from that of the parents and nurse. But of course it does need infinite patience and care, and one of the main difficulties for the mother or nurse is to be sufficiently loving and just to the visitors without giving cause for jealousy to one's own child.

Perhaps the writer of the first letter can now take heart and realize that it is bound to take time, and that if she can go on doing her best to make the situation easy for the little host, and being patient with his misery, he will in the end come to be glad that he has some playmates. It would probably be better not to *ask* him to do things for his cousins. That is probably more than he can stand; and it would be just as well, too, to give him as much of herself as she could possibly spare. I don't think the solution lies in more toys, but the learning to read and write, which the cousins won't be able to do, may give him a refuge in pride and self-respect. He will probably get over the difficulty with consistently cheerful firm handling and the assurance of steady affection and understanding.

VII. PHOBIAS AND ANXIETIES

Q. My little boy, nearly three, used to go to sleep quite happily as soon as he was put to bed, but now as I leave him he calls me back, "Cos Goo-goo comes". He doesn't seem very frightened of this imaginary creature, yet it keeps him awake, and he calls me again and again to tell me about "Goo-goo". At first I told him there was no such person when he said "Goo-goo bites the windows all up, and bites the door and bites everything", but he insists that there is, so, thinking he might get worse fears through repressing it, I encourage him to talk about it. I suggested Goo-goo was a little boy, and little boys didn't bite windows, etc. only nice things like biscuits and apples. But that was no good. Then he called me in a more frightened voice, and when I told him to shut his eyes and go to sleep, he said, "No, if I shut my eyes Goo-goo will come and eat me". I know the origin is not from any frightening fairy tales, as I have not allowed them yet. I think it is entirely his own invention, but that the idea of "biting" and of anything frightening comes from the influence of a maid I had recently, and who I discovered was using old-fashioned and wickedly alarming and untrue threats to make him be good. Luckily she had very little to do with him. I don't think he dreams about it, as he does not appear frightened if he wakes during the night. I'm afraid I do not always keep the calm and cheerful attitude you constantly advise, and which I know so well is rig'ıt. But it is very difficult to avoid scenes sometimes when he persists in doing a thing after I have forbidden it and explained why I don't want him to do it (e.g. dragging a chair to the sink, turning the taps full on, and putting Vim, Lux, basins, anything he can get hold of, into it, and getting frightfully wet). I know it must be fun for him, but it's wrong that he should persist when I ask him not to, and that we should end with a skirmish and tears. He has plenty of outlet for his energies, as he helps with dusting, washes his own socks, etc., and helps to lay the table, and he never tires of his bricks. It is difficult for me to manage him patiently at present, as I have got very run down and, I suppose, a bit nervy since my next baby was born, and through having to look after them both. I have been careful that he should feel no jealousy of the baby, who is now eight months old, and I am sure he does not, although he is inclined to touch her carelessly and might hurt her by mistake if I left them alone.

A. I think you may be right in putting down the acuteness of your little boy's fears to the maid who frightened him, but it is not necessary to look to her for the idea of biting. Such fears of things that may bite—for example, animals or imaginary creatures do come to little children quite spontaneously, and are not at all uncommon. They really spring from the child's own primitive ways of anger. The tiny infant very often shows his own anger by biting, for example, people's fingers or mother's breast, and then they naturally fear that this may be done to them. This imaginary creature, "Goo-goo", of whom your little boy is frightened, is simply his own naughtiest self, which the child feels not to be his *real* self. He wants to be a good and loving child, and is terrified that he may not be able to be so, but may bite you or his little baby sister. I think we cannot avoid the conclusion that the onset of this fear is due to his jealousy about the baby which he has managed to control and conceal when he is with her. Now, as to treatment. I think you are quite right in letting him tell you about "Goo-goo", and it would be a great help to give him a little time every night to talk about this and to enjoy the comfort of your presence in keeping these fears at bay. He may lose the fear within a few months as he gets more used to sharing you with his little sister and gets more sure of his own affection for her. I should, therefore, not be in a hurry to cut down the time you sit with him after he is in bed. Later he may be able to do without it, or with less of it, but for the present I think he really needs your support. The naughtiness with the sink is probably again connected with the same inner difficulties. You are quite right in being firm in not letting him do that. There is no reason why he should be allowed to do something that is really a nuisance to you, especially as you let him help with the dusting, and washing his own socks, etc. If, however, you could let him have water to play with in some way that would not be too messy for you, that would be very worth while. It will, of course, be easier when the warm days come and he can be outside with a pail and wearing mackintosh drawers. I understand how hard it must be to be altogether patient when the child is so trying and you are not well yourself, and the baby too needs attention. I am sure the solution lies in finding things that he can do without bothering you too much.

Q. Susan (three years) has been a model child except for one thing—when she was cutting her last four double teeth she started waking during the night and we found that she needed the comfort of somebody there so her nurse started to sleep in the same room. But Susan went on waking up at various times in the night. Then we decided to make the break and still Susan went on waking up—and we had to go to her every night and sometimes two or three times during the night. This has been going on for over a year and I have tried everything I have seen recommended. The doctor put her on bromide for a while. She always goes to bed happily—we stay and have stories with singing, etc., and I always stay with her in the night if she really seems to need me. I take my mattress and sleep by her. But usually she is content if you go and tuck her up and sing one song to her. I feel that she is not getting enough sleep. She is very well and very forward and intelligent. We never try to teach her anything because she started to stutter once when she was saying nursery rhymes at two years old. On the nights I stay with her I have noticed she keeps waking with tremendous starts just after dropping off to sleep. I am afraid it is now a habit and I am so worried because I wonder if it is starting a habit that will persist into adult life. Some nights she appears to go to sleep quickly, other nights she stays awake a long time and looks very tired in the morning.

A. It is not very often that a child continues waking with this night anxiety for so long as your little daughter has done. But it does happen sometimes. I cannot tell from your letter what the continued reason may be. Obviously the difficulty began with teething. On the whole it would appear that the difficulty is getting less, since she usually falls asleep if you simply sing one little song to her. I don't believe that the difficulty is a habit, and *certainly* you need not fear that it is a habit that will last into adult life. If it were a habit it would be there all the time. The fact that she sometimes can go to sleep very quickly and on other days stays awake a long time shows there is some state of anxiety in the child's mind, which has been stirred up probably by some event during the day. I would try to find out whether you can make any connection between the general conditions of her life during the day or any special happening, and those nights when she has an extra degree of anxiety keeping her awake for a longer period and needing your continued presence. I don't think you need worry about the actual amount of sleep, since she is in other ways healthy and happy. As I have so often pointed out, children differ so enormously in the amount of sleep that they can take, and one cannot force a child to take more than favourable conditions and a pleasant friendly atmosphere of content will induce. I am wondering whether you yourself worry too much about the child's waking up and not sleeping, and communicate your anxiety about it to her. Children are very sensitive to the state of mind of grown-ups and I am inclined to feel that if you yourself worried less about it and somehow conveyed to her that it did not matter very much even if she did not sleep, that might soothe her and relax her mind more. You will probably find the problem getting easier within the next year. The tendency to stammer a year ago shows that there is incipient mental tension, and you are very wise not to deny her the comfort you have been giving her. But I am sure you are worrying unnecessarily about the relative lack of sleep.

Q. My little son, aged five, has formed the habit of waking during the night and calling for nanny or me. On going in to him and asking what he wants, he stares blankly in front of him and will not answer; if I go out of the room he starts to scream and call again. I once went in to him four times during one hour. I try suggesting something he might want, and having supplied all possible and trivial needs and talked to him about his toys or his story books, I leave him apparently contented, only to be called again soon afterwards and to meet with the same blank silence on asking what he wants. As he sometimes wants the door open (I do not encourage this because of a direct draught, as his window is always open) or the light left on, I wondered if he was afraid of sleeping alone, and suggested he might like to sleep in nanny's room in place of his younger brother. But he would not hear of this. Inevitably I have sometimes become annoyed and scolded him and punished him (by some deprivation), but neither this, nor the giving of some reward when he doesn't *call seems to have any lasting effect. When I say that I cannot help him if he will not tell me what he wants, he invents some silly requirement such as, "Tuck this in", when he is already tucked in everywhere, or, "I want a hanky", when he has one, sometimes actually in his hand. I am worried as to whether his brain is all right; or is it just naughtiness? and how can I stop it? I feel that there is something wrong about his waking at all in the night. He seems a fairly normal child, not thin, but rather pale and pasty looking. His appetite is good; his last meal being at 4.30. I wondered if he needed something more before going to bed. He has usually a serious look, and is more inclined to play by himself than with others (he is the third of six children), but when he does laugh it is a very infectious chuckle, and I think he has a very keen sense of humour. He will be starting school next Monday. I think perhaps it will do him good to have different occupations.*

A. Your boy probably wakens up from some nightmarish kind of dream and lies in a state of anxiety until you go and re-assure him. He probably does not himself really know what is the matter, or what he wants, except that he needs the comfort of knowing that you are there. There may have been some happening in his daily life that has stirred up this difficulty, but that I cannot tell from your letter. It would be helpful if you met the situation by saying that you understand that there is something that he is frightened about, but that you feel confident he will soon be able to get over it. I should be inclined to leave the door open and the window nearly closed, or rearrange his bed so that it is not in the draught between the door and window, if having the door open would prevent the difficulty. I would also leave the light on if that would help him to lie quiet and not have to call you or to scream. It is quite possible that if you could arrange to have the door open and a night-light left, he might be able to get over his anxiety without calling for you. I should certainly try this, and also should let him know that you understand that there is something that frightens him in a dream, but that you feel sure he will be able to get over it with this help of having the door open. It is probably only the sense of not being altogether shut away from communication with you that he most needs. There is no reason whatever to think that his brain is disturbed. Many children have terrors and anxieties in the night and they are by no means "just naughtiness". They come from some inner difficulty in emotional development, which they grow out of, provided they have the help they need at the time. It is possible that a warm drink when he went to bed would help him. Children differ in this, just as grown-ups do. There are many who cannot sleep if they are a little hungry and others who sleep better if they are. It would certainly be worth while trying. It is possible that starting school will be another help. Indeed, in the long run, it will be sure to be a help, but the strain of adaptation may for a time increase the child's anxiety and make him all the more in need of the comfort of feeling that you are not far away in the night.

Q. I am writing for your advice as regards my little charge of sixteen months. He is perfectly well and happy and just full of life. My one problem is that if I attempt to take him out to tea, or into any strange rooms or house, he just cries and screams until we leave again. Do you think we should take him out at all, or should we wait until he is older? I am rather worried about this matter as baby will be very likely going to the sea for a month and then on to stay with Granny, and then to a new house later on. Last week I put him into a fresh place to sleep in the garden and he screamed and worked himself into such a state that I had to put him back into his usual place. I don't think it is necessary to take him out to tea, only would like your advice as regards his fresh homes. He is such a good boy in other ways, and goes to sleep with no curtains to his windows even when it is light. He is not a placid child by any means and when he gets these attacks he nearly screams himself into hysterics and sobs for quite a long while afterwards, so I do hope you will be able to help. He will go to any strange person quite happily.

A. I should certainly not try to force your little charge to go out to tea or to go to strange places. Many children of his age dislike strange places, and are rather frightened of them, and there is no reason to force him to try to overcome something he will grow out of quite naturally during the course of the next year. It would be far better not to take him into any strange house, but of course there are times when this cannot be helped, as will happen when you go to the seaside and then to stay with his grandmother. In circumstances such as these you will just need to accept the fact that he will be unhappy for a time, but that with patience and comfort he will get over his fright of the new house and settle down in a day or two. I would tell him before you leave for the seaside that you are going, if I were you, and tell him something of the nice things he will see there. I would also try to take with him as many of the familiar things from his own room as you can manage—small things, for example, his own toys. Any object to which he is attached, and that could be carried with you would serve to make a link for him, so that the new place would not be entirely strange. I wonder if you could possibly show him a picture beforehand of the place you are going to, say a picture postcard? This would, of course, be more help with a rather older child, but the suggestion may help you to think yourself of some other way which will make the change less extreme for him. It is a very fortunate thing that his fear of strange places does not also attach to strange persons. Many children are nervous of both at this age. He will grow out of his fear of strange places within the next year, provided you can ease the situation for him in the ways I have suggested, and as he slowly learns that it is possible for other places to be pleasant and interesting, as well as his own home.

Q. My son, C., aged two and a quarter years is a very big child who walks and talks well, although backward up to eighteen months. He is very impatient and passionate by nature, like his father. He is evidently very sensitive about some things. For instance he is sometimes clumsy with his milk, as all children are, and I may say, "Oh C. what a mess!" or if he has knocked it over in temper, scold. Yesterday I knocked over my own cup near his chair and said slightly scolding: "Naughty Mummie". After a long pause and struggle he burst into violent tears and was quite upset for the rest of the meal and shuddered when he looked at the cloth, although I laughed about it and said, "We've dried the place now and the table is better." To-day after another slight accident at table I said something half under my breath about being clumsy and he said, "Naughty Mummie" and again was starting to cry, and of course I cheered him up. He cries rather easily, about having to leave his toys or his bath or his little games outside, although we try to tell him beforehand. Another thing that has worried him for six months really and is becoming worse since we came back from our holidays is the sight and sound of the vacuum cleaner. When it is carried upstairs he cries unless handled carefully and while I am using it, or the maid, somebody has to keep him interested in another room. If he is in the room with it he is really upset and bursts into tears. Occasionally he looks round the door fearfully, and even before breakfast while we are dressing and the vacuum is on, two floors below, he tells me about it and always says when it stops: "No more cleaner now". He is really interested in things that work, especially wheels, and I have tried playing with the wheels and asking him to help me to push it about and my maid or I always talk about it when it is going to be taken upstairs or switched on—quite casually, of course, but he really hates it. He helps with the beds and mops and dusts and **loves** *picking up the bits or "Puts away" as he calls it, with the* **carpet sweeper** *every other day when we don't vacuum. But I tell him* **the vacuum** *takes bits and dust away too. He disliked the noise* *as a baby and I suppose hates it now. Can you advise me about it? And also, about the question of "the dark". Since at bedtime it is dark now there is bound to be a sense of surprise and loneliness I think when the light is switched off, and as I leave the nursery he has started saying, "Don't go away now", or, "Where's the light now", or, "Teddy sleeps with Roy", showing his loneliness. I say the usual things—"Roy sleeps now", etc. and go, but I fear he is feeling it a little more each night. What should I do? I must add in self-defence that I am* not *fussy about spoiled tablecloths or clothes but only make a remark about being more careful or something harmless.*

A. You seem to be handling this difficulty of your little son very well. Many children of his age are sensitive about particular noises such as the vacuum cleaner, but grow out of it naturally with further development. Don't you think one can understand how mysterious and frightening a vacuum cleaner can be for a little child? It must look rather like a great big mouth that can suck everything up into it, and it is quite likely that he fears that it will suck him up, especially if he is messy and dirty. And don't you think too that the noise the vacuum cleaner makes *is* rather an unpleasant one? It has such an insistent quality! Lots of grown-ups dislike it, although we put up with it because we know what a useful servant it is to us. The little child, of course, cannot appreciate this and cannot see what real advantages it has. I should go on as you have been doing, not refusing to consider the child's difficulties, but on the other hand, not taking them too seriously and refusing to use the cleaner. Your own rather matter of fact but sympathetic attitude will help him to overcome his fears of it. It would do no harm actually to say, "You know, the vacuum cleaner does not suck up little boys, only bits of fluff on the carpet". Again, don't you think it is understandable that he should be distressed at your scolding yourself and becoming, a "naughty Mummy"? Especially *if*, like his father, he has a natural intolerance of messy things. It would be a serious handicap if you too were an anxious or intolerant person, but as you are naturally balanced and sensible about these things, and will be careful not to over-emphasize any objection to clumsiness, he will grow out of this difficulty as well. Have you ever let him try switching the vacuum cleaner on himself? It is just possible that that might help him to get over the trouble, by letting him feel more active towards it and less passive. I would not force this, but I would give him the opportunity to switch it on and off occasionally. With regard to the night time trouble, I would try staying with him for just a few minutes after the light is switched off. Just a few minutes' quiet and holding his hand, sharing the darkness with him and then quietly leaving him, might be a greater help than disappearing from his room in the very moment that the light goes out. If you stay with him in the darkness for a few minutes, he may then feel that he keeps you in his memory and imagination beside him, and that the darkness does not, as it were, swallow you up.

Q. My eldest child, aged just five, is not a difficult child to manage, though very highly strung and excitable, but very sensible as a general rule, and most affectionate. The only time when he behaves really idiotically is when he has to take any medicine, or patent food such as emulsion or cod-liver oil. He shrieks and shrieks, and becomes quite hysterical, and the only way to get him to take it is to force it, and then, of course, most of it gets spilt. I feel this cannot be good for him, and it worries me, because if he were really ill it would make him so much worse. He has never been given nasty medicine, and the stupid part is that after he has taken two or three doses he doesn't mind, and will take it without any bother, though if it is left off for a time and then started again—such as cod-liver oil, which he only has in the winter—we have just the same fuss for the first day or two. He is just the same, if he cuts himself, at having a bandage put on, though there again, after the first time, he does not mind having it dressed. It is really a fear of anything unknown, and he does not seem able to trust one when one tells him it will not hurt, though he has never been deceived, I know, and is really very brave over other things, such as bumps and knocks. At the moment I have just been forcing him to take the things that are really necessary, but I hate doing this; yet what else can I do?

A. Your boy's fear of medicine and bandages has no special importance in itself, although it is, of course, a considerable nuisance from the practical point of view. As regards the best way of dealing with it, I don't think there is any alternative to making him submit when it is really necessary. You say that after he has once or twice been *made* to take the medicine he is no longer frightened and fussy about it. This is often true of such hysterical fears of medicine or of having cuts attended to. It sometimes seems as though, once a child has got into the grip of such fear, he simply cannot get out of it without our support, and no amount of mere coaxing or reasoning will give him a hold on himself. But perfectly firm treatment that, whilst not ignoring his fear yet treats him as being able to control it, is a greater help to the child.

I have found this more than once with a frightened child when having to dress an abraded arm. So long as one coaxes and reasons and says persuasively, "Now, don't be frightened", the child will go on shaking and trembling and being unable to deal with the situation. But if, whilst being quietly sympathetic, one yet takes a firmer line, saying, "I know it will hurt a little, but it will be very soon over, and it must be done", or "I know you don't like it, but it won't take a moment, and it has got to be done; so here it is", then the child can very often screw himself up to it and get it over quickly. The relief which he usually shows is proof that this firmer handling has been a real help. He feels then that he *has* been brave and so can respect himself. I don't think, therefore, that there is any harm in forcing medicine upon your boy without much preliminary coaxing, when it is really necessary for him to take it. I would, of course, give him the choice either of being sensible and taking it himself, or of having you actually put it into his mouth. But I would not reproach or scold for the fear, since that makes too much of it. The best help is for him to have the actual experience that after all it does not really hurt and the relief of having got it over. When, however, it is something that *will* hurt, such as having a dressing removed, then, of course, I should not tell him that it won't. It is very important that children should not be deceived about these things, because then a complete loss of confidence in us is added to the terror of the actual pain. But this you are well aware of, I am sure. And the difficulty is sure to get less as he grows older.

Q. My little girl who is just three years, has developed a fear of noises. Since birth she has always been "highly strung". When she was about eighteen months old she had a fright when playing alone in the nursery. The window-cleaner bumped his ladder against the window-sill and mounted it and appeared suddenly at the window giving her a very bad fright. It took some little time to settle her nerves and we were obliged to take her to the doctor. She has always disliked excessive noise, becoming obviously agitated. We have never tried to be unduly quiet about the house, at the same time have avoided making unnecessary noise. During some recent severe thunderstorms she was obviously terrified, and it has brought things to a climax, for since then, whenever the wind blows round the house, or a tram goes by, or someone moves heavy furniture she works herself up into a state of agitation even when someone is with her. She goes rigid, and screams, "I don't want to hear it", and it is impossible to reason with her or to explain. Until recently she has gone to bed in a room by herself without difficulty, but in the last fortnight she cries and screams when we leave her and though we have tried to break her of it, we have been compelled to stay with her until she goes to sleep. If she wakes up in the night we have to do the same, for she was getting into such a "nervy" state. I realize part of it may be due to naughtiness, but it is obviously more than that. We try to keep her as quiet as possible and avoid undue excitement and do not ourselves get agitated. None of us is afraid of thunder. Is it a matter for the doctor or for the psychologist? Or is it a phase out of which she will eventually grow?

A. Most little children would be frightened by the sudden appearance of the window-cleaner in that way, together with the bumping of the ladder against the window-sill, when the child was alone in the nursery, and certainly the thunderstorms this summer have been very trying for anyone who is affected by them. All the same, I think you can be sure that this excessive sensitivity of your little girl's is a phase of development. She is at the age when all emotional tension is the most acute, and every half year should bring an improvement now in increasing self-control and sense of reality. If there is no improvement before the autumn, it would be very sensible to get first-hand advice about her from a medical psychologist. Meanwhile, I would try to handle her rather more firmly when there is a noise that frightens her, letting her get a sense of confidence from the fact that you see no reason for her agitation. I don't mean that I would scold her or speak sharply, but I would speak in a firm rather than a coaxing or persuasive way. I would say, "There is no need to be frightened. Please don't make a fuss." A firm appeal of that kind will sometimes help a child when coaxing and pitying will not. On the other hand I would not pretend that the thunder is nothing to be frightened of. Sometimes when we pretend that things are less dangerous than they are, that does actually frighten a child more; for example, when we have wounds to dress or iodine to put on, or when the child is going to the dentist. Very often the child gets more frightened if we say that he is not going to get hurt than if we say quite frankly and honestly that it is going to hurt, although not a very great deal. Some of my medical friends have told me how the child screams all the more if they assure him that it is not going to hurt, but stops screaming and becomes confident and trustful if the doctor says, "I am going to hurt you, but it will do you good, and it will not be more than you can bear". The same is true with regard to really frightening happenings outside. One ought to admit to a child that a thunderstorm can be dangerous. If one pretends that there is no danger at all the child feels we are not to be trusted, we don't understand the danger, or that we are not honest about it. When a tram goes by the house I would take the child to watch it, and say, "Look, it is the wheels going round on the lines that make the noise. But that does no harm." Frank explanation and matter-of-fact talk about these things will often do more good than mere assurances. It is possible that in your wish to keep the child quiet and avoid excitement you overdo it and suggest fear to her without meaning to.

Here are two letters, both raising the same rather unusual problem.

Q.1. My little boy of twenty-two months is terrified of having his hair washed. I have always done it myself, so I know he has never slipped. I do it exactly the same way as I did when he was tiny, namely, with him lying back on my arm in his bath, and it seems to be the lying back that distresses him so much, because as soon as I start getting him into this position he screams and clutches my arm and stiffens himself all over, which makes it very difficult, besides being very bad for him, I am sure.

I have tried everything I can think of to distract his attention, but so far have found nothing sufficiently attractive to make him forget what I am doing. I tried making a game of it by trickling just a little water down the back of his head as a preliminary, but he didn't like that either. After I have got his head wet I always let him sit up while I soap it, but I have to lay him down again to rinse it, otherwise the soapy water would get into his eyes. He is too young to hold his head over a basin, as he would be sure to bump his face on the edge of it. One day he was playing in his bath quite happily, and I started talking to him quite quietly and cheerfully and said, "Now will you let Mummie wash your hair?" He immediately burst into tears, so I didn't do it. Also I have tried putting him in the bath with no water and with all his clothes on, and a thick towel on the bottom of the bath, just to see if he would lie down if there was no water, but he refused emphatically.

It's very worrying, as he must have his hair washed sometimes, though I dread the scene I know is in store for me so much that I only do it about once in six or eight weeks. He seems to get worse and worse every time.

I was talking to a hairdresser about it the other day, and she told me that some people use a liquid "dry" shampoo for their children, that you sprinkle on the scalp and then wipe off with a damp sponge; but it doesn't seem to me that it would be wise to use that sort of thing for a baby. What do you think about it? But, on the other hand, I feel if I could somehow manage to do without actually washing it for a good time—say, six months or so—he might by that time have forgotten about it. He is thoroughly healthy, although very sensitive, but on other points where we have disagreed I have usually managed to win him round by means of persuasion, although he is a very determined little person.

Q.2. My small son is aged three and a half. For the last six months we have a scene and screaming every time his hair is washed. He really seems frightened and it upsets him very much for the time being. He has it done in the bath, and until lately he was perfectly good and held a towel over his eyes tightly to keep the soap and water from running down his face, and never cried at all. As a small baby he always cried, but seemed to get over it. I am nearly always there when it is done, and, to my knowledge and as far as my nurse can tell, he has never had soap in his eyes or been frightened.

We have tried coaxing and bribes, all in vain. We also tried to make a game of it with a watering-can, and got him to kneel over a basin and pretend we were making his hair grow like the flowers. That was a success the first time, but useless afterwards. Would it be better if I took him to the shop where his hair is cut and let them do it over a basin, and so break his associations, as it were?

He is perfectly easy to manage and as good as gold about everything, and very reasonable. If he wasn't I would not think much of it; but I am quite sure he is frightened, and he won't tell me why he doesn't like his hair washed. I don't think he really knows. Both his nurse and I dread hair-washing nights. Can you advise me what to do?

A. In both these cases it would appear the child's fright is not due to any rough handling, or slight accident, or any real happening of any kind. It is rather one of those *phobias* of early childhood of which I have spoken on other occasions. The fear arises from deep hidden imaginings in the child's own mind which are quite inarticulate and uncontrollable. Q.2 says that her little boy won't tell why he doesn't like it. **He almost certainly doesn't know why, but just feels a great** overwhelming fear of the situation. In the case of these two little boys there is evidently something particularly frightening, either about the helpless position or about the actual wetting of the head. In both cases mother and nurse have tried all reasonable methods to help the child get over the difficulty—coaxing and bribing, making a game of it, and varying the situation, so as to get round the main trouble.

The only thing to do now, therefore, is to leave the whole matter alone for some time, finding some other way of keeping the child's head clean. Q.1 quite rightly suggests that if she could manage without actually washing her little boy's head for some six months or so he might by that time have got over the phobia or forgotten all about it. Many of these strong childish fears are temporary. They do fade away if rightly handled. But if an attempt were made to force the child to do the dreaded thing, this might make the fear settle down in a permanent phobia or cause severe general strain.

I would therefore suggest to both enquirers that they should get a good hairdresser to suggest a reliable dry shampoo, making sure that there is nothing in it injurious to the delicate scalp of a little child. If this can be done for a time, the child may then be able to submit to having his head washed without any difficulty later on.

Q. R., my small boy, nearly three, is in most ways a normal child. He has, however, lately been passing through phases of contrariness and tantrums which seem to afflict most children, more or less, of his age. Unfortunately, my husband's job entails a great deal of travelling for all of us. Of course this has frequently to be done by train, and R. has a perfect horror of them, and mainly of stations. He is very sensitive to noise, and I am sure this is at the root of the trouble, because once he is in the train he is perfectly all right. About ten days ago we had to move, and R. was taken by his father and his nurse to the station. I was not there myself, but nurse said she never heard him sob and scream so much until he was safely in the train. We are faced with another railway journey in about five weeks' time. How can I best prepare him for it? He knows we are doing the journey as we are going to his grandfather's. He loves the prospect, but says he is going by tram or 'bus, which is quite impossible! I think he is inclined to be nervous. For several weeks after Christmas and its consequent excitements he developed a habit of constantly blinking. Fortunately this has cured itself to a great extent. Is there anything I can do should it recur? I tried to take no notice of it.

A. This is a very difficult problem, since your circumstances are such that you cannot avoid it. You may be right in feeling that the boy's horror of noise has a good deal to do with his fear of trains and stations, and yet it cannot be simply that, since, after all, there is a great deal of noise inside the train. It must also be the sight of the engine and train themselves which, of course, must look very much larger and more impressive to a little boy than they do to us. Does he have engines and trains to play with? That might be a help to him. I would suggest your playing out a railway journey with him before the next time when you have to make a real one, either with a toy engine and coaches on rails, and little wooden people, or by making a train with chairs and pretending yourself to go the journey with him. You would probably find that this would help; and you could make the noise of the engine too, not of course in a loud way. I should also let him understand that you know how frightened he feels, and I should suggest to him that probably the engine looks very big to him. I should describe the journey to him, and the things that he will perhaps see on the way, and at the end when he gets there. The difficulty will, in any case, pass away as he grows older. He is very small for such frequent changes of life, although this cannot be helped. If the blinking recurs, you cannot do anything about it directly. You are very wise in not taking any notice of it. It is much more likely to fix itself into a habit if you speak about it. It is simply an expression of his general nervousness and will be relieved by helping the boy over his general problems. When it actually comes to the point of the journey, and you have to take him to the station, I should tell him that you are going, and say, "Perhaps you won't like it at first, but you will find there is really nothing to be afraid of". At the time itself, I should do my best to help him by distracting his interest, for example, letting him look at the fireman and engine driver, and even speak to them. All these different ways of making the child more familiar with trains, and helping him to play out his phantasies about them will gradually ease his terror of them.

Q. My charge, a little girl of four years, has suddenly developed a fear of horses. Molly is a fine sturdy child and very intelligent. About six months ago she started this terror of horses. We live in the country where there are several riding schools close at hand, so naturally Molly has always been accustomed to seeing plenty of horse-riders all day and every day and was delighted in watching them, and has been quite thrilled when they galloped over the common. No child could have been more fond of horses than Molly was, and why her love for them should suddenly turn to fear I am at a loss to understand. Now I dread taking her out each day, because at the first sight of a horse she screams herself nearly into hysterics, and nothing will pacify her until I have taken her inside someone's garden gate or make for home. I am sorry to say she is getting worse, for now she screams if we see a stationary horse with a cart by the side of the kerb, and nothing I say to her will persuade her to pass it, and we always have to turn and go the opposite way, or cross over on the other side before she will stop screaming. The walks are simply a nightmare, for I am dodging constantly down side-turnings, or Molly is running into gates the whole time we are out. Of course, the child is becoming a bundle of nerves, and most unhappy. I am certain she has not been frightened in any way. Her mother, I know, is not fond of horses, but surely that could not have any effect on Molly especially when she was so fond of them?

A. Such an acute phobia is very difficult indeed to deal with. There probably was some event which changed the child's attitude to horses, but it may not have been any happening that would seem to be frightening to an adult. It is also probable that she has been influenced by the mother's attitude to horses, as children are very sensitive to these things in adults. The difficulty will pass away in time, as most of these acute phobias in little children do. The age when these special fears are felt most intensely and frequently is between two and five years. But meanwhile it is very difficult to know how to deal with the child. I think a firmer handling than you seem to have been adopting would probably help. That is to say, whilst I should avoid any walks where you know you are *sure* to meet horses, yet when you do meet them, as for example in the ordinary streets, I should not turn aside for them or try to circumvent them, but should simply carry the child past them in spite of her screaming. I should speak to her soothingly and quietly, not scolding or say that she is foolish, but nevertheless showing her very clearly that you do not feel there is anything to be frightened of, and that you believe she will be able to get over this fear with your help. Life will become quite impossible for you if you go on trying to avoid them altogether and turn home every time she sees a horse; and it seems to imply that you too are afraid of them. She cannot help her fear. These things spring from very deep sources in the mind, but the fact that you yourself behave as if there really was nothing to be frightened of, and show a confidence that she, too, will be able to learn that attitude, whilst yet you understand her fear and do not reproach her for it, will be the best help you can give her. If, however, the difficulty does not lessen at all, then I think it would be a good plan to get the little girl's mother to take her to a wise physician who understands these psychological difficulties. It is quite likely that a skilled psychologist could discover the specific cause of this fear fairly readily, and help her over it. If the little girl's mother would like it, and you will let me know, I will suggest a competent consultant for this purpose, who has helped many other children in similar difficulties.

Q. I have a little nephew, and should be so glad of advice that would enable us to help him to overcome a great fear that he has of balloons and crackers. He is four years old this month and an only child. About a year and a half ago a balloon burst near him, which frightened him very much. Since then he has been terrified of anything which will make a bang, i.e. fireworks, crackers, and balloons, in case they burst. My little boy of two loves those things, and we hoped this Christmas that A., seeing his little cousin playing happily with them, would help him to get over his fear, but if anything he is worse. Explanations are useless. Do you advise keeping him away from everything like that, which means parties? He is a highly strung child, intelligent and rather tall for his age, and it is very distressing to see him so frightened.

A. I would certainly think it desirable to keep your nephew away from frightening things like fireworks and crackers for the present. He will overcome his fear of such things far more readily if he is not forced to endure them at his age. It always takes time before a frightening experience of that kind can be mastered by a child in these early years, but very often the child grows out of the anxiety which has caused it after he is four or five, and he does so the more readily if he is not forced into further experiences of the same unpleasant kind. He is very likely to feel better about these things within the next year or two. Children change so much after five years in many of these respects. There was a very remarkable photograph in one of the daily papers a little while ago, showing a group of children standing round a Punch and Judy show. The group happened to include children of various ages from ten years or so to about four, and the striking thing was the change in the expression of the childrens' faces according to their age. The eight-and-ten-years-olds were heartily enjoying the show, the six-year-olds were doing so, but with a considerable reserve of expression, whereas the four-year-old was unmistakably frightened and suspicious. Your little boy is still at an age when these things are so often very disturbing, but greater maturity will make a big difference to him.

Q. I have a very nervous little girl of three years, three months, a very poor sleeper. One would call her excitable and rather highly strung—but on the other hand a very sturdy, healthy, fresh-coloured child with a good appetite. All through her second year, when I was getting in and out of bed at night to go to her, finding her sleepless or crying, I told myself she was teething; but the teeth came all right and the trouble has been gradually getting worse. It is most disappointing that with development and getting older she gets more puzzled and frightened over things. For instance, at one time whenever Daddy and I spoke to each other about anything J. would say, "Mummy—what did you say to Daddy?" She would be so persistent that I would have to explain simply to put her little mind at rest. At another time she got to talking in such a quick anxious way, determined to be heard, that she started stammering a little, but this passed off. When she has said anything, that she is obviously pleased about and we agree to, she immediately dances for a minute or two, showing her very high spirits. At night it is rather pathetic that J. does so try not to call me—even though I have always been patient and gone to her when she needs me. Lately she has been awake for sometimes three hours, and then goes to sleep from about 5 to 8 a.m. when she should be getting up. She has her own room and has never seemed to want to come into my bed. I have been giving her a tonic, but as the poor child was strung up to-night and could not get off to sleep until eight o'clock, I fear this is working off and proving useless. I encourage J. to tell me of her little fears, which she does do—the dark, strange lights, etc.—and I explain that as she gets bigger she won't mind these things. If, when carrying the child, one has known nerves and fears, does this make it rather deep-seated and hopeless in its cure? For instance, when my girlie was coming very little things upset me and I cried hysterically quite a lot—a thing I have never done since. Is it advisable or not to put the nervous, sleepless child with the placid child, who needs lots of sleep, in the same room? My little boy of thirteen months sleeps well and needs lots of sleep. On the other hand, he isn't a heavy sleeper, and I fear that J.'s talking and calling out would wake him up and encourage the same attitude in him. Do you think J. will grow out of this nervousness? It seems a very long phase, which has certainly not improved with time.

A. Such nervous symptoms as you describe—the sleeplessness and excitability—very often occur at the age of your little girl, in children whose later development is quite satisfactory. In fact, some emotional difficulty showing itself in one form or another can be considered perfectly normal in the early years of life. Since your little girl is healthy and sturdy and has a good appetite, I would not worry about her emotional development; for, in the later years of childhood, children tend to become much more stable, provided the general conditions of their lives are satisfactory. There is no evidence to show that if a mother has nervous symptoms when carrying the child, this has any direct effect upon the child's later emotional life. In the early years of the child's life, however (after birth), the mother's anxiety, if she is worried about the child, does tend to communicate itself to her. The best help you can give your little girl, therefore, is to be as matter-of-fact as possible in your attitude to her. With regard to the sleeping difficulty, I think I would try the plan of putting the two children to sleep in the same room. This does sometimes help a sleepless child. Then, I would certainly let her sleep on later in the morning if she will do so; it would be a pity to wake her if she has been sleepless for two or three hours in the night. I should not think it advisable to let her come into your bed. Hot drinks at bed-time sometimes help temporarily, but often they do not have a lasting effect for, as I have suggested, the sleeplessness arises from some emotional difficulty. I would, however, continue to give her the drink, but would try changing it from time to time. It is very disappointing when a difficulty persists as this one has done in your little girl; but even so, she is still within the age when sleeplessness is a very common symptom. The recognition of this fact may help you to be patient a little longer, and to continue to give her the help which she needs. If she does call you in the night, I would go to her and sit beside her for a few minutes, talking quietly and soothingly. Since, however, she does not cry, I would not stay with her in the night for very long since your own rest is, of course, also very important. The behaviour you describe, of her wanting to know what you said when you and her Daddy spoke together, springs from curiosity and jealousy. The child is afraid of being left out of things, and that you and Daddy have something which she cannot share. This again is a very natural feeling. If her Daddy when the child is present, would say, "We will talk to you presently about what you want to say", it would make it clear that she is not shut out. And if possible I would explain the matter to her in simple words, as you have been doing, so that the child can share in the situation. You do not say whether she has any little companions to play with. If you could arrange for her to have some free play with one or two other children regularly, every day or two or three mornings a week, this would be the greatest help for her all round development, and in easing the emotional conflict which gives rise to the child's nervousness. I would provide the children with plenty of materials which will interest them and help in the development of skill—drawing, building, modelling, cutting out, jumping, climbing, dancing or running to music, materials for dressing up, and give them as much opportunity as you can for free, imaginative play.

Q. I wish you would give us an article on the child who has already been frightened, justifiably. So many people write to you about a child's fear of the dark, or of some imaginary trouble—all real enough to a child, I know. But what do you advise when a child has been subjected to real terror? How can we erase the fear from the little mind, and see to it that it does not grow secretly? My child was in a motor accident, but was not seriously hurt. He adored motoring, both before and after the crash, but for many months the sight of a car that had crashed being towed along, or even a car that had punctured or had a bent and battered mudguard, turned him white and faint. He himself was not afraid to motor, but all his sympathy was arouse ond behalf of a broken car, and it was sheer terror to him.

This phase is passing off now. Another child of mine has always loved dogs, and gone fearlessly to strange dogs, stroking and petting them most lovingly. And then an enormous hound, twice his size marched up to him, barked like a thunderstorm, and proceeded to lick his face. Charles thought it meant to eat him, and in the terrors that followed away went all his love and trust in dogs. Very, very gradually we are trying to coax it back.

There are many children who have been in a bad motor smash and seen blood pouring out like water, or been present at a horrible accident. How can we erase from their minds these memories, so that they shall not brood over them? One does not always feel that because a child has ceased to speak of something he has necessarily forgotten it. As a child I once saw a drowned man washed up, and I suffered from one or two other alarming experiences that I could not tell to others, since putting them into words recalled more vividly than ever the horror and terror they caused me. A sensitive child shrinks from the sight of a cut finger; the sight of an injured person lying in a pool of blood may cause a secret horror that will remain with him always. Why do most of us dread the sight of blood? Why should one cut person send half a dozen sane people into faints or hysterics? Could this frame of mind be prevented in childhood? And if so, how?

A. I quite agree with you that this is a very acute and difficult problem. I don't think there is any short and easy way of dealing with the terrors of a child who has actually had some dreadful experience. One can only be ready at all times to listen when he talks about it if he wishes to do so, and to give him the quiet understanding that will help him to gain restored equilibrium.

The two things which really ought to be avoided, I am sure, are the extremes of refusing to talk about it at all, saying perhaps, in a brisk and breezy way, "Oh, don't think about it, you will soon forget", and so on; and the opposite, perhaps less common fault, of forcing the child to talk of it whether he wants to or not. The former would be the commonest sort of error on the part of well-meaning people, but the latter is a mistake sometimes made nowadays by people who have read a little psychology and got hold of the idea that "repression" is bad. I know of a particular case of this, where an otherwise sensible and motherly woman tried to compel a little girl whose sister had died to talk about her loss, when she did not in the least want to. It would be hard to say which of these two mistakes was the worse, and both are to be avoided. We must somehow convey to the child by our voices and manner that we *will* talk freely about anything *he* wants to discuss or ask questions about, that we are not afraid of his fear, nor shocked by it, nor forcing upon him a shallow sort of courage that merely covers up genuine terror. A mere pretence at courage has, of course, no real value, and when a child has seen a terrible thing like an accident it would be mere pretence to say that there was "nothing to be afraid of".

With regard to the dog, the help that could be given would, of course, be the true explanation that the dog had not been going to hurt him, but had meant to be friendly, and only seemed dangerous because it was so big and noisy.

In the latter part of your letter, as to why we all feel so terribly disturbed by an accident or the sight of blood, you touch upon very far-reaching psychological questions which would need many pages to deal with. Put very simply, however, it is that the accident stirs up fright in all of us that goes far beyond what the real danger or injury usually justifies, because it links up with the deepest and most phantastic terrors of childhood that have very little to do with reality. The worst thing about a real experience of this kind in childhood is that in the child's mind it links on to his imaginary terrors and confirms them.

He could deal more successfully with the real situation if he were free from terrifying phantasies. That is why the same experience will have different effects on different people.

You ask how one can deal with this problem in childhood. Within ordinary limits, sensible, firm understanding by the grown-up, who sympathizes with the child's fear without being himself afraid of it, is the best help; but with an over-sensitive child, one who is already neurotic, nothing can help but proper psychological treatment.

Q. I am wondering if I have been too rigid in the upbringing of my baby who is almost nine months, has gained well, and seems very happy, and sleeps exceedingly well during the evening and night, but has an abhorrence of strangers picking her up. Is this a normal attitude at nine months or do you think it is the beginning of a "bad habit" which I ought to take steps to correct without delay? I think she has always been inclined this way, but a really bad occasion took place last week. Her grandmother came to spend the day, bringing with her two friends, one of whom was almost stone deaf. The deaf lady picked baby up and immediately started asking me questions in a loud voice, to which I had to reply by shouting. All our remarks had to be shouted, and in a few seconds baby was screaming in the most alarming manner. I thought it must be her gums (she has no teeth yet) or her tummy troubling her and gave her to her grandmother, whom she has always treated as a second mummy, while I fetched water, etc. But nothing availed, and the screaming lasted for about half-an-hour, until I took her myself in order to relieve her grandmother. Almost immediately the screaming ceased, except for a few choky sobs, and in a very few minutes she was laughing and smiling at everybody. Unfortunately, that was not the end of the trouble. The same state of affairs continued throughout the day. Directly any of the strangers attempted to pick her up she screamed, and went on doing so until I took her. Do you think it would have been wiser for me to leave her with the strangers to scream until she was used to them? I did not do so, as I felt probably the shouting was the cause of the upset. Her grandmother was furious with me, saying it was all that could be expected of a baby brought up "by book", that I ought to have allowed people to nurse her more, and taken her about more. I have not nursed her a great deal myself as she has usually been so happy, laughing and kicking in her pram, that it has not been necessary, and as I have baby and the house to manage without any help whatever, I have been most glad that she was so good. I have never given her to other people a great deal, as I think that unless people are real baby lovers they just feel awkward and embarrassed by having someone else's baby suddenly thrust upon them, but I now let her see as many people as possible, though she does not seem shy. When we are out and neighbours lean over her pram to talk to her she usually smiles back in a highly delighted manner—but do you think it would be wise to start taking her for journeys where she would be more likely to get accustomed to seeing several people at once? I am afraid elderly relatives are not very helpful to a young mother, as they seem to forget entirely what their own children were like in babyhood.

A. It does not seem to me that your mistake has lain in being too rigid in your general routine, but in not understanding how very painful and difficult an experience it must have been for a child of nine months to be picked up by a stranger, and to have shouting going on so near for some time. There was nothing whatever abnormal in the baby's behaviour. All little children are more sensitive to sudden, very loud or very ugly noises than they are to any other painful stimuli. It is a general and normal characteristic of infancy. Many little children retain this sensitivity even up to three and four years of age. With your little daughter, there was not only the sudden violent stimulation of the loud sounds almost in her ear, but, of course, also the fact that she was picked up in this way by a stranger, a thing that should never be done. A child of nine months is perfectly well aware of strangers as such, and if we think what we should feel like if we were suddenly subjected to some rather violent experience that left us completely helpless, by someone we had never seen before, it may enable us to get somewhere near in imagination to what the experience must be to a tiny child. I will say quite frankly that I am really very surprised that you did not understand how painful the situation was for your little girl. Why you should have to think that it must be her gums or her tummy, I do not know. It was the simple experience of being picked up by a stranger and then having this violent stimulation of the ear. It would have been astonishing, indeed, if the child had not screamed and been frightened. Of course she would go on being frightened of any attempt of any of the other strangers to pick her up, because she would fear that the same violent noise was going to occur. In any case, one should not expect a child of this age to be willingly handled by any stranger that comes along. No real lover of children would want to force an infant to be handled in this way. It does not take long to win the affection and interest, even of a child of nine months, if one is content to sit quietly by and make no violent movements. It is just the same with babies as it is with animals, one has to give them proof that one is not going to hurt and is to be trusted. One sees exactly the same thing with children of two and three years, either single children in the home or a group in the nursery school. Let a stranger, who fusses and tries to make any of the children talk to her or like her, go into the nursery school, and soon she will be avoided, or there will be two or three children crying in her vicinity. But let anyone who is quiet, and shows her friendliness not by trying to force the children, but by being gentle and passive, go and sit amongst a group and be content to watch their play, and within ten or fifteen minutes two or three or four mites will come and sit quietly beside her, and bring a toy, or look at the visitor's bag or apparel or comment on her beads or buttons. I have watched this over and over again, and have been struck with the certainty with which you can predict the reaction of the children, even at three and four years of age, to a fussy, anxious visitor, as compared with a quiet and gentle and passive one. But this is infinitely more true of the child under a year. I have great respect for the wisdom of grandmothers, and have often pointed out in these columns many ways in which the mothers of a generation ago understood things about little children which we have rather tended to lose sight of; but in this case your little daughter's grandmother was quite wrong. Possibly, if your little girl had seen more people she might more readily have accepted this situation, but I think the shouting into the ear of the deaf woman who was holding her would have frightened the great majority of children, even if they had been used to being nursed by strangers. But in the case of your little girl, who has seen so few people and been used to entertaining herself in her pram, then this was quite a severe trial. It seems to me you are unduly sensitive to what your visitors may feel. You are sympathetic with their feeling awkward and embarrassed by having to hold a strange baby, but not quite imaginative enough about what the baby herself feels in being suddenly handled by a complete stranger. There is no reason why you should not occasionally take her for journeys and let her see more people, but I should be perfectly firm about not letting any stranger attempt to force her liking, and about not subjecting her to a sudden violent stimulus such as the one you describe. I quite agree that elderly relatives very often forget what their own children were like in babyhood, but surely it is part of the true function of a good mother not only to be sympathetic and understanding herself to the child, but to protect the child from people who are unimaginative and a little stupid, as, alas, only too many grown-ups are with babies.

Q. My little girl is just four years old. At fifteen months she fell over and cracked a nail right across and got a lot of dirt right under it. Our doctor poulticed it for me, but the nail eventually came off. This seemed to make a terrific impression on A. She remembered it for quite a year, and used to point out her "poor finger". Unfortunately when she was two and a half years old she caught the same nail in a gate and pinched it badly. (It eventually turned black and again came off.) On this occasion she was very nearly mad with hysteria, absolutely uncontrollable, and in the end (I felt a perfect brute) I had to give her a sharp slap. This sobered her at once, and she allowed herself to be undressed and put to bed. When she was three she had 'flu, and the doctor came to see her once. She got rather worked up about it, trembled with nerves, and screamed most of the time he was there. At three and a half I took her to a dentist, but she refused to open her mouth and got into such a terrible state that I simply had to take her away. Six months later, I took her again, and she behaved in exactly the same way, only she was very much worse. My trouble is this: firstly, she will not go near a doctor or dentist without making a terrible scene, really the poor child is trembling with fear. So far this has not mattered very much because she has not been ill, but I am beginning to wonder what would happen if she were really ill. In the case of the doctor, his two little girls are great friends of ours, and she frequently meets him socially without a qualm. Secondly, she seems to have developed an absolutely hysterical horror of blood—her own, not anybody else's. She can watch her small brother bleeding from a bad cut quite calmly, but if she has a minute scratch and it bleeds, we have shrieks and nerves for hours afterwards. Fortunately she has never had anything but the most superficial graze so far. What is the best way to deal with her when she behaves like this, and how can I help her to get over it? She is extremely interested in her own body and how it works, and I have tried to use this interest to help her to take a more normal view of these everyday things.

A. These hysterical reactions to actual experiences of bodily injury are always very difficult to deal with. When such accidents happen at an age when the child cannot understand them, and cannot know how unimportant they are in bodily reality, they always do leave a very considerable emotional impression. The child cannot have any sense of proportion about these things when they occur at so young an age, because she has not the experience to put them into proportion, and give her security. Nevertheless she will probably grow out of her violent reaction to such happenings within the next year or two. She is well within the period when most little children have very strong and unmanageable feelings. But within the next year or two they gain so much more emotional steadiness that you are likely to find she feels these things rather less.

With regard to the dentist, so much depends upon the way in which the child is handled. I wonder whether you or the dentist made the mistake of assuring the child that it "would not hurt her"? That is always a great mistake, even with children who have not had such painful happenings as the injured finger that your little girl had. The child never believes the doctor or mother or dentist who says: "It won't hurt you". But if you say truthfully and frankly: "It will hurt you a little, but the pain won't last, it will soon be over", the child can then control her hysteria, because she feels that you are telling the truth and she can trust you. When you say, "it won't hurt", she knows that you are not telling the truth, and it is her distrust that makes her feelings so unmanageable. **Many wise mothers and many of my medical friends dealing** with little children confirm me in this view. With more than one child who has had to have a cut or a grazed arm dressed, and who worked himself into a hysterical dread of the process, I have found that if one takes no notice of the child's fear, but goes quietly and firmly on, so that the child knows it is going to be done, he gets much calmer and ceases to fuss about it. If he finds that his cries and protests have an effect upon us, it confirms his fears that it is going to be an unbearable thing. But if we just go steadily ahead, it means to him, far more plainly than words can do, that the pain will not be unbearable, and that the whole thing will soon be over. I should like to know whether this mistake was made with your little girl. A quiet, firm, confident handling that is neither fussy nor dishonest is the best help to the child.

When the child shrieks in terror at the sight of her own blood, the best way, again, would be to keep quite calm about it yourself and treat the situation good-humouredly, helping her to wash the cut herself. Getting the child to attend to herself often calms her more than verbal assurances. Giving her knowledge about the parts and processes of her own body at other times certainly will help her in the end, but it takes time for this to produce any effect. I would like to repeat again that if any situation arises in which you have to take her to a doctor or a dentist, it is really important not to let her feel that pain and injury may happen without foreknowledge. That must have been the frightening element in the two incidents with her finger. It is the feeling that anything may happen in the world at any time, without one knowing beforehand, that is so unbearable. To be told that one is going to suffer pain and to have the grown-ups go straight ahead with the business, showing in their actions that there is nothing to fear but the momentary pain, is a far greater help than coaxing and assertions that, "it won't hurt".

VIII. DESTRUCTIVENESS AND AGGRESSIVENESS

Q. My son aged two years has suddenly developed a very vicious tendency which at first I put down to the last big teeth coming through. These tendencies are not becoming less, although his teeth are practically all through he will suddenly approach any person near him and setting his jaw, will strike with whatever toys he has in his hand, or sometimes he will pinch and scratch. On one occasion he nearly injured a young baby I had on my knee. I feel sure it was not jealousy because he was playing quite contentedly with some clothes pegs when he suddenly set his jaw and ran with his arm upraised to strike the baby's head. Luckily I gave him a push with my spare hand and averted the accident which might have been very serious. I have tried to tackle this difficulty sensibly, but it is not always possible to be placid when I see him inflict scratches and weals on his grandmothers and aunties, who are always kind and gentle with him. Sometimes I take him on my lap and say, "Michael, Granny can't love you if you are a naughty boy—you mustn't hit her because it hurts", and he will laugh and say "Michael—naughty boy", and take no further notice of anything I might add to this; or alternatively I have sometimes said, "Oh—Michael, look how you've hurt Mummy", and he has put his face against me very sweetly and said, "Love her".

I should be very glad to know whether this is a phase with which you often have to deal, or whether you think it may spring from some nerve trouble. Perhaps you would tell me how I should tackle the problem.

A. The sudden attacks on other people are by no means unusual at your son's age, and do not necessarily mean that he will go on doing it when he gets older. The fact that he was apparently playing quite contentedly with the clothes pegs before he made his sudden attack on the baby who sat on your knee is no indication that he was not jealous. Indeed, the sudden attack is a clear proof that he was jealous and very acutely so. Evidently his jealousy of other people and fear and suspicion of them only shows itself in these sudden attacks, which seem to spring out of nowhere. Doubtless they are due to the tension of feeling accumulating within him and suddenly bursting its bounds into open expression. It would be a pity to deny him the companionship of other children altogether, because such companionship is the best means of helping him to learn control and develop confidence in their friendship. But it is quite clear that when you do have them you should supervise their play very carefully, so as to be quick to safeguard other children from these sudden attacks. That is the best way of dealing with the difficulty, not by scolding or punishing when he does it and then expecting him to be able to control the violent impulse another time, which he obviously cannot do just yet; and is not likely to be able to do for the next year or two, until he is out of the period of the most acute emotional conflict. It is better to direct your attention to preventing actual harm, acting as a guide and control for him, and most carefully avoiding any situations which will stimulate his jealousy and violence—for example, by taking another child on your knee. Probably you could get the boy's grandmothers and aunts to co-operate with you in this by avoiding any situation which might stir up this violence. It would be better *not* to say, "Granny can't love you if you hit her", because that is one of the things he is afraid of—the loss of love. It helps more to say, "Please do not hit Granny, because it hurts her", but not to frighten him with the threat of loss of love. I should make sure that he has lots of opportunity for big vigorous movement, running, climbing, jumping, throwing, hammer-

DESTRUCTIVENESS

ing, and so on. Robust and healthy boys of two to four or five years always get more difficult emotionally if they have not plenty of this vigorous physical activity. If you can ensure these general conditions, you will find that his liability to make such sudden attacks will get much less during the next year and will pass away altogether by the time he is three or three and a half.

Q. My daughter, aged five and a half years, presents rather a difficult problem in connection with toys. I have always taught her to be tidy and clear up after playing, but, of course, very often I have had to do it, as is often the case with young children. She has had plenty of toys, and a very large number of dolls, but after a week or so most of the toys and the dolls are spoilt. Though not wilfully destructive, she seems to break the legs or arms of the dolls, ruins the clothes, usually by undressing them and using the clothes for other purposes; clothing the dolls again in all the old pieces of rags and papers that she can get hold of! Boxes of puzzles and bricks are all mixed up, the boxes broken, and she has a perfect mania for wrapping up most of her toys in endless parcels. It seems that, instead of using the toys in the orthodox way, she has a "special" method of her own, but the trouble is, though having had plenty *of toys, she never keeps anything intact for long; hence she possesses mostly rubbish! I have shown her how to tidy her cupboard, and she does this to some degree upon occasions, but in a day or so there is the same old muddle, and the usual cry, "I cannot find anything to play with". Books come adrift from their bindings, plasticine gets mixed up with bricks, dirt, or wrapped up in paper! She is a very intelligent child, and very sensible for her age, and I cannot understand this trouble, except that my husband thinks she has been given too many toys in the past, and suggests I start letting her have one thing at a time. This, of course, would to some extent take her back to the baby stage, as I should have to take the toy cupboard away from her and "dole" the toys out. Naturally she helps herself, and often she is alone in the garden or room playing, so I do not see how all the toys get so mixed and spoilt, but I am quite sure it is not done wilfully.*

A. The behaviour of your little girl with her toys certainly presents a difficult problem. There is no doubt that it should not be looked upon as mere naughtiness or wilfulness, but as an expression of inner emotional difficulties of a neurotic type. I don't think the trouble can have come merely from her having had plenty of toys, although it would be a good thing not to give her too many. It may possibly be that she feels she has more than other children that she knows, and feels guilty about this or it may be her way of avoiding any wish to hurt people. You don't say whether she has any brothers and sisters or playmates of her own age. It is quite likely that one way of helping her to take care of her possessions would be to suggest her giving away some of the toys to children who have fewer than she has, or perhaps none at all, and helping her to mend them up for this purpose. At any rate, I would suggest your trying this, though not in any formal or didactic way. If you know any children or could make acquaintance with any who are short of toys, and try her reaction casually to this, and then one day suggest that some particular toy that she has could be mended up and given to these other children, it is quite possible that might help her. I would begin quite slowly with this, and not make too much of it. Otherwise it would be better to leave her alone as regards this difficulty, since it clearly springs from some deep emotional conflict and is not a question of mere habit. It is an expression rather than a source of difficulty. So long as she does not injure anyone else's possessions in the same way, other people really have nothing to grumble at in the child's messing up her own belongings, although, of course, one wishes to help her over the difficulty that gives rise to this. And it would be better to try to develop her interest in mending things than merely to scold her for messing them up. For example, if you could give her the means for mending the boxes, such as paste or seccotine, and help her to develop an interest in *making* clothes for dolls rather than giving her ready-made things, that would be a help, too. And helping in a real way in the house—washing up, putting her own clothes away, sweeping and dusting her room—i.e. giving her opportunity and encouragement for these things, not demanding them.

Q. My son aged four and a half years is very wilful at times and most difficult. Twice recently he has cut his small sister's hair, and though I pointed out to him how dangerous it was, it seems to have had no effect. In fact, he either will not or does not want to listen when he is corrected. Another trick he has is to tear the wallpaper from the walls. I put him to bed for some hours for this, and it seemed very effective for a time, but I was told this was wrong. When I asked him if he had done either of these things he said, "No", but after much coaxing he admitted it. At one time he was smacked, but I have stopped this for some time, as I felt it was not right. I try putting him in the corner, but he will only stay there for a minute or two. He is very highly strung, and I try to avoid a scene as much as possible.

A. I should very much like to help you with your boy, who is clearly passing through a difficult phase of development.

But I should like to speak quite frankly, if you will let me. I think the difficulties must have arisen because you have not been quite sure in your own mind about what was the best way to treat him. You are anxious to train him well, but do not feel any confidence in the cruder forms of punishment, and yet do not quite know what to use in their place. There are many people who find themselves in just that position to-day. As our treatment of children has grown more humane, we do not feel it right to whip them and put them to bed and yet we have to find some way of helping them to behave well. Now, we can only find out what the best ways are by learning something of the general ways of growth of children's minds and what healthy growth depends on.

When we understand these, it is easier to find constructive ways of training them. Help does not really come from special recipes for this, that and the other problem, but only from knowing something of the general principles of child training. Particular problems will often solve themselves, or never arise, if our general attitude to the child is right.

There is one thing I can suggest now. If the boy cuts his sister's hair and tears the wallpaper it is almost certainly because he has not enough things to occupy him actively, and upon which he can express his destructive energy.

Whenever you find the child pulling off the wallpaper it would be best to say, "I don't want you to do that; but here is a bundle of newspapers—you can cut those up as much as you like". You could show him how to make a "Red Indian's" headdress by making a deep fringe on a long piece of paper with scissors, or by tearing it. Or he can make all sorts of exciting patterns in a large piece by folding it up several times and tearing out small holes. It is quite thrilling to see what design is going to appear when the paper is unfolded! Or he could stuff pillows for his sister's dolls by tearing or cutting up sheets of paper into small pieces; or make decorative fringes and streamers for his nursery for Christmas, either colouring the newspaper with water-colour paints or using coloured tissue paper. Then, again, why shouldn't he help you chop up the coal and wood for the fire? Once one has got the idea that a constructive method of using his energy and enterprise is best, many ways can be invented, and the question of punishment will hardly arise.

DESTRUCTIVENESS

Q. I do so want my little girl, aged two years four months to be kind and considerate to animals, but we have a dog and she is a positive little horror to him. He is devoted to her and most patient, but she really frightens him, either by pushing her wooden horse or doll's pram into him and after him, or by chasing him with something that squeaks (which he hates at all times), or by treading on his paws or prodding him with sticks. This wouldn't be so bad if she weren't serious about it, but she seems to take a fiendish delight in plaguing him. I have talked to her. I have shut the dog away from her, and I have gone so far as to treat her in a similar manner, but without avail, and I am at a loss to know how to proceed with her.

A. This problem of the little child's cruelty to animals is a fairly common one, and I think it is rather surprising that (as far as I remember) yours is the first letter which has raised the question in my columns. Most little children in their earliest years show occasional impulses of what amounts to cruel behaviour towards animals, although it is not always cruel in the sense that the child really wishes to inflict pain. Sometimes, and especially in the second and third years, it is simply lack of understanding that certain actions cause pain. But it is not always this, at any rate after the end of the second year, and it sounds to me from your description as if your little girl did really wish to hurt the dog. I happen to have made a fairly detailed study of this particular problem in my own observations of children between two and seven years of age, and I have found very few children who did not show the impulse to hurt occasionally, although some children do so very rarely, and others much more often. But what is clearly striking is that one very rarely sees a child who has not equally strong impulses of tenderness and sympathy with animals. According to the mood they are in, they will be tender and cherishing or hostile and unkind.

Now, since these impulses are so general there is not any need for you to dread that the child will necessarily be cruel when she is a little older. She is at just the age when the impulse is often at its strongest, and when there is the least imaginative realization of what she is doing to the dog. What I found was the best way to educate children in humane behaviour to animals was to encourage their interest in animals as independent creatures with their own lives and their own histories. This is, of course, easier with children a little older, but I think it could be done even with one so young as your little girl. I should, of course, forbid her to hurt the dog, and, in so far as you possibly can, refuse to let her do it, by shutting the dog away, by holding her hands firmly, or by depriving her for the time being of the wooden horse or the doll's pram which she bumps into him. I should say to her, "If you use these things to hurt the dog, I won't let you have them", but I should not go beyond this, nor should I treat her as she treats the dog. This last method has definitely been shown to be harmful, not helpful. So much for the negative methods. Now for the positive. I should tell her or read to her plenty of animal stories—e.g. The Beatrix Potter tales, which are suitable for her age, and any simple stories of animal mothers and children that you can get hold of. And I should let her have more pets to keep. This should be fairly easy as you live in the country. A rabbit makes quite a delightful pet for a child of this age, as the soft fur is so pleasant to touch and the child can help to feed the animal. Is there a farm anywhere near where the child can be taken to gain an interest in the sheep and cows and horses? Would it be possible for her to keep a hen and chickens, and be told about the eggs and the way the chickens grow and come out of the eggs? This, at any rate, is the sort of education which is most likely to win her from her cruelty by building up a lively sense of the personality of animals and the natural history of their lives. But with all this you will, of course, have to give the child time to grow out of her love of power in hurting and not be too distressed if she does not respond at once.

Q. What can you do about a child who persists in throwing her beads on the floor instead of threading them and yet goes on asking for "beads to thread"? Whenever I give her a box of beads she threads a few, but seems to get suddenly tired of them, and deliberately throws them on the floor. She is just over four.

A. Most little children do this sort of thing from time to time and some of them go through a phase of doing it so often as to be very irritating to mother or nurse. It can be a nuisance; and we are liable to be annoyed by it, even if it happens only occasionally, because it seems to us a purely destructive and perverse action.

But it is worth while stopping to find out, if we can, why the child does it. Although in itself a simple action, it may have a lot of meaning for her.

There are, of course, destructive elements in it; but even these have their meaning. It may be that throwing the beads down is an act of direct defiance because the child is cross or generally disgruntled. But if the disgruntlement takes this particular form, one would at once suspect that the child is probably not getting enough free movement of the larger muscles and joints of the body, of the shoulder and hip and wrist, in running and jumping and climbing and throwing a ball. Threading beads, sewing, writing, and so on call for fine co-ordination of the smaller muscles and joints with the eyes; and in the early years these involve a much greater nervous strain. Explosive actions, like knocking or throwing things down, are a definite relief to nervous tension; and the need for this relief is greatest when the child is encouraged to do things that are unsuitable for her age. Perhaps the beads are too small; they ought to be quite large, with large holes, for a child of four years. Then there is always the possibility of defective eyesight; that, too, should be inquired into. If, however, her eyesight is all right and the beads are really large enough, then the impatience that leads to the explosive action of throwing them down might pass away if the child got more general active movement of the body as a whole out of doors.

On the other hand, throwing the beads on the floor is not *necessarily* an act of mere impatience. It often has a positive pleasure and positive values. We know well how the child of a year and a half or two years of age will throw a spoon or a doll down over and over again if an obliging adult will keep on picking it up for him. His laughter and shouts of delight show that this is very far from an act of defiance. It is an experiment—an experiment partly in action and power of movement and partly in cause and effect, an inquiry into the way things happen. This particular pleasure does sometimes last on until the child is four years of age. (The vast delight there is in the act of throwing is shown by the enormous place which this occupies in our adult ball games.) The child seems also to love to watch the way the beads scatter and roll on the floor—in much the same way as we like dribbling sand through our fingers on the beach.

Now, there is obviously no reason why the child should not have this interest. It is not in itself an undesirable thing, and it would seem to be a pity to turn it into something merely "naughty". And yet, of course, we have to find ways of limiting it, as we can hardly have beads and other things about the floor all the time!

If, then, she does sometimes throw the beads down, it is more likely to be a direct pleasure in the act of throwing and in seeing the way the beads roll and lie. Now, this we could let her have occasionally, *on the condition that she picks them up again*, or helps to pick them up if she is quite small. But even before urging this condition we could show her that we understand her pleasure in the way the bright, shining things have rolled about. We can treat it all as a matter of genuine interest, and avoid suggesting "naughtiness" by our manner. Then, having laughed with the child, we can say gently, "Now I'll help you to pick them up", taking it for granted that she will help to do her share, and making this, too, into a pleasant game. We can then let the child clearly understand that we expect that she will pick up the things she spills or throws down, although, if she is as small as four years, we are willing to help in this, if she does her share, provided we are not too busy with other things. And sometimes it would be as well if we *were* too busy! And we can quietly comment on how much longer it takes to pick things up than to throw them down! This sort of way of going about things is far more effective in helping the child to gain understanding of the results of her own actions, and the self-control and consideration for others that rest upon understanding, than mere scolding.

The particular instance may seem to some people a trivial one. But the child's day is made up of small matters, and our relations with him in the end depend upon the way we deal with the trivial problems that arise.

Q. Our youngest son, Brian, aged two years seven months throws anything anywhere at any moment! Toys, ornaments, books, cutlery, they all go the same way. Many times Brian gives absolutely no warning at all that he is going to throw. This can result in nasty accidents to people within his range, as you can imagine. Normally he is very fond of his brother Ben, aged four years seven months, but just recently he seems to make a set attack on his brother at every conceivable moment, especi-

ally at meal-times. Brian throws his spoons, plates or even mugs across at his brother for no apparent reason except for the delight of hurting him. You can imagine how disturbing the meal times are—if Brian does not actually throw he threatens to do so holding the article above his head and of course scaring his brother a good deal. Brian also will pinch or kick his brother, again for no apparent reason. This all seems so strange because Ben is really fond of his young brother and is very kind to him, sharing most of his toys and pleasures with him. Ben is a very sensible little fellow for his age and I have asked him not to hit or hurt Brian in return, as Brian does not really mean to be unkind to him, it is that he does not quite understand yet, but will do so when he is a little bigger. We are just wondering if this is an unwise course to have taken, and venture to suggest that Ben should hold his own against Brian occasionally. But "an eye for an eye, etc." is not our policy! To-night when I was tucking Ben in bed he said he didn't like Brian any more because he hurts him so much and that Brian must go away somewhere. You can appreciate the little fellow's point of view, can't you? The two boys share a bedroom together and are in each other's company a great deal except for two and a half hours in the mornings. I should add that Brian has very restless nights, waking sometimes four or five times in the night. He is soon comforted, but getting out of bed and going into another room so often is very tiring to me. These bad nights are caused, I feel sure, by Brian's emotional upsets during the day. When Brian has been corrected for throwing, etc. he throws himself into a terrific paddy, lying on the floor, kicking and screaming, finishing up by tearing his shoes and socks off—then crying for me to put them on again. Normally Brian is a very loving and lovable child—talks very well and is highly intelligent and robust.

A. This is not a very common problem, and certainly a difficult one. I would try to deal with it by giving Brian the opportunity to throw as much as he likes at certain times and in certain places. I would give the two boys separate tables at meal time, or even let the younger one eat alone for the present. I would arrange this without scolding or reproaching him, but say in a simple, direct way that you do not want him to throw spoons and mugs, etc. and perhaps soon he will be able to prevent himself from doing this, and meanwhile you think it would be better if he had his meal at his own little table by himself. Then I would give Brian definite periods, either in the nursery or in the garden, or both, when he can turn his throwing into a game which is shared with his brother and with you. Let him even throw a brick, so that it may be caught and thrown back, but when throwing it back you will have to be very careful not to let him feel that it is being thrown *at* him by way of punishment. Turn it into a jolly game for everyone to share in as soon and as often as you can, and preferably of course let him throw balls. But give him ten minutes or quarter of an hour as soon as possible in the morning, for example, immediately after breakfast, when he can have a really good throw, and again when he is out for a walk and so on. Then at other times try to watch very carefully and stop the throwing in time, before he can do any damage.

As regards your policy for the older brother, I fully agree that the "eye for an eye and a tooth for a tooth" attitude should not be encouraged. On the other hand, it is certainly undesirable to expect a boy of four to be completely disinterested and not protect himself against attacks by his younger brother. That would be to put a terrific moral strain on a child of this age. I would suggest your letting him defend himself, but trying to find a way by which he can do it without hurting the younger brother. It would be better for the younger child not to feel that he could attack the older with complete impunity. The strain of being so very self-sacrificing might very easily make the older boy hate the younger one. You already have a hint of that. Little boys, and even bigger boys, can actually struggle and fight quite a good deal in a good-tempered way without this arousing real bitterness and hatred. But to compel the older boy to be victimized by the younger one would easily arouse real resentment and hatred that might last until he was grown up. It would probably be better for both of them if you did not interfere, but left the older boy to find his own equilibrium in the matter. Brotherly enmity can be very acute in early childhood without spoiling the relationship later on. I have known many instances of acute rivalry between boys who in their later childhood and youth became splendid friends. They have more respect and affection for each other if they have fought it out between themselves in a natural way, and since your elder boy is obviously of a friendly disposition you do not need to fear that he will hurt the younger child.

Q. My small nephew, aged two years four months, is a constant worry to his mother. For the last six months or so Peter has been biting other babies younger than himself. He has lately bitten baby Pat, aged five months. Peter is a lovable child and very good apart from this. But it worries his mother so much that she is making herself ill. We can think of no reason for his biting unless it is because he came nine years after marriage, and his daddy used to love him very hard and used to pretend to eat him. The other day he bit the hand of a baby, who was standing at the gate. He has been smacked a lot for it and also kept indoors, but we cannot go on doing this as it is bad for the child always to be in disgrace. His mother has tried biting him but it makes no difference. We are still hoping that he will grow out of this, but it has been going on for so long now.

A. The impulse to bite other children is often quite strong in little boys of two to three years of age, although in your little nephew this impulse is unusually strong. Very often one can tell from the child's behaviour that the biting is a form of love. Like his father, the child is actually saying to those for whom he feels affection, "I love you so much I could eat you", only, being a little child, he cannot say this in words, nor does he understand that he should only play at biting. He has not the self-control and the imagination necessary to stop before he hurts. We cannot doubt that it is so marked in this little boy, partly because his father has so often expressed his own strong feelings of love by pretending to eat the child. It is always very frightening to a little child when grown-ups do pretend to eat him. The tiny child cannot distinguish between pretence and reality, and is really afraid that he is going to be eaten in fact. Your little nephew's present ways then will be partly an expression of love of the same kind as he has learnt from his father, but with the difference that comes from being himself a tiny child, and partly an expression of his own fears that his daddy is going to eat him. I have found that the best way of dealing with this difficulty in a child of this age is not to scold or whip the child; this often makes him bite all the harder and more frequently and certainly *never* bite the child himself. This would always increase the tendency in the child, because it confirms his view that that is what grown-ups do to children and so it is what he must do to those smaller than himself. If, however, when the child has bitten anyone, we speak very clearly and firmly to him, without scolding and frightening him in any way, and say that we do not want him to bite because it hurts: we know that *he* does not want to be bitten and would not like his daddy or mummy or another child to bite him, and as *he* does not like it, perhaps he can remember that and not do it to other children. I should let the child understand that you appreciate that he bites partly out of love, not only in anger, and I should say to him that it would be better to kiss the other child instead of biting. And then I would kiss him and show him how much pleasanter kissing is than biting. One little boy of three (who is now twelve years of age and the most delightful and admirable boy you can imagine) was very much addicted to biting in love, and I was able to help him out of this habit by firmly and quietly saying, "No, thank you, I do not want to be bitten: I do not want to be hurt, and I am not going to let you do it to me". He would then say, "Well then, I shall kiss you instead". It is very important, however, not to scold or reproach or frighten, but to let it be a quiet comment, accepting the love but not the biting, which is the crude way of expressing love. A child with this tendency to biting needs very careful supervision, of course, while the phase lasts. I would be very careful not to leave him alone with another child whom he might hurt in this way. It is not fair to the other child to subject him to this biting and hurting, and it is not helpful to the biting child to find himself constantly in the position of having hurt another. For a time, therefore, I would suggest very careful supervision and watching, and this quiet, loving training. It is important to make sure that the child has plenty of affection and happy activity in every direction. But I would strongly urge you to give up entirely smacking and the biting and the punishment. You can be sure that he will go on biting as long as you do this.

IX. VARIOUS SYMPTOMS OF DIFFICULTY

Q. I have twin sons of eighteen months, normal, healthy children. Number Two is a calm young person, and whatever the excitement of the day, he sleeps quietly in the same position all night. Number One goes to sleep quite happily at six and sleeps rather restlessly. About 2 a.m., however, he wakes up, apparently quite rested, and until four or five jumps up and down, making a terrible noise as the cot springs move. While doing this he laughs and sings and goes over all the words and phrases he knows. When he has tired himself out he falls asleep until his brother wakens about 6.30. This has been going on for five out of the seven nights for several weeks. I have tried: (a) putting him down to sleep gently with his favourite rabbit; (b) whispering that he must sleep just like his brother; (c) giving him a different animal to take to sleep; (d) lifting him out of the cot for a few minutes and sitting quietly beside him. Daddy has tried saying firmly, "Alan mustn't make a noise with cot". To all methods he smiles charmingly, says, "No, no, no" and continues playing.

We always try to let the children play quietly before bed and we have definitely tried not to stimulate Number One these last few months. He has always liked people and had an audience, tried to repeat all I say and wants to be praised all the time. Because of being twins, they have had the usual amount of admiration on their daily walks and from babyhood he expects passers-by to smile to him.

I feel this cot-banging cannot be good for his nervous system and it is certainly very bad for his parents. Little brother sleeps through it all.

A. In the second year of life these habits of banging the cot or their own heads and bodies are by no means uncommon, particularly amongst boys. A year or two ago I had a great many cases of such automatic habits described in letters. One of the conclusions the letters I received made very clear was that no method we can use, persuasion, appeal, scolding, punishment, whatever it be, can *prevent* the child's movements, as long as he feels this urge. It is something very deep and intense in its urgency, and simply does not respond to any attempt to stop it. On the other hand, there is not the slightest evidence that it ever does any real harm to the child himself. It is disturbing and annoying to the grown-ups, and may be so to other children, but for the child himself it provides a means of maintaining nervous equilibrium, which would suffer very considerably if we forcibly prevented his movements by, e.g., tying him down.

Psychologists have come to understand a good deal about the meaning of these movements to the child in his second year, but I could not hope to make the explanations clear and convincing in the space at my disposal. I would strongly suggest that you do not try to do anything directly, but leave the child to grow out of this necessity, as he certainly will do, probably within the next twelve months, provided his general emotional needs are satisfied. I would clothe him in such a way as to make quite sure that he will not get cold, and I would try to give him a cot which would not make quite such a disturbing noise when he moves. And then I would try to sleep through the disturbance, so as not to be affected in my own temper in dealing with the child. It appears to be the child's normal development and the satisfactions he gets in his waking life, through play and gaining skills with his hands, and in speaking and companionship, and all the varied activities of the life of a child of three or four, that renders this particular type of activity at night unnecessary. I would allow him to have even **more** bodily **activity than** his brother during the day, e.g., running and climbing, rather than being pushed in a chair; and I would be quite unsparing of open signs of affection with such a child. It is very fortunate that his brother is so placid, but it is not in the least necessary to worry over this boy's development either. It is obviously going to be on different lines, but it does not follow that it will not be quite as satisfactory in its own way.

Q. My small charge is eighteen months old. He is exceptionally forward in all ways. He is very strong and healthy, and is not in the least a "nervy" child. About one month ago he started to bite his nails. He generally does it when tired, and if ever I go back into his nursery after he has been put to bed at night I always find him biting his nails. When told he is not to do it he promptly pushes his fingers down his throat so making himself "retch". Occasionally, on being corrected for some misdeed he will attract my attention by some sound and then bite at his nails hard as though he knows it will annoy me. This made me think that he did it just to attract attention, but if he does it when alone (and he always does when put to sleep) I think it is more of a habit. The only way I can stop him is to stay by him and hold his hands until he is asleep, and as I have only just taught him to go to sleep alone I do not want to have to stay with him again.

A. I think you will find that indirect methods of treating this difficulty will be much more effective than a direct attack. The child's response to the direct prohibition is an unusual one and distinctly neurotic, even though he may not seem to be "nervy" in other ways. It is quite clear that he does not mind injuring himself if by doing so he can make you cross. Now unless you are prepared to stand over him all the time and be very severe you will not be able to cure the habit by scolding or command. The methods that are so often tried—of bandaging the fingers or putting on bitter aloes—practically always fail. In the meantime, whilst they are being tried they simply serve to make the child more nervy and irritable and to prevent his using his hands in ways that would help his growth. For these reasons the only direct method I would try is rubbing olive oil into the nails. This will ensure that the nails are soft and not brittle nor ragged, and so the temptation to bite them will be lessened. But otherwise I should leave the whole matter alone, beyond, perhaps, an occasional cheerful encouragement on any days when the boy bites his nails less frequently. I should rely upon the indirect ways of seeing that he has plenty of happy occupation for his hands and suitable things to play with and plenty of chance to run about freely in the open air. As regards the biting at bed time, does he have a favourite toy to cuddle? That might help too. But if you are very anxious that he should not bite his nails when falling to sleep, then I do not think you have any alternative to staying with him and holding his hands. It would be very unwise to bandage them or tie them down in any way. The one certain thing, however, is that the more attention you give to the biting, the more fuss you make about it, the more likely it is to settle down into a permanent habit.

Q. My little boy, aged two years eight months, has a habit when in bed of turning over on to his hands and knees and rocking violently backwards and forwards, banging his head each time against the top end of the cot. He has done this off and on for more than a year but lately the habit has greatly increased. He does it sometime during every night. It does not always wake him. If it does he does not cry and seem unhappy—rather the reverse—often getting quite flushed and excited. I feel obliged

VARIOUS SYMPTOMS OF DIFFICULTY

always to go in to him, as if I did not I feel convinced he would continue for a long period. I feel this would almost certainly be very bad for him. I have padded his cot, so that I do not think he can actually injure his head. I think there is still a little trouble with his teeth, nothing much. He is the picture of health and perfectly normal and jolly otherwise. There is no trouble in this way during the day.

A. There is nothing you can do directly with regard to your boy's habit of rocking and knocking his head on the end of the cot. It was very sensible to pad the cot so that he cannot injure himself; but you will find the habit will pass away during the next year or so if the general conditions of the child's life are happy and his development in other respects is satisfactory, as it seems to be. It is not a common habit in children, but it does occur now and then, and chiefly in boys. It rarely persists after the fourth year, however. Whilst the child feels the need for it, interference does much more harm than good. It is an expression of anxiety, by which the child maintains his emotional equilibrium in other respects. There is, therefore, no reason for you to feel any special worry about it, unless it increased very considerably or showed no signs of passing away during this next year, in which case I would advise your getting first-hand advice from a medical psychologist who would be able to diagnose the underlying difficulty.

Q. Peter, one year nine months, is a very healthy and contented boy. We have been having considerable trouble with him lately, however. On going to bed, he gets on to his hands and knees and makes a regular thumping movement for hours on end. He goes to bed between 6.45 and seven o'clock, and often it is nine o'clock before he goes to sleep. During the night he is often awake for an hour or two, and always he is doing the same thing. He does this even when he is thoroughly fatigued, and continues although he seems to be half asleep. We have tried everything to stop him. We have talked to him, and punished him, and tied him in his cot, but nothing seems to cure him. This has been going on for three months. I was away with him a few weeks ago, and he had to sleep in a single bed then, and I hoped the different bed and surroundings would make a difference to him, but there was no alteration.

A. This practice arises from very complex processes in the child's mind, the explanations of which would be far too long to enter into here. It is a solution which the child has found for himself for certain kinds of mental conflict, and in itself it does no harm. It is not this habit which disturbs his sleep, but the anxieties underlying it. The bumping or thumping itself is an attempt on the child's part to get rid of the anxieties which are disturbing his sleep. I am not at all surprised to hear that you have not succeeded in stopping the child by scolding or punishing him or tying him in his cot. You could only stop it by extremely severe treatment that would do a good deal of harm to the child's emotional life. There is, however, no need for you to worry about it at all, since it will certainly pass away itself with the child's normal development. It is in the second and sometimes third year of a child's life that one chiefly hears of this habit, and very rarely does it occur or persist in later years. It might, of course, continue in a child who was very badly treated, and very unhappy, but otherwise you can feel quite assured that it will cease of itself as the child grows out of the inner difficulties which give rise to it.

I should rely upon keeping him happy by play and suitable occupations and a friendly relation with him, both during the day and at night when he is going to sleep; and I should certainly avoid any scolding or reproach about the thumping.

Q. My small son is twenty-two months. He is a strong, healthy child, full of happiness and vitality, but he developed an extraordinary habit some five months ago. When put down to sleep, he turns on his tummy and bangs his head on the pillow for fifteen minutes or so, without a pause. He does so with tremendous force, and I feel very worried about it. Someone suggested strapping him on his back. This to me seems rather an unwise procedure with a child of his temperament, and I should feel happier if the habit can be cured less drastically. He gets plenty of exercise, and when unable to romp in the garden, I myself play a game of football indoors with him. I have tried coaxing, and have adopted a severe attitude, without any satisfaction. Friends tell me he will grow out of it, but it seems to have continued for such a long time, and I feel it cannot be good for his head, that I want to take immediate steps to cure the habit.

A. I have had several letters dealing with this particular problem. This banging of the head is not quite so common as thumb-sucking and nail-biting, but still it does often occur. It is of the same psychological nature as thumb-sucking and nail-biting, but whilst it is perhaps more dramatic and distressing to watch, it has in fact less possibilities of real harm than either of these other habits.

The idea of strapping the child on his back is, of course, wholly wrong; "wrong" is, in fact, hardly sufficient condemnation for the idea! I am very glad that you felt yourself that such a method would be unwise and senseless. On the other hand, I don't think it is the least use your adopting a severe attitude towards him. If you succeeded by scolding in preventing his doing this, you might very well cause him to bite his nails or stammer, or have night terrors, or break out in any other of the nervous habits which children of this age so often have. Since, apart from this habit, the child is so strong and well, full of happiness and vitality, I should leave the whole matter entirely alone. You may be sure that it serves some definite psychological end in the child's mind. It acts as a safety valve for some imaginary wish and self-punishment, and there is no reason at all to think that it can do him any harm. If he is happy and well and contented, he will grow out of it in a year or two.

Q. I should be so glad of advice with regard to my small daughter of four years old. She has developed a dreadful habit of sniffing, and pulling faces; she has no nasal obstruction or catarrh, so I am quite sure it is a nervous habit. She is a very highly-strung child, and much too sensitive for her own good. I feel that she is rather misunderstood, and am not sure how I should treat this new habit of hers. She has a small brother of two, who comes in for a lot of attention, being of a sunny, friendly, disposition, but I do not think Jennifer is at all jealous of him, in fact she plays very sweetly with him. J. sucks her fingers too, but she only does this in bed.

A. I would suggest that you do not comment upon your little daughter's habit, and do not pay any direct attention to it. These little habits often occur, in the years between three and five. They are an expression of emotional conflict and are usually best relieved by indirect remedies, that is, by finding out what the chief source of the emotional conflict is and making sure that the child has normal satisfactions in play and companionship, and secure affection. The sniffing may well be the one way in which J.'s jealousy of her little brother is expressed. She evidently manages to control her feelings in her direct relation with him, and to be affectionate and helpful. But difficult feelings do force themselves to expression, if not in one way then in another. With plenty of affection and plenty of play and companionship, however, she will grow out of the difficulty, and the habit will pass away all the more readily if you do not take any direct notice of it.

Q. *I would be very grateful if you could help me over a little nervous trouble which has just started with Pamela, who was five years old last week. She has always been perfectly healthy, and never has given me a bit of trouble right from babyhood. In March of last year she caught bronchial catarrh. Under the doctor's care the catarrh left the chest but since then there has been some sort of slight catarrh in the right nostril. About ten days ago she caught her first winter cold. She threw it off remarkably fast, but the cold was followed by two styes on her eyelids, one of which came on her left lower lid, and was right inside the lid, and of course kept irritating the eye itself, with the result that she kept screwing up her left eye with the pain of it. After two bathings the sty cleared, but the nervous habit remains of screwing up that eye. I don't know how to deal with it. Should I mention it to her or would that make matters worse? Do little nervous habits clear off in a short while?*

A. It is most probable that this eye twitching will pass away before very long. Such habits arising from a particular physical difficulty do usually pass away, but they take a little time. Whether or not the habit would become worse if you spoke of it to her depends very much upon what you said and how you went about it. Scolding or criticism would certainly make it worse. But it would probably help if you said to her that she seemed to be screwing up her eye as if she was not quite sure that the sty was better, and suggested her bathing the lid herself with some warm boracic solution, so that she could be quite sure that there is nothing painful growing there. It would be better to get her to bathe it herself than for you to do it. I think you might try this method, and otherwise take no particular notice of it. It will then probably pass away with time and growth.

Q. My wife wrote to you about our boy, aged nine then, who was sucking his thumb and had damaged his teeth and mouth through it. We thought that you would be interested to hear that for one year he has not attempted to suck his thumb. The cure was effected by myself in the following manner and was absolutely complete in four weeks. During the Easter holidays I gave him riding lessons. This kept him in the fresh air and occupied his hands. Then, every evening as he was falling asleep, I suggested to him that he disliked sucking his thumb, and that it tasted bad. In the mornings I compared his thumbs, and showed him the change (imaginary at first) which was taking place in the sucked thumb. He took a personal pride in this change and at the end of four weeks he was cured. His health improved out of all recognition, his mouth improved, and his teeth have resumed almost the normal.

A. I have no doubt that the effective influence in this cure was the father's interest in the matter, and above all, the riding lessons. These must have meant to the boy that his father wanted him to do something good with his hands, wanted him to become a skilful and clever boy, and took pride in his physical prowess. This would act in the boy's mind, both as a permission to grow up and do things like fathers do, and as a direct spur to those activities suitable for his age. I do not believe that the attempt at suggestion would have had the slightest effect unless it had been accompanied by these more positive fatherly encouragements, and indeed, I do not doubt that the latter would have acted perfectly well without the other.

This letter is a valuable hint of how much help fathers can

VARIOUS SYMPTOMS OF DIFFICULTY

give to boys of this age by taking, not an attitude of punishment and anger, but one of positive teaching and encouragement in manly pursuits. I am very grateful to the writer for taking the trouble to put his experience at the service of other readers. I have no doubt that fathers could help more than they sometimes do in these problems, with children of even earlier ages than nine years, if they would take this positive line and prove themselves willing to hand on their own good knowledge and skills in an encouraging way.

The following three letters deal with thumb-sucking, the third one making a protest against one of my previous suggestions.

Q.1. My little boy, aged twenty months, is perfectly healthy and full of vitality, but has formed quite a nasty habit of continually sucking his first finger and at the same time putting his other hand to his ear and pulling it. He does this more frequently when feeling tired, and though I have tried wrapping his finger up, he always manages to pull the bandage off or puts in another finger.

Q.2. I should be so grateful for your advice for thumb-sucking and nail-biting. My son is an only child, four years and four months old. He goes to a kindergarten school, the full school hours, as I think he needed a companion.

Q.3. Who calls herself, "Horrified". On reading through your reply to another enquirer about finger-sucking, I was astounded that you, after having suggested points whereby one might not interfere with the psychological and the physical well-being of a child at fifteen months, should descend to such bathos as prescribing boiled sweets before finally tucking up for the night. You must surely be aware of the cause of decay in teeth as far as is known to dental science, that this method of treatment is providing an ideal field for decay to commence. When is this form of treatment going to finish? It simply means that the child will not go to bed without a sweet in its mouth. It is a pernicious form of bribery and corruption. Another point: Boiled sweets are extremely slippery and much too easily swallowed—even by grown-ups—to be safe as a bed-time palliative to a baby who has little muscular control. My little daughter of eighteen months finds much comfort in her fingers, but has her teeth cleaned most carefully before she is put to bed at night, and no amount of finger-sucking will ever drive me to boiled sweets as a cure.

A. I should, of course, agree with the writer of Q.3 that it was better to leave a child to find comfort in her fingers if that helped her to go to sleep. I have often suggested that the distress which most people feel about thumb- and finger-sucking is quite unwarranted. In itself there is nothing to worry about, and the habit does not deserve to be called "nasty". Many children don't seem to be able to go to sleep without this particular satisfaction, any more than many of their fathers and mothers nowadays seem to be able to do without a comforting pipe or soothing cigarette! And those mothers who don't give themselves the pleasure of cigarettes do, as a rule, indulge in tea-drinking, which, of course, can hardly be described as a real necessity and has much more the quality of an indulgence. Most of us need some such innocent pleasure to keep our tempers even and our characters agreeable.

In his thumb- and finger-sucking the little child simply shows that his needs are much the same as our own. But there are two difficulties which have to be faced with some children and some parents. The first is when they fear that it is indulged in too freely that it damages the gums and alters the shape of the mouth. I myself would not want to interfere with it forcibly and directly even then, but it is not at all easy to make everyone understand that the psychological harm of forcible deprivation may be more serious and lasting than the hypothetical effect on the teeth or on sore fingers. Then, even apart from the question of spoiling the teeth, there are a great many mothers and nurses who feel so strongly about thumb-sucking that they cannot refrain from interfering with it by some sort of method, no matter who says it is better not to!

Now, the point about the boiled sweets was that I wanted to make it as clear as I could that if parents do feel the thumb-sucking habit to be so objectionable that they simply must try to get rid of it, then they have to recognize the fact that the child will need some substitute gratification. It is unwise to take one comfort away from the child without giving him another in its place; and we must try to choose one that will do as little harm as possible. When I suggested the boiled sweets I took it for granted that no one would be so foolish as to give a sweet to a child after he was lying down, when it might slip down his throat and choke him. I, of course, fully agree with what Q.3 says about this, but thought everyone would understand that I meant mother or nurse to see that it was safely disposed of before the child lay down to be tucked up. As regards dental decay, I know that sugar has long been regarded as very harmful to the teeth, but I am given to understand that the latest scientific research on this point has led to a change of opinion, and that sugar is not, in fact, harmful for the teeth—at any rate, in moderation. Starch is bad, but sugar is now (I understand) not considered to be. After all, there is plenty of sugar in the apple, which is supposed to be such an excellent thing to clean teeth with!

As I have suggested before, when one is dealing with a child who is a very persistent thumb-sucker one is up against a very difficult problem for which there is really no perfect solution: it is entirely a matter of balancing possible evils against each other.

But I would like to suggest again in reply both to Q.1 and Q.2 that the wisest way to go about the whole problem is not to make any direct attack upon it. I should not, for example, try to wrap the boy's finger up. No harm can be done with a healthy child who only sucks his fingers when he is tired or going to sleep. Even the nail-biting is best left alone, unless definite psychological treatment by a properly trained person can be arranged for. The indirect method of providing plenty of active interests, companionship in play, and pleasant things to do with the hands is the only really satisfactory way of dealing with the problem.

Q. My daughter, aged three and a half years has sucked her thumb from the time when she was a few days old. I have done many things in an effort to stop it, but all in vain. When she was two years of age we decided it had just got to cease, so first I tried bitter aloes, which somehow was rubbed off, and then I tried putting gloves on at night, and she would not rest, so those I was obliged to take off. Worse things happened, for I found that she was biting her nails in the daytime—this only when she did not suck her thumb. I asked my doctor what to do, and he said, "Do not worry her—try to ignore what she does". This I did, but I fear the thumb-sucking still goes on. After she had turned three I tried reasoning with her, explaining that she was growing up, and, although little babies did such silly things big girls did not. For a child of her age she is very sensible, but, I regret, terribly sensitive. After my talk with her she would lie awake night after night until nearly eleven o'clock, and then I have had to scold before she will sleep. Yet if she had been allowed to suck her thumb she would have slept almost as soon as her head touched the pillow. This I have proved. And now I have had to commence bribery! She has been promised a new dolly's pram, or a large tricycle on her fourth birthday, only if she refrains from thumb-sucking. Although it is not done in the daytime, I rarely go into her room after she is asleep but I have to remove the thumb from her mouth. It worries me in more ways than one. I have always been very careful never to make rash promises, neither have I ever (knowingly) broken my word, so I feel I must somehow break her of this thumb-sucking business before her next birthday in February. Some say, "Oh, don't worry her; she will grow out of it". I have but little faith in such words. I have a niece who is now nine years of age, and who has persistently sucked her finger since her arrival, and I dread my little girl should continue to do so. Do you think it is at all harmful to her that she keeps awake so long? I have felt tempted to try the gloves again, but I do not want to make her ill through loss of sleep.

A. I wonder why you feel so strongly about your little girl's thumb-sucking, especially seeing that she only does it when she is going to sleep? Few people like to see it when it happens in the daytime, but there really is no good reason why we should feel so strongly about it when it is merely the child's way of comforting herself to sleep. I don't know whether what you fear is that the child's teeth and mouth may be pulled out of shape. No good grounds have been shown for believing that thumb-sucking does permanently deform the mouth and teeth. I think you have probably made it ever so much harder for your little girl through starting punishment and prohibition so early. It is very rarely that the bitter aloes, or the gloves put on at night, or tying the hands, does cure this habit. I have had case after case reported to me in which these methods have been useless. I expect the reason why your doctor's advice to leave the little girl alone about it did not work may have been because you were not really convinced about the wisdom of doing so, and so the child still sensed your distress and disapproval, and therefore still felt guilty about doing it.

And three years of age is very young to be appealed to as a "big girl" to give up such a habit. The fact that she lies awake so long at night when she tries not to suck her thumb shows how very sensitive she is about your blame. I see no good grounds for distressing a tiny child about an innocent habit so as to make her lie awake night after night in this way. And I wish very much that you had not got yourself in such a quandary about the birthday promise. There isn't any way that can be guaranteed to break her of the thumb-sucking before her next birthday, in February, unless it were something that would terrify the child, and thus be infinitely worse than the thumb-sucking could ever be. With regard to the habit dying away later on, this does happen with the great majority of children. A thumb-sucker at nine years of age is quite unusual, and I should say, needs psychological treatment—at any rate, if the child does it in the daytime. If it were only when going to sleep I should not worry about it even then. But the age when the child most naturally and easily gives up this habit is between five and seven years of age, when many other important psychological changes are going on, and babyhood and the nursery are left behind. It is useful and legitimate to appeal to the "big girl" idea if the habit is not given up by six or seven, but it is disproportionate to do this at three years of age. Now, don't you think the best way of dealing with the problem about the promise would be to transfer the emphasis to the child's *attempt* to give up the thumb-sucking? That is to say, to let the pram or tricycle be the reward for the *effort* to give it up? I don't see how you can wisely make the present contingent upon the actual *success* in giving it up. I would comfort her by saying, "I know you have tried hard, and we won't mind about it at present, as I am sure that when you *are* a big girl and go to school you won't feel you want to do it". I think you will find that such an attitude of understanding and sympathy would be far more helpful to her.

Q. My small only daughter, aged one and a half is a perfectly healthy normal child in every respect, and is usually in very good spirits, but at the moment she is cutting double teeth, and I am quite certain that this is the cause of two trying habits which she has recently developed. In the first place A. is constantly putting her finger into her nose. When she does it I have tried to make her play a game—pinching her nose and saying, "moo" for cow. This she enjoys, and it makes her forget about putting her finger to her nose, but as soon as she is alone it all starts again. I cannot think how this habit has developed. The second habit—due to teething, I am sure—is one of whining for everything she wants: she says, "Ta, Ta", or "Please", followed by a nasty whine.

A. I am sure you are right that the child's emotions and nervous strain caused by the teething process have given rise to this habit. The cutting of teeth is almost always an experience which causes anxiety, whether in the tiny child or the older one who is getting his permanent set. It would be far better not to take any particular notice of her little habit of fingering her nose. It will pass away as she gets active skill with her fingers and more security in her interests in the real world. Sucking the tongue or the lips, always tends to be more persistent than sucking the fingers or such a habit as your little girl's fingering her nose, because the natural diversion of the hands to activities, in building and modelling and sewing and using them generally in handling objects, presently distracts the child from the pleasure of sucking them. The whining, too, will pass away, provided you take no special notice of it, but just go on handling the child with quiet confidence. In general she seems to be developing very well, and some little difficulty of this kind occurs in the development of every child. There are so many important crises in the child's experience—weaning, teething, getting on to solid food, learning to face strangers or traffic, learning to bear inevitable partings, dealing with jealousy of a new baby—that some form of expression for the difficulties which these events bring during the process of adjustment are bound to occur. But mostly they pass away as the child passes through the main crises of these early years, provided she has steady affection and opportunities for making and doing and learning and playing.

Q. My little girl is five years old next August, and ever since she was about a year old she has gone to sleep sucking some part of her clothing or bedclothes. For a while I gave her a handkerchief, as these could easily be washed through every day and were preferable to her sucking her woollen coat or cover. I then tried as she got older to make her give up the hankie, but it was hopeless, and if I did not give her one she would get out of bed and get something else—any old thing she could find—doll's dress, etc. I put sheets on her bed after doing away with the hankies, and those were sucked at night. During the winter she has had no sheet, top or bottom, and I had hopes as she was getting older that she would not like to stuff the blanket into her mouth. However, it is just as bad, and I feel quite hopeless about it. Every night after she is asleep I go up and remove it, as I think it is making her mouth large and a bad shape. When she is lifted at 10 p.m. she does not wake up properly, so goes off to sleep again then till 8 a.m. with nothing in her mouth; but should she wake in the night and not be able to go to sleep at once, the blanket or whatever is handy will be pushed into her mouth. I have tried everything I can think of to get her to stop it, but nothing seems to be any good, though I do think she tries not to do it sometimes, and then the habit is too strong for her. She is a healthy child, full of high spirits, but very excitable and strong-willed.

A. I don't think I should try to take any definite steps to

break your little girl of this habit. The need for something to suck is obviously so very strong that any direct attempt to break it off would, if successful, almost certainly result in other symptoms of a probably more distressing kind, such as nail-biting or stammering. After all, this is a very innocent habit, much less likely to be in any way harmful than sucking the thumb, as the small piece of soft hankie or sheet cannot injure the teeth or jaws. She may very well grow out of it, as your friends suggest. But she may not! She may be like a woman friend of mine, now in middle age, a very fine person intellectually and morally, doing splendid work in the world, and happy in all her relationships who nevertheless to this day cannot go to sleep without rubbing a little bit of flannel between her thumb and finger, and sucking one finger-tip! But this does no harm to herself or anyone else. I see that you say that the blanket stuffed into the mouth is spoiling the shape of your little girl's mouth, and, of course, a piece of blanket is much more likely to do this than a piece of soft linen handkerchief. I should be inclined to let her have a handkerchief, as that could so easily be kept perfectly clean. There is, of course, no reason why you should not from time to time suggest that now she is getting a big girl perhaps she might be able to do without this.

Q. My little boy, aged three years, puts everything in his mouth that is given him or rubs it along his lips, especially pieces of paper. Can you help me to rid him of this awful habit as scolding has no effect?

A. This too is a difficult problem. Scolding never does prevent it. On the other hand you need not worry about it too much, since no particular harm will result from the habit unless the child is in circumstances that would make infection likely. In an ordinary household, with normal standards of cleanliness, there is no particular risk of such infection. I should, of course, watch that the child does not put anything dirty to his lips, but little pieces of paper will do no harm, will they? It is a habit comparable to thumb-sucking. I would try to make sure that he has sufficient pleasure in his food. A habit like this is always connected with other things in his mind and sometimes it indicates a greater need for the pleasures of the mouth in some form, for example, more sweets (which should of course be well chosen). You would help the boy by playing little games with his fingers and giving him plenty of play material that will occupy his hands and at the same time plenty of nursery rhymes and songs, to develop the pleasures of speech. But he will grow out of the habit in time if all these other needs are satisfactorily met. I would advise you not to try to stop the habit by direct means such as scolding or even commenting.

Q. My small girl of six years has just started school, and I am afraid, although only being at school for two days, her habit of sucking her tongue has been already made conscious to her. From a baby she has sucked her tongue, especially if she is doing anything which requires effort, or if she is thinking or if tired. I have at different times tried my hardest to interest her so that she forgets it, but in the end she usually reverts to it again. She is bright and intelligent.

A. There is no definite step you can take to help your daughter get over this habit of sucking her tongue in a short time. It is very likely that the other children at school will show that they notice such a habit, and although this may be painful to her for a time, it will probably be the best help to her in overcoming it. It will do no harm to say in a perfectly quiet and matter-of-fact way: "Do you know that you suck your tongue when you are doing so-and-so? I daresay that now that you are getting a big schoolgirl you would like to know about it, because you would probably rather not do it. But if you can't stop it all at once, don't worry about it: you will grow out of it as you get older." Otherwise I should not worry, but leave time and growth to help her out of it.

Q. My little boy began finger-sucking at the age of about a week, in spite of all the efforts of the nurses in the Home where he was born, and for months nothing would stop him. I was almost in despair when I discovered he was being underfed, and as soon as I put this right the sucking entirely ceased, though I am certain that hunger was not the original cause. Now at nearly thirteen months he has suddenly begun again. I am pretty sure that the trouble this time is teething, which in his case has been very late and very painful; at eleven months he had no teeth, and the four he has now have caused us all weeks of misery and given rise to every imaginable kind of difficulty. Most of them I have managed to get around in one way or another, but I do not know what to do about the fingers. It is no use trying to distract his attention, because when his gums are hurting he will not look at any toy; nor will he suck or bite anything else except hard crusts, and I feel sure that to be constantly eating between meals is a worse evil than the sucking. The only thing is to pick him up and carry him about, and I am far too busy to do this for long at a stretch. I am very anxious not to draw his attention unduly to the habit by punishment or any kind of restraint, but it gets dreadfully on my nerves and sometimes I simply cannot help pulling the finger out of his mouth. I do my best to give him extra attention, but he has to spend a good part of the day by himself, and that is when the sucking goes on. Perhaps if I take no notice he will give it up when the tooth trouble is over, but I would far rather prevent it, as I am so afraid of its becoming a permanency.

A. I wonder why you feel so upset about your little boy's finger sucking? What is it that makes it "Get so dreadfully on your nerves"? It is an extremely common, almost universal, practice amongst little children, and one which gives them a great deal of comfort from all sorts of mental stress. Don't you think that the picture of the nurses in the home making tremendous efforts on the one hand to stop the baby comforting himself with his finger, and on the other, letting him be underfed, is just about as bad a combination of mistakes as might be made? As you found when you began to feed him properly, the sucking was his refuge against the nervous irritation and distress he was suffering through no fault of his own. The same thing is true as regards teething, which is being exceptionally painful for your boy. I cannot see why, when the child is suffering such acute distress with this painful teething, you should be so anxious to stop his getting the comfort that he finds from sucking. What harm do you feel that it will do? When you say you are afraid of this becoming a permanency, you do not mean you think he will go on sucking his finger all through life? It is true that grown-ups find sucking of some sort a comfort, as for example, smoking cigarettes or pipes, but we do not, as a rule, think that we ought to make a fuss about that. Why should we want to deprive children of a type of pleasure that we ourselves so often find helpful? The little child has far fewer sources of pleasure and comfort than we have, and far fewer ways of dealing with any temporary anxiety or irritation. Especially in the case of a boy like yours who has already shown how desperately he needs this particular comfort, I cannot see why you should want to deprive him of it. If you keep him satisfied in other directions, for example, do not stint him of affection, let him have plenty of suitable playthings and plenty of opportunity for sharing in your activities when he crawls or runs about, plenty of laughter and good-humour, he will gradually wean himself of the sucking as he grows and finds more satisfactory things to do with his fingers and more expressive pleasure in speaking or singing with his mouth. I would urge you to exercise self-restraint and not pull the boy's fingers out of his mouth, but let him have this help for the present teething crisis, relying upon the process of normal and happy development to wean him from the sucking later.

Q. My little boy, aged five, has a horrible habit of pulling his finger nails till they are torn off to the quick. I wonder if you could give me any advice as to how to stop it. If I scold him he seems unable to stop, and hides his hands behind his back till he has finished.

A. I wonder if you have tried applying olive oil to your boy's finger nails? This is the method I have found most successful for nail biting, and it is quite likely that it would work with the pulling of the nail as well. I should trim them very carefully, so that there are no ragged edges, and then put a little olive oil on them each night to keep them smooth and soft. I think you will find this will help considerably.

Q. I should be so grateful for your opinion and advice about a little girl of four years who continues to bite her nails in spite of many methods of prevention. She bites them at any moment and also at night when she can remove the gloves, which latter garments enrage her terribly. This poor child was forcibly stopped from sucking her thumb at the age of two years, and she im-

mediately commenced to bite her nails. I have always contended that this was the real cause of it, as all my experience with children leads me to believe that many children must have some habit or other which they grow out of when they can be reasoned with. The brother of the little girl stopped thumb-sucking at two and a half years when he was reminded of Father Christmas's impending visit, fortunately he did not acquire another habit, but he is still rather afraid of the dark. The little girl had a difficult time as an infant owing to whooping cough at four months, and I did not try to prevent thumb-sucking, as it was a great comfort to a nervous child. Her parents do not believe it is a nervous habit, and they insist that she wears gloves almost all the twenty-four hours which makes her very miserable and also cunning, as she will find a way to hide herself and bite the nails. I have tried olive oil and cold cream, also promised to paint her nails pink, etc. so if you have any helpful theory to offer I shall be very thankful. I have never failed with a child before, and she is very dear to me because I was present at her birth and brought her up under great difficulties. I must add that the child has plenty of occupations and interests, she is youngest of three and is clever with her fingers, fond of drawing and tries to sew.

A. It seems likely from your letter that the trouble is so persistent just because so much fuss has been made about it, and above all, because of the parents' insistence on the child's wearing gloves. Nothing could be more unfavourable for a little child's development than to have the natural use of her hands interfered with by the wearing of gloves. I note that you say that treatment with olive oil has not relieved the trouble. I suspect that this is because, on the one hand, the gloves were still insisted on, and the general attitude of the parents is so much one of disapproval; and on the other hand, you have not persisted long enough with the olive oil. I would strongly urge that the gloves are discarded, that nobody scolds the child or bothers her about it, but that you dress the finger nails with olive oil at night and two or three times during the day, and let the little girl do this for herself if she possibly will. Above all, try to develop in her a positive attitude to her finger nails and the uses that can be made of them. But once such an unfavourable attitude has been built up it is bound to take time to relieve the trouble. There is no good expecting the habit to be cured in a few days or even in a few weeks.

Q. My little girl was three on December 4th. She is healthy and happy and very active and alert. About three weeks ago Elizabeth started a distressing habit of pulling little pieces off her finger-nails, making them look as if she had been biting them, although I know they have not been near her mouth. I tried to coax her out of this habit by saying she was making her hands ugly. Although she takes a great interest in her clothes and appearance this has no effect, so I tried binding up the fingers of her left hand. This was too great a hardship for her, as she loves using her hands, so I had to remove the bandages. She generally plays with her nails in bed, so I see that she always has her dolls at twelve and when she goes to bed at night. I think most mischief is done on waking in the morning, but Elizabeth has her own room and is always perfectly quiet until after the postman has been at 7.30, so we do not know when she wakes up. She never gets out of bed until she has called to me and I have given her permission. She loves stories, songs, crayonning, and helping in the house. So far she is an only child, but she plays with other children as often as we can manage it, and she is not yet spoilt. I have a young "lady help" who plays with Elizabeth and takes a great interest in her.

A. Your little girl's attack upon her finger nails is one of those small symptoms of emotional trouble that occur so often between two and four years of age—if not in this form, then in some other. The further my own experience widens, the clearer it becomes to me that the children who do not have *any* nervous symptom of any kind in these years are so rare as to be almost non-existent. Tantrums, night terrors or wakefulness, particular fears, finickiness about food, shyness of strangers, teasing or hurting of other children, thumb-sucking or nail-biting; one or more of these signs of emotional stress are practically certain to appear. Habits such as the one you describe are a safety-valve for the child's feelings. It is very probable that she hurts her nails in this way because they seem naughty to her—they might scratch and hurt someone else when she was angry if she did not punish them and herself in this way! I know how ugly and distressing the habit seems to other people—but it is seldom that it persists into later childhood and grown-up life. Of course, it does so sometimes; but the number of grown-ups who have these habits is far, far smaller than the number of children who show them in the early years. And it is by no means always the *direct* means we take to effect a cure that do, in fact, bring it about. Indeed, it is often the reverse—the grown-ups or older children who bite their nails are often the ones who have been punished or scolded for it in their childhood, or about whom a fuss of some sort has been made because of it. The indirect means are usually far more effective—helping the child by letting her have appropriate material to play with and make things with, letting her help in the house, as you do, and enjoy the shared delights of song and story; helping her to find outlets for her wish to be independent and to assert herself in useful ways, whilst at the same time fostering her sense of secure affection and understanding. You were very wise to abandon the binding of her hand—that would inevitably have increased the need to hurt her nails by exasperating her and giving her an angry sense of frustration.

Have you tried soothing the nails with olive oil applied at bed-time? And trimming them very carefully so that there are *no* irritating rough bits or jagged edges? I should do this, and I should tell her that you know she feels cross with her nails because they sometimes want to do bad things—but after all, they can do good things too, and she will find more and more good things to do with them as she grows older.

X. SEX EDUCATION AND "WHERE DO BABIES COME FROM?"

Q.1. My little boy will be three and a half when a second child arrives in the autumn. I'm afraid he may feel the change in the family life rather acutely as he has been so much alone with me. His father is away all day, and it is only recently that we have even had a maid with us, except in the mornings, so that he is rather a "mummie's boy". However, he thinks babies are dear little things, and is pleased that we are going to have one of our own. He says he is going to help bath it and dress it. He asked me a great many questions about where it was coming from, so I have explained a good deal of this. What is really worrying me is that I have to go to a nursing home for the event and I am afraid that W. will be very upset at my leaving him. His Granny and the maid, with both of whom he is quite happy, will be here to look after him. He is used to being left with Granny for an afternoon occasionally; but if he knew I was not coming back at bedtime he would be very distressed. Would it be best to say nothing about not coming back that day, and leave him to get used to it gradually? I thought of leaving a parcel with a new toy in it to distract his attention when he first begins to worry about my absence. What would be the best attitude for his Granny and father to adopt if he keeps on asking for me? I thought of telling him that I have to go to a nursing home for the baby to be born because it will be so little at first and will need a doctor and nurse to look after it, but that very soon it will be strong enough for us to look after ourselves. Would it be a good idea for him to have a photo of me in the nursery while I am away and for me to write him little post-cards from time to time, or would it be better for him not to be reminded of me? I intend to come home as soon as I can get up—at a fortnight, I hope, and have a nurse in the house for a week or two. I imagine that a child must not be allowed to think that the baby has made his mother ill? But as I am bound to spend the mornings in bed at first, would it be all right to explain that mothers are a little tired after growing a baby?

Q.2. Perhaps you would be good enough to tell me what general steps to take to prevent what appears to be the inevitable awkwardness of a three-year-old when her baby brother or sister is born? D. is already (about a month before) going through a nervy phase, which I partly blame on an attack of measles which, though very light, was a bad experience for her as she had been lucky enough never to have had to stay in bed for even one day before. She is quarrelsome with other children, wanting her own way all the time, and has become afraid of noisy bikes, trains and large animals, such as horses, cattle and large dogs. We have discussed the new arrival in the hopes of sparing her the disappointment that the new baby will be rather useless as a playmate for some while. She is most interested in learning that she was very new once, and is always asking to be told about what happened when nurse was here to bath her, etc. I have wondered if she is already sub-consciously jealous of the new arrival. Are all first children awkward when a second arrives, or can this trouble be avoided?

A. There is no method by which we can *altogether* prevent the first child's feeling of jealousy. Jealousy is too deeply rooted in human nature for such a typical and essential situation as the arrival of a new baby not to evoke it. But we can certainly make it very much harder for the child to bear, or help him to master his jealousy, by the way we prepare him beforehand and deal with him afterwards. It is always worth telling the child that a new baby is coming, because he then feels that he is not shut out of the magic circle of the love between his parents. It lessens the frightening sense of mysterious events in which he can have no part, as well as increasing his sense of love and confidence in his parents. It is worth while answering any of the questions that he may put as to where the baby is coming from and how it begins to grow, for the same reasons. It is doubtful whether we can give the young child much real understanding of what happens, however, even if we should wish to. Very often we find that children of ten or twelve years who were told quite fully about the birth of babies when they were small are just as ignorant of the matter as children who have been brought up on stories of gooseberry bushes and storks. But it is equally true that children who were told about things have benefited, not through the *knowledge*, but through the sense of sharing with their parents and trust in them. They do not get so strongly a feeling of secrecy and evasion on the part of the parents. The idea of telling the children the truth about babies, however, will not work as a panacea for all ills; it will not solve all the child's problems. A sense of proportion has to be kept about this, as about everything else to do with the education of children. If the child prefers not to ask questions or shows reluctance to talk about the matter, then it is best not to force explanations upon him. But this is very seldom the attitude of the quite small child. It is shown more often by the child of over six or seven. The small child who has an affectionate relation with his mother does feel privileged and pleased to be told by her about the event, since he will in any case have surmises and wonderings about the changes he sees in his mother and in her activities and plans. With regard to the best way of dealing with the actual arrangements for the birth, e.g., the mother's leaving for the nursing home and having to be careful of her health when she returns, Q.1's suggestions are all excellent. Q.1 has evidently realized how lost a little child may feel when the mother leaves home in this way, and how much it will help him to have constant and solid proofs of her continued love and interest in him. The plan of leaving the parcel with a letter and new toy in it, and of letting him have a photograph and sending him post-cards are all excellent. It will certainly be far better to do this than to leave him without any reminder. There is certainly no reason why children should not be told that mothers want a little extra rest after growing a baby, and need the help of doctors and nurses to achieve so important an event. As regards the actual day of leaving, it probably would be best, with so young a child, not to tell him beforehand, but to leave a little note behind and a picture or a toy for him.

The same steps would be very helpful for the little girl. I have no doubt that the child is already aware of some impending change, although her feelings and ideas about it will hardly be conscious. Children even younger than this notice the change in mother's figure, and are often afraid that it means something harmful, not only to them (they cannot e.g. sit on her lap comfortably) but also to mother. She will, however, get over the difficulty if she is sure of the mother's continued affection and interest, by consideration along the lines suggested.

Q. I am expecting my new baby next month, and before the event I would like to feel prepared to deal with the effect on the first baby aged nineteen months. Jean is now becoming a problem to me. She had an unfortunate weaning—she was a normal baby at birth, and I fed her (breast) successfully till six months, when we moved house. I had a strenuous time—and it was very bad weather as well. After that I began to worry, and my milk was not sufficient. My doctor would not agree to weaning completely, but suggested supplementing. From the beginning it was not a success. Baby literally fought *against it—would not take the supplement, and she lost weight and vitality to such an extent it became alarming. I thought I should lose her, and at last the doctor suggested taking her to an Infants' Hospital for advice, at nine months. To my great distress they kept her for a week—but were unsuccessful in getting her to take milk in any form, and she was put on a meat juice and vegetable diet. She pulled through somehow but has never liked milk and still objects to it. She now has a lovely colour, boundless energy, generally sleeps well, and "pot" trouble is non-existent. But she has frequent "tantrums"! Two months ago my niece (aged sixteen) came to live with me to help with baby until after the next is born. She is a kind girl, fond of babies, and Jean loves her, and I hope that when I am away with my second baby, Jean will not miss me so much with Barbara and her Granny, whom she loves, to care for her. I still do a number of things for Jean, but Barbara is now with her more than I am—am I doing right? Or is this, do you think, contributing in any way to these sudden tantrums, which are mostly connected with feeding times? It is, "No! No! No!" to everything offered, and if thwarted in any way sudden stiff rages—and the plate and cup are thrown overboard deliberately. She will do this suddenly with some toy she may have. I have provided her with as many outlets for her age as I possibly can. She used to play out in the garden on her own, but began to want to be with us, so now she, "helps", round the house. Jean is very intelligent for her age. She speaks remarkably well—easily understands and makes herself understood—sociable with other children and strange adults—does not seem nervy at all. How shall I deal with these tantrums? I have wondered if I am keeping her in the "baby", stage too long. She is so active she has to be strapped in her high chair at meal times. Is she old enough to sit on an ordinary chair, to have a single bed instead of a cot? Perhaps she feels "kept back" in some way. Also how shall I set about preparing her for the new baby?*

A. Your little girl will be rather too young, of course, when you have to go to hospital to have your baby, to understand specific explanations of the reasons, and of the necessity for your going away. In the moment of parting from her before you go to hospital you might say to her that "Mummy has to go away for a little while, but she will soon come back to Jean". I would tell her that Granny and Barbara are going to take care of her while you are away, and that then you will come home, and how lovely it will be when you come back to her again. It will be a help to the child that she has had time to get to know and to love Barbara beforehand, and also that she loves her Granny. I would do as another correspondent did with her little girl, and before you go away give Jean a doll, and perhaps a doll's pram or cot. Then I would show her the baby's little garments and the cot (you could give Jean some similar garments for her doll), and say, "Mummy is going to bring you a little baby to play with". Another suggestion, which I have made before and which has been found helpful, is with regard to your first meeting with Jean after your return from hospital. On this occasion, do not let her see you first of all with the baby in your arms. I would greet Jean first, warmly and lovingly, so that she has no doubt of your affection for her, and give her a little time all to herself. And when she first sees the baby, let it be when someone else is holding it, or when it is in the cot. It is a very difficult situation for the elder child if she first sees her mother on her return with another baby in her arms, which the child thinks has taken her own place. I would not worry about the tantrums. They are very understandable, considering that Jean is still having trouble with teething, that she has had the feeding difficulty from such an early age, and that there are changes connected with the coming of the new baby, for example. Barbara is now doing more for her than you are and she must be aware of the changes in your body. She will grow out of these tantrums in time, with constant love and patience on your part. But you may have difficulty with her for some time, and especially since she will soon have to deal with the presence of the new baby; for however careful you are, there is bound to be some jealousy and emotional upset. I would continue to share with Barbara the care of Jean, and if you cannot do so many things for the child now as you have been doing, I would show your love for her in other ways. With regard to the feeding difficulty, I would try putting the food in front of her, and if she refuses it, leave her to eat it in her own time, without pressing or urging. Give her the kind of food which she likes best and let her pick it up in her fingers and eat it in her own way. I would not reproach her if she does not eat it, but would give her plenty of time, and offer it to her again if she refuses it at first. It may increase her interest in eating if you give her more independence in the matter; but I would be encouraging in my attitude, and help her if she wants help. You say that the child is strapped in a high chair. It might be a good plan to try a low chair, of a kind which can now be bought, with a movable food tray which can be adjusted in front. The novelty of the new chair, and the fact that she could get in and out of it herself, might also be of assistance in overcoming the feeding difficulty. She is perhaps a little young to have a bed instead of a cot.

Q. Should one make a definite effort to see that a child has more or less clear knowledge of birth, etc.? My eldest child was three when the younger was born, and though I answered her questions, I don't think she understood much, and though we have had many new baby friends born, it seems to need this exciting thing to happen in one's own family to get that steady stream of questions that would show me where the gaps lie. Would you advise reading to her some such book as How a Baby is Born, *or just to wait till the questions come? The child is now seven. I would much rather tell her myself than let her hear in some stupid manner from another child.*

A. Experience has shown that the most helpful plan is to answer the child's questions on the subject of birth at the time when they are asked, as you have done with your little girl. Young children of, say, from three to five years of age, often ask such questions spontaneously, whereas older children, of from seven to eight years onwards, are more shy and less openly interested in these matters. Indeed, boys and girls in the later years of childhood are sometimes embarrassed and awkward when talked to on this subject. I think your little girl may know more than you imagine about the origin of babies, since there is a younger child in the family and you have answered her questions as they arose. Children do ponder about this question, and they seem to have a spontaneous knowledge about it, although this is not explicit, but half-conscious. One can understand that the arrival of a new baby in the family is an event of vital importance to the child, and it would be strange if his mind were not full of, sometimes secret, sometimes open, ponderings about such a happening.

I should certainly give your little girl a copy of *How a Baby is Born* as a present. The delightful illustrations would be very likely to start a number of questions, and you could then either answer these yourself or read her the text of the book—whichever seemed to her the most interesting. Can she read at all yet? If so, you could let her read parts of the book aloud to you, and could then explain anything which was not clear to her. I quite agree that it would be better to tell her about it yourself than to let her hear in some secret or frightening way from another child. But I would not read the book to her in a solemn or didactic way. Let her have the book and follow her interest in it in whatever form it takes, making clear anything she wants to know in a simple and frank way, and telling her that you would like to answer any questions she wants to ask about it.

Q. We hope to have a new arrival in the spring—it is a good time off yet but I wondered how to prepare my two children for it. The girl is five and boy three. Several months ago my little girl asked how she was made and I told her she started like a tiny seed and then grew as big as an egg and grew and grew until she was a baby. That satisfied her. I have not been well and have made the excuse of an operation I had some time ago. How soon before the event is it best to inform the children and is the boy too young to tell? At the moment he rather resents babies coming to the house but the girl is very fond of them—is always saying she would like one of "her very own". She is not very good at keeping a secret and, of course, may inform everyone and perhaps mention it at school to children brought up on the "Stork" story. I have a very good book "How a Baby is Born", and thought of showing her one or two of the pictures in it.

A. The little book which you mention, How a Baby is Born by K. de Schweinitz (Routledge, 2s. 6d.), is one of the best helps to the mother who wishes to deal with this problem intelligently and in a friendly way. The pictures are delightful, and the letterpress can be read even to quite young children. I do advise mothers to tell their children about the happy expected event, two or three months beforehand. Tell it as a secret, by all means—but a *good* secret, to be shared by all the family as a special family happiness—not as a solemn affair with a tinge of shame which "ought not" to be talked about. I should tell them how much you want another little child, just *because* you love those you have, and because they bring *you* so much happiness. Tell them that you know that they, too, will be glad to have a brother or sister to play with, even if it seems a little strange at first. Tell them you know it may feel strange, and that perhaps they *may* even imagine you don't love them quite as much as you used to, when they see you doing so much for the new baby. But that you want them to share the helping of the baby, and all its love and the pleasure of its coming. And then later on you will be able to play together, and sing and laugh together and have great fun. But that when babies are *very* small, as they, too, were once, they have to have such a lot of care—to be washed and kept warm and fed in a special way by mother herself—just as little kittens and lambs are. I should certainly not try to keep the breast feeds from the knowledge of the elder child, as is sometimes done—it helps her far more to let her see it, and try to understand it. Tell her why it is the best thing for the baby—and how she had this happiness, too, when she was a baby. And when *she* is grown up and a mother herself, she will have the delight of caring for her own babies in the same way.

I should also tell the older children that mother and father have together helped to make the new little baby, and that they both love it just as they love the children who are already sharing the family joys. And that it lives for nine months in a special place inside mother's body, to be kept safe and warm while it grows big enough to be able to come out and feed at mother's breast and open its eyes and learn to see and hear its brothers and sisters. I should say that being born is so important and such a change that both baby and mother need to be taken care of specially for a time by nurse and doctor; that hospitals can help because they often have mothers and babies there and so know just what to do and how best to do it; that mothers are not usually ill but very tired and needing special rest for a time. But emphasize how lovely it will be when you are all at home together again and baby is learning to play and grow.

Q. We have one child, a girl eight years six months. I think she is above the average in everyday intelligence and general knowledge, as she has always asked many questions which we have answered fully, showing her when older how to look up things for herself. She is very fond of animals and younger children, and has spent various Easter holidays on a farm, but has never asked anything about where the young animals appeared from. About a year ago I read her, "How a Baby is Born", recommended in your pages. I should like to know if other mothers reading it to eight-year-olds found it seemed a little beyond them? I have always read a lot to E., but felt this book didn't seem to interest her at all. When I had finished I told her that unlike most things I read to her it was all true, and asked her if she had understood it all. A funny, "shut", look came over her face and she said, "No, I don't understand it at all, I think it's a very difficult book". She ran very quickly from the room as if to avoid discussion of the subject. I let the matter drop, and a few months later we met our neighbour buying a pram. On the way home E. asked why Mrs. Jones was buying a pram as she had no baby. I replied she soon would have one. "Oh," said E., "how does she know?" I asked if she didn't remember me reading that book about babies. The same odd look came over E.'s face as she said, "That was the difficult book I didn't understand", and ran quickly ahead again as if she didn't want to hear any more. A short time ago I told E. her favourite aunt was to have a baby. She was tremendously excited—did I think it would arrive in the holidays, would she be allowed to wheel it in the pram, and could she start knitting a vest now? I next suggested that as someone she knew so well was having a baby and as she was older we might read the baby book again. It struck me further perhaps I had made a mistake reading it all at a sitting, so I suggested we read a chapter a day. She listened without comment to the first chapter. The next being a busy school day, there was only the last fifteen minutes which we always keep for reading. When E. saw I proposed reading the baby book in her precious time she was so upset it seemed useless to continue. Her father often seems to understand her better than I do. He feels confident she understands as much as she needs, and if she doesn't care to speak about it, we must respect her reserve. Do you advise me to leave it at this or must I go on till I am confident she does understand? She goes now all day to a big High School and is in a large form with a good many girls older than herself, and as she has a very sociable nature goes out a lot, and I wouldn't like to feel I had sent her out badly prepared to face any question that might arise.

A. It is not uncommon for children of your little girl's age to resist information about the origin of babies. The spontaneous interest is usually shown very much earlier, at three or four years, and even in children who have been given correct information it often happens that after six or seven they turn right away from the whole subject and refuse to show any interest in it or to listen if any information is given to them. With your little girl, I think that there is no doubt that the book was read to her not too early, but too late. The book is itself very simply written, and no intelligent child of eight years could possibly fail to understand it unless there were strong emotional reasons inhibiting understanding. With a child of over seven, it would be far better to give the book into her hands and let her read it herself. It is quite likely that she wants to know and understand, but is frightened about getting this information from you. I should certainly not read it to her again, but I should leave the book where she could get it herself and read it if she wanted to. I should not refer to the subject at all unless she asked questions about it, and if again she did ask you about friends or neighbours having babies I should answer her simply and directly yourself in your own words, not by reference to the book. It is quite a different matter to try to compel the child to be interested in what disturbs her, from answering her spontaneous questions directly and simply at the time when she puts them.

Q.1. Our son aged thirteen, is going to his public school for the first time next term, and my husband wishes to tell him of the facts of life before he goes. Can you tell me of a book that would give him some idea of the best way of explaining things to a boy of that age? He was quite interested in the arrival of our baby girl about three years ago, and we answered all his questions quite frankly. But they only touched the fringe of the subject, and since then he has never asked another question on these matters; so we feel a little puzzled as to the best way of opening the subject again.

Q.2. I should be very glad of your help about a subject that has been worrying me for some time. My eldest girl is now ten years old, and I am wondering when I should tell her about menstruation. I notice in most books on "how babies are born", they do not mention this subject. J. is a very intelligent child, but rather highly strung and nervous, and I do not want to her be worried about something which might not happen for a year or two. On the other hand, I do not want her to learn about it at school—as I did! Should I tell her now?

A. There are two books I would recommend to both these correspondents, not necessarily to be put into the hands of the children, but to be used in the first instance for the purpose of reference and illustration. The first is, *What is Sex?* by Dr. Helena Wright. This is definitely not a book for the children themselves, but one that discusses the whole problem of the biological development of children and the best ways of dealing with the problems that arise in adolescence, and is an extremely useful book for parents to read. It gives other sources of reliable information, as well as discussing difficulties in a sensible, straightforward way. The other book, which could be given either to the girl of ten or the boy of thirteen, is *The Human Body*, by Dr. Marie Stopes, published at 3*s.* 6*d.* by Putnam. There is nothing in this book about birth control, with which many of Dr. Stopes's other writings have dealt—nothing in it a parent need hesitate about in giving this book to boys and girls in their teens. It is a straight-forward and workmanlike account of the anatomy and physiology of the body as a whole, including the reproductive processes. It grinds no axe of any sort, and confines itself to a clear statement of the simple facts, leaving it to the parent to give guidance in the emotional and moral aspects of the family relation. These aspects of sex education—namely, the emotional and moral side—can, of course, never be dealt with by giving the child a book to read. They are essentially the parent's own responsibility, and what parents teach is bound to be an outcome of their own personal attitudes and fundamental beliefs on these matters. It is clear, however, that my correspondents have in mind not this aspect of sex teaching, but the basic physiological facts, whether of the reproductive process itself or of the fundamental physiological changes connected with growth and development in adolescence, and it is desirable that these basic facts should be given in a scientific and intelligible way to the child of these ages. If the boy of thirteen is likely to be, as so many children of his age are, rather sensitive about discussing these points, it might be best simply to place *The Human Body* in his hands and leave him to ask any further questions about it which he wishes, just telling him that you want him to know where he can get such knowledge if he is interested, and that you want him to feel that he can discuss such things with you if he wants to do so. As regards the age at which it is best to tell a girl about menstrual periods, that does partly depend upon circumstances. It is not too early for a girl who is mixing with girl friends older than herself or one who is away at a boarding school, since she is so likely to get mysterious hints about it and be rather puzzled and frightened. It is a great help to a child when the periods first begin to have been given some correct information about the physiological meaning of the process. So many girls are really frightened by its first occurrence, and it is highly desirable that the girl should be helped against the emotional stress that is part of the ordinary development of her life at that time, by having sound knowledge of the fact that the process in itself is not in the least abnormal and has nothing whatever to do with illness. I should be careful to avoid any suggestion of forcing knowledge upon the child that she does not feel ready for, but I should be equally careful to let her feel that there is helpful information when she wants it, and that you are only too glad to give it to her when she feels she needs it. The process is explained in its proper setting in *The Human Body*, and that is the best way of giving information about it.

REFERENCES FOR FURTHER READING

Aldrich, A., and Aldrich, M.:	*Understand Your Baby.* Black, 1939.
Bowley, Agatha H.:	*The Natural Development of the Child.* Livingstone, 1947.
Chesters, Gwen:	*The Mothering of Young Children.* Faber and Faber, 1943.
Cummings, Jean D.:	*The Incidence of Emotional Symptoms in School Children.* British Journal of Educational Psychology, Vol. XIV, 1944.
do.	*Follow-Up Study of Emotional Symptoms in School Children.* British Journal of Educational Psychology, Vol. XVI, 1946.
Gesell, Arnold:	*The First Five Years of Life.* Methuen. (Undated).
do.	*The Child From Five to Ten.* Hamish Hamilton, 1946.
Goodenough, Florence:	*Anger in Young Children.* University of Minnesota Press, 1931.
Isaacs, Susan:	*The Nursery Years.* Routledge, 1929; Schocken Books, 1968.
do.	Chapter on "Habit" in *On the Bringing Up of Children.* Edited by John Rickman. Kegan Paul, 1936.
do.	*Some Notes on the Incidence of Neurotic Difficulties in Young Children.* British Journal of Educational Psychology, Vol. II, 1932.

Klein, Melanie:	Chapter on "Weaning" in *On the Bringing Up of Children*. Kegan Paul, 1936.
MacFarlane, Jean Walker:	*Studies in Child Guidance, I. Methodology of Data, Collection and Organization*, Society for Research in Child Development, National Research Council, Washington, D.C. 1938.
Gruenberg: (Ed. by)	*Parents' Questions.* Child Study Association of America. Gollancz, 1947.
Shepherd, Flora:	*Weaning*. Home and School Council, 109, Fulham Palace Road, London, W.6. March, 1937.
do.	*The Baby Who Does Not Conform to Rules*. Home and School Council.
Tudor-Hart, B.:	*Play and Toys in Nursery Years*. Country Life Ltd., London, 1938.
"Wise, Ursula":	*Habit Training*. Benn Bros. (Undated).